BUSINESS SENSE

BUSINESS SENSE

Exercising Management's Five Freedoms

Dan Thomas

Foreword by Jeffrey M. Wilkins

THE FREE PRESS

New York   London   Toronto   Sydney   Tokyo   Singapore

The Free Press
A Division of Simon & Schuster Inc.
1230 Avenue of the Americas
New York, N.Y. 10020

Printed in the United States of America

printing number
  2 3 4 5 6 7 8 9 10

Library of Congress Cataloging-in-Publication Data

Thomas, Dan R. E.
    Business sense: exercising management's five freedoms / Dan R.E.
  Thomas.
      p.   cm.
    Includes bibliographical references and index.
    ISBN 0–02–932444–0
    1. Strategic planning.   2. Success in business—Case studies.
  I. Title.
HD30.28.T467   1993
658.4′012—dc20   93–18521
                                                            CIP

Credits

Contents

Chapter 1: What Is Business Sense?   1

What can management do to make the most difference between success and failure in a business? Management has Five Freedoms that, if exercised effectively, can create and sustain success.

Freedom #1:
Choosing the Right Business

When you have the choice, the single most important thing you can do is choose a great business—one with growth, profit, and diversification potential. Some businesses are lousy businesses. They don't give you much chance to be successful. It's important to be realistic about your business' potential.

Chapter 2: What Is a Business?   15

Contrary to popular belief, "transportation" is not a business. It is a sector of the economy that contains over a hundred businesses. Many managers underdefine their businesses and make serious strategic mistakes that lead to poor performance, or failure.

Chapter 3: How Much Growth Potential Is There?   33

If you can only have one positive factor in your business, choose growth potential. Growth is the elixir of business. It can free you to make many mistakes and still succeed.

Chapter 4: What Is the Profit Potential?   53

Profit is essential. But profit comes in many forms and you may try to make the wrong kind. In assessing the profit potential of a business you need to understand its profit model and financial structure.

Chapter 5: Where Is the Diversification Potential?   73

No business lasts forever. When your current business matures, you need to know what your next one will be and have a clear path to it.

Freedom #2:
Creating the Right Strategy

The right strategy for your business is the one that will take maximum advantage of its potential. That's true whether you are in a great business or a lousy one. A brilliant strategy can make you a winner in even a mediocre business.

Chapter 6: What Is a Business Strategy?   87

"Strategy" is the most overused and least understood word in the English language. A practical, operational approach is required.

Chapter 7: What Is the Future of the Industry?   123

No crystal ball is necessary. You can predict the future of any industry by using structural analysis. Tear it apart, put it back together, and you'll see how it works.

Chapter 8: How Good Is the Strategy?   153

The old strengths and weaknesses test didn't work very well. Instead, you must apply nine tests to thoroughly evaluate any business' strategy. Failure to apply all nine could cause you to miss a golden opportunity or fatal flaw in your business.

Chapter 9: What Are the Alternative Strategies?   175

What is the "performance envelope" of feasible alternative strategies for your business? Tighten your seatbelt, we're headed for the outer reaches.

Chapter 10: What Strategy Should We Follow?   189

Effectively selecting a strategy from the many alternatives available is a challenge. To do so you will need to understand the boundary and specific objectives for your business. All objectives are subjectively created, but there are some guidelines.

Chapter 11: What About Missions and Visions and Such?   **205**

Missions and visions are all the rage in management books and articles. Every company has to have one or both. An examination of a few shows that most look alike—the generic mission or vision statement. To be effective a mission has to go somewhere, and a vision must be visionary. When they are, they are great bridges between your strategy and its implementation.

Freedom #3:
Developing the Right Systems

Most management information systems contain excellent information on yesterday's business. Unfortunately, many lack crucial information on customers and competitors. Since systems provide the navigational information for your business, it's important to have the right ones.

Chapter 12: What Systems Do We Need?   **219**

"Systems" are routine ways of doing things in your business. They include information, decision making, and incentive systems. The most dangerous systems are the incentive systems. They're dangerous because they often work too well—and get the wrong results in the process.

Freedom #4:
Designing the Right Organization Structure

The right organization structure for your business is the one that uses the systems to create and implement the right business strategy. To be fully effective, the structure must be linked directly to your systems and strategy.

Chapter 13: How Should We Be Organized?   **243**

There are only four ways to organize any business. There are, however, a number of combinations, permutations, and, some would say, mutations of these four that add complexity. Ideally, the business' strategy and systems should drive the organization's structure. Unfortunately, in most companies it works the other way around.

Freedom #5:
Getting the Right People

The right people can make all the difference between success and failure. If you don't have the right people, it's impossible to turn the right strategy into actions that get the results you want.

Chapter 14: What About People?   259

Many managers believe that their biggest problem is getting and keeping enough good people. It can be, but it is much less of a problem if you've exercised your first four freedoms effectively. Great people flock to great businesses with brilliant strategies, systems that support the work they need to do, and clean organization structures. If you've exercised your first four freedoms, you can get and keep all the great people you need if you know how to assess their motivation as well as their skills.

Conclusion   275

The key to keeping your Five Freedoms in great shape is to exercise them regularly. If you don't use them, they won't do you much good.

Foreword

I have known Dan Thomas since 1976 and during that time I have seen him work with many businesses, including several of my own. His techniques truly are common sense for business—applied in an uncommonly powerful way. The title of this book, *Business Sense*, is an excellent description of what the author possesses and what he has put into this book.

Let me tell you how I came to know Dan Thomas and his *Business Sense* approach.

Many years ago, fresh out of graduate engineering school at the University of Arizona, I started a computer services company that eventually became CompuServe. Like most 25-year-olds, I had few clues about how to build a company. What I did have was an intense desire to succeed and a willingness to seek out help and knowledge anywhere I could find it.

After a few years of hard work, and the good fortune to pick a growth industry, I was introduced to YPO, the Young President's Organization. YPO members are company presidents who reached that position before the age of 40. I quickly learned that one of the greatest benefits of YPO membership is the frank and honest business discussions that focus on real problems we all face as executives. In the mid-1970s, early in my YPO experience, I attended a week-long seminar at the Harvard Business School specifically tailored for YPO members. The classroom work and discussions covered a number of standard topics including marketing, finance, and strategic planning. During the corporate governance discussions, one of the professors put forth the idea of utilizing younger faculty members as consultants and board members. The idea intrigued me and I interviewed several candidates, including professor Dan Thomas, who had taught the session on Strategic Planning. The selection of Dan Thomas was one of the most important business decisions of my life.

Like other business executives charged with increasing shareholder wealth, I was well aware of the large body of consultants and firms standing by to assist in the creation of a "strategic plan." But, as a member of the board of directors of other companies, I had seen firsthand the largely ineffective results from such efforts. I knew intuitively that external advice was not enough; what was needed was for the management team to develop its own strategy, its own "strategic process." I wanted my executive team to expand its business perspective and its ability to manage "strategically." Again, I looked to Dan Thomas for help. He began to coach the team, using his unique approach to strategic management. As I observed Dan's progress, I was amazed. I saw talented people who had largely been concerned with "local optimums" begin to see the "bigger picture." They began using common vocabulary, relating their own concerns and ideas to those of the whole team and in the process gaining respect for each other. Decisions became easier and the outcomes more predictable. Dan had led the way in successfully transforming a group of individuals into a team with a common vision and established the strategic management process I had envisioned.

Over the years, I recommended Dan to many companies that prospered and grew from his efforts. But, all too quickly, the demand for Dan's services began to outstrip his ability to provide them. Frustrated, I saw many companies with a strong need for access to his strategic management process cut off from the option. When I became aware of Dan Thomas' efforts to put his philosophy and approach to business management into a book, I saw a solution to this problem and became an enthusiastic supporter. I volunteered to serve as sounding board and critic and to help spread the word. The result is the book you have before you, *Business Sense*. Its pages are replete with Dan's knowledge and experience and—equally important—with Dan's style. Using familiar language and concrete examples, *Business Sense* provides today's manager a practical road map for understanding and practicing true strategic management. I am sure you will be as pleased with the result as I am. In fact, I expect this book will be so well received that there will soon be an outcry for sequels, *Business Sense: The Workbook* and *Business Sense: The Video.*

Jeffrey M. Wilkins
Columbus, Ohio
February, 1993

Preface

I have been incredibly fortunate in my business career. Since 1972 I have been an entrepreneur, manager, consultant, educator, and corporate director. During that time I have had the opportunity to participate in or directly observe over five hundred businesses. I've been involved with many successes, and a few failures.

Throughout my adventures I have been fascinated by the fundamental processes that make the most difference between success and failure in a business. Those processes, and what I have learned about them, are the subject of this book.

THE PERSPECTIVE IN THIS BOOK

This book is written from the perspective of the general manager and the key members of his or her team. A general manager is usually defined as someone who is in charge of one or more businesses in an organization. General managers have many different titles, depending on their organization's structure and their responsibilities. A general manager might be the president of the company in one case and a division manager in another. He might be a sector manager or a product manager.

The general management team includes all direct reports to the general manager. In the simplest organization, this would typically include functional managers such as those individuals responsible for marketing, production, finance, and research and development.

As I discuss the Five Freedoms that management has and how to exercise them, it will be most useful if you put yourself in the role of someone running a business. From that perspective, and not the perspective of an owner, customer, competitor, or interested observer of the business, you will gain the most from the insights in this book.

WHO SHOULD READ THIS BOOK?

This book is not for everyone. If you don't have an interest in the management of the total business, either as a participant or an observer, this book is not for you.

If you are interested in those management activities that make the most difference in the success or failure of the total enterprise known as a business, then the Five Freedoms will give you a powerful perspective.

The most obvious target for the contents of this book are members of the general management team, as defined above. Others, both above and below the general management team, can also influence the exercise of the Five Freedoms. Boards of directors, in their role as representatives of the shareholders, must be vigilant in their oversight of management. When they observe management that consistently uses good Business Sense appropriate rewards are in order. When management shows poor Business Sense through the improper exercise of the Five Freedoms, then it is probably time for the board to encourage swift corrective action or make some changes.

Subordinates to the general management team can also learn from honing an understanding of the Five Freedoms. Presumably, many people in management aspire to the top ranks, at least in one of the management functions such as marketing or finance, if not to the management of the total business. Since one definition of an effective subordinate is someone who makes his boss successful, an understanding of those general management activities that make the most difference between success and failure in a business is probably essential.

Interested parties like investors, customers, and students of management will probably find the Five Freedoms a novel scorecard to use in rating the management of specific companies.

WHAT ARE THE SOURCES OF THE EXAMPLES IN THIS BOOK?

All of the examples in this book are from real companies. None of them are fictional or creative "composites." They are the real situations. I participated in or observed directly all but a few of them.

In many cases, clients have graciously allowed me to use their stories for the educational value they provide. Several of the examples, particularly the ones that show management at less than its best, are disguised. By disguising the examples enough to eliminate my clients' risk of public embarrassment, I have been able to use their mistakes as illustrations for others. Whether I was directly involved or not, when a story has been covered in the public press, I have often used that story to illustrate a point and avoid the complex process of getting a release.

This book is not just a book of stories about famous companies or managers. Companies and people do populate its pages, but that is not the book's purpose. You can read all of the stories you want in the daily and weekly business press. The purpose of this book is to share with you what I have learned about management's Five Freedoms and how you can use them to improve your results.

WHY ARE THERE SO MANY QUESTIONS IN THIS BOOK?

Before you read further, it is important that you know about one of my fundamental beliefs. I believe that the quality of your management is directly proportional to the quality of your questions.

If your management is working well, then I'll bet you are asking some very good questions. If it isn't, you probably need to ask better questions.

You will find a lot of questions in this book. They are the questions I've asked that led me to define and learn about the Five Freedoms.

Acknowledgments

This book is the product of over twenty years of two of my favorite activities—learning and having fun. Along the way, I have had a lot of help.

Most of what I have learned about business I learned from my clients. I have been fortunate to be able to count a number of great companies and brilliant managers among them. Since our working relationship assures their anonymity, I cannot publicly acknowledge them. To all the companies and their managers who have enriched my knowledge about general management, I thank you for the education.

Among my long-time clients, Fred Wenninger and Jeff Wilkins were particularly helpful in the creation of this book. As CEOs with experience in multiple companies and businesses, they were exceptional sources of ideas.

As a business school professor I have been privileged to learn from a few thousand graduate and executive students. They thought they were learning from me, but the process really worked in both directions. I will continue to teach as long as I continue to learn.

The entire project could not have been possible without the support and encouragement of Bob Wallace, vice president and senior editor at The Free Press. Lisa Cuff, associate editor, did an outstanding job educating a naive author on his first effort at publishing a book.

Throughout the intensive writing process, Nathan Tacy has served as a personal creativity consultant and trainer. Whenever I got stuck, I would call Nathan and he would have just the right mental exercise to get me back on track.

The people at FOCUS, The Management Process Company did yeoman duty on several key dimensions. Lisa Hudson was the lead Research Associate who spent countless hours tracking down facts, figures, and stories, only a few of which eventually made it into these pages. Steve Ellis, Phil Mosakowski, Andy Ordoñez, and John Schroeder critiqued every chapter and provided excellent suggestions for changes to the manuscript.

Susan Squires Cox, my executive assistant, has taken on every job I have requested of her in the last decade. Assisting me in the preparation of this manuscript, no matter how many weekends or evenings it took, was just one more of her excellent performances.

Finally, my thanks to my spouse Jeannie who not only critiqued and proofread the manuscript, but was supportive in a hundred other ways so that I could take the time to have an outstanding experience, writing this book.

While the writing of this book was truly supported by a team effort, I bear sole responsibility for its content.

BUSINESS SENSE

Chapter 1
What Is Business Sense?

"What is the one thing every manager wants?"

"I don't know. Can there be one thing that every manager wants?"

"Of course. Every manager wants better results!"

Better results may mean more results, more consistent results, faster results, or even different results, but they are somehow better than the current results. It's the job of general management to get better results.

What is it that managers do that consistently makes the most difference in results? What are the ongoing management processes that literally cause success?

My search for answers to these questions was a process of discovery, and I found the richest source of knowledge in my own experience.

The answers I found there surprised me. They weren't as complex as I expected. The answers were so obvious that I am surprised that no one has written about them before. But no one has.

There are just a handful of things that successful managers do consistently that make the most difference in improving results. These five are the common sense of business. Each of the five is something that management is free to do.

Managers with *Business Sense* exercise *Five Freedoms* that create

1

better results. By exercising management's Five Freedoms you can take the most effective actions that will have the greatest impact on results.

Freedom #1: Choosing the Right Business

If you have the option, the first effort you should make is to choose a business that gives you the best chance for success.

Are there lousy businesses? Businesses in which you just can't win? Absolutely.

To understand what factors create a lousy business, we must first understand what a good business is. In a capitalistic world, a good business is one that has the potential to increase shareholder wealth. Period.

Lousy businesses have characteristics that are likely to decrease shareholder wealth. In some businesses you can't win.

No business is an automatic success, and there are more ways to lose than to win. The best a business can do given its essential characteristics is to have *potential*. Good businesses have three kinds of potential: profit potential, growth potential, and diversification potential. Any one of the three is a positive thing to have. Taken together they are dynamite. They maximize the potential for success by creating a field on which you can play and really have a chance to win.

Lousy Businesses

Lousy businesses are all around you. Take a look.

Businesses that have low barriers to entry tend to become fragmented because more and more people go into them until the shareholder returns are no longer there. Take any of the cottage industries like shoe repair, dry cleaning, or delicatessens (especially in New York City!). You can make a living, but not much more.

Look at all those businesses that you can enter fairly easily, that let you work twelve to fourteen hours a day, six or seven days a week, and your return is the same salary you could be earning by working eight to ten hours a day, five days a week for somebody else. But you do get to be your own boss! Big deal. They're still lousy businesses.

Businesses that are associated with things that people love to do can also be lousy businesses. How many sailboat manufacturers make money on a consistent basis? Why do restaurants have the highest annual failure rate of any business? It's because of all those people, known officially as "stupid competitors," who like to sail or cook more than make money.

Even businesses with significant barriers to entry can be lousy businesses when they become over-hyped as the "business of the future." During the 1980s venture capitalists invested in more than fifty startups that made disk drives for personal computers, a business that requires significant capital and technology. How many are still around?

Sometimes businesses do not develop because of limitations in technology. One of my clients once described gallium arsenide semiconductors as "the business that is now, always has been, and always will be the business of the future."

In effect, lousy businesses have so little profit, growth, and diversification potential that it doesn't matter what actions you take, you can't do much that will improve results.

Great Businesses

As noted previously, good businesses have three fundamental characteristics: profit potential, growth potential, and diversification potential. Which one should you look for first? Growth potential!

It is almost always easier to be successful in a growing business than in a declining one. Growth means that customers want more of the value that the business provides. Therefore, multiple competitors have the opportunity to be successful while avoiding fierce, direct competition.

Growth can hide a multitude of sins and often does. Business history is replete with examples of companies that were successful for years until the market growth slowed and real management skill was required.

Because growth potential is such a powerful factor, it tends to attract competitors. The number and type of competitors directly affect the profit potential of the business. Profit potential is directly proportional to the suppliers' ability to provide value to the customers in excess of the cost to produce that value. The profit potential of any one competitor in a business is directly proportional to that competitor's ability to create and sustain a significant advantage over the competition.

No matter how good a business is today, it will eventually mature and decline. Every business, like every person, has a life cycle. One of my seminar participants once challenged a group of sixty high-level executives to name the businesses that had not changed significantly in the last twenty years. It was, and is, a very short list. Virtually all businesses are constantly changing.

Constant change is the reason for the third requirement for a good business: diversification potential. You need a new business to jump to before the old one dies.

Instant photography and video games are two examples of businesses that had terrific growth and profit potential but little or no diversification potential. The results were stalled or failed companies (e.g., Polaroid and Atari). Without diversification potential, you had best know when to get out of a business. Otherwise you may see a lot of that shareholder wealth you have created disappear. We will see whether Nintendo finds more diversification potential in computer games than Atari did.

An example of a business with excellent diversification potential is personal computers. Not only do the computers hook onto lots of other things like laser printers that you could also produce, but a personal computer is a "scalable product." Increase its "scale" (i.e., its power and capabilities) and you have the "engineering workstation business." Decrease its scale and you have the "home computer business."

When growth, profit, and diversification potential are all excellent, it's much easier to get good results. Some businesses are so good that you have to try hard *not* to be successful. In the early 1990s networking of personal computers and graphical user interface software for those same computers are examples of great businesses. The demand clearly exists, the profit potential is huge, and the diversification potential is significant. Any company with competitive products and services should do well.

In order to evaluate the business' potential, you have to *define* the business first. What is a business anyway? How do you know whether you are in one, two, or twelve businesses? Chapters 2 through 5 in the first part of this book, "Freedom #1: Choosing the Right Business", show you how to define a business and evaluate its potential.

Freedom #2: Creating the Right Strategy

The ultimate strategy is to create a legal, unregulated monopoly in a growth business. Most of us have to settle for something less. So what is the right strategy?

The right strategy for a business is the one that will take the best advantage of its growth, profit, and diversification potential in order to increase shareholder wealth. That's true whether you are in a great business or a lousy one.

Creating the right strategy becomes even more important if the growth, profit, and diversification potentials of the business are somehow limited.

A brilliant strategy can transform a business.

Discount retailing was not a very good business when Sam Walton started growing Wal-Mart in the mid–1970s. There were already too many companies in the field, with too many stores. Cutthroat competition was fierce among the major discount chains. Several firms, including W.T. Grant, were in bankruptcy or in the process of going there.

But Sam Walton had a better strategy. He wouldn't compete with the other discount stores. He would compete with the small downtown merchants in rural towns who couldn't match his buying power and resulting low prices.

A lot has been written about Sam Walton's devotion to his "associates" in his stores and his fanaticism toward customer service. Both of these elements were critical to Wal-Mart's success, but I doubt they would have been enough to allow him to compete head-on against the large discount chains when Wal-Mart was small. It was his location strategy and his careful targeting of weak competition that enabled Wal-Mart to overtake Sears as the world's largest retailer.

For Sam Walton, an avid lifelong hunter, it was a turkey-shoot.

Creating the right strategy is the second most powerful thing you can do to improve results. Chapters 6 through 11 take you through the process of creating the right strategy.

Freedom #3: Developing the Right Systems

The right systems are those that provide the right information in the right form at the right time to the right people so that they can make and implement the best possible decisions.

Some companies use systems to gain significant advantages in their businesses.

Frito-Lay knows how many bags of which kinds of their chips are sold in each retail outlet each week. If sales decline, they can pinpoint where to look for new competition or changes in customer preferences. It is no accident that they are the only significant national competitor in the snack-food business.

IBM routinely reviews its suppliers' performance with each supplier. Detailed measures of quality, quantity, and timeliness are regularly tracked. Some suppliers have been embarrassed to learn that IBM knew more about their performance than they did.

The sophisticated casinos in Las Vegas, Reno, and Lake Tahoe know who is winning and losing how much money at which games of chance each day. They have complicated formulas to enable them to know how much to "comp" (i.e., make complimentary) rooms, food, and drinks for "high rollers." The profitability of each customer relationship is carefully tracked.

"System," in the context I am using here, refers to any routine way of doing things. The common characteristic of all systems in a business is that they are information driven. The three fundamental types of systems are information, incentive, and decision-making systems. The right systems provide the navigational processes that gather and process the information that management needs to guide the enterprise on its course.

Perhaps the single most important system in any organization is the incentive system. The amazing thing about incentive systems is how well they work—either to help or hurt a business.

The effectiveness of Sears' incentive system in its auto repair operations created a national scandal and a black eye for the company.

Sears' auto repair service advisors were paid a commission on the amount of parts and services they recommended to customers. An investigation in California by the State Department of Consumer Affairs alleged that Sears was selling unneeded repairs "90% of the time at the 38 Sears service outlets that were investigated."[1] Subsequently, the states of New Jersey and Florida entered the fray with their own investigations and allegations. When the dust settled, the chairman of Sears accepted personal responsibility for the problem and eliminated the incentive compensation system. The total damage to the company's reputation was difficult to calculate, but in the short run, auto repair business fell by 23%.[2]

Dynamic competitive environments require that management teams be prepared to shift strategies in mid-course. The right systems provide the information that enables them to do so. Chapter 12 gives you the fundamental tools for developing the right systems.

Freedom #4: Designing the Right Organization Structure

Designing the right organization structure is the fourth freedom management can use to improve results. The purpose of the organization structure is to provide a framework in which management can access and use the information necessary to create and implement the right strategy.

For some reason, changing the organization's structure is the first method most managers choose as the way to improve results.

I have seen too many situations where a narrow focus on the organization's structure has caused more problems than it solved. One company reorganized its business every six months for two years because it wasn't performing well.

Performance didn't improve.

The problem wasn't the organization structure, it was the strategy.

Frequent reorganizations can be a sign of a company using reorganization as a substitute for effective strategy development. Even very large companies, where a reorganization affects tens of thousands of people, can fall into this trap. Digital Equipment Corporation (DEC) reorganized its $14 billion business twice during the first four months of 1992.[3] Could DEC have been trying to fix a strategy problem by reorganizing?

As management is required to deal with constant change, organization structures are becoming more organic and less structural. Perhaps this means that companies will reorganize less often in the future.

How many ways are there to organize a business?

Most managers, when asked this question, believe there are thousands. In actuality, there are only four. Chapter 13 shows you where to use each to match your strategy and systems.

Freedom #5: Getting the Right People

The right people are the ones who have the combination of skills and motivation that will allow them to use the systems in the organization to effectively and efficiently implement the business strategy.

Many managers who run businesses think that their number one problem is finding, hiring, and keeping the best people. In many ways, getting the right people is the toughest challenge. Because there is more variability among individuals than among the factors in any of the first four freedoms, there is more room for error in getting the right people.

The problem is not that there are not enough good people. The best companies either find enough good people or somehow turn average people into good people in order to sustain their performance.

Examine any company that has a track record for exercising the first four freedoms effectively and you will see a company that good people seek out. Hewlett Packard is an example. HP is a company that has been in over a hundred different businesses since its founding. While the company has made some mistakes in its exercise of the first four freedoms, the mistakes have been few and generally corrected quickly.

When HP hires people, do they pay exorbitant premiums to get the top people?

No. In fact in some markets, such as the market for business school graduates, they pay salaries at the median. How do they get good people? A great track record for choosing the right businesses, creating the right strategies, developing the right systems, and designing the right structures is a powerful recruiting tool. Chapter 14 shows you how to get the right people for your business.

EXERCISING THE FIVE FREEDOMS

It is the general management team's right and obligation to exercise the Five Freedoms. Exercising these freedoms *is* general management.

The freedoms cannot be exercised just once, or even occasionally. Exercising the freedoms is not like exercising your body. Going to the gym three or four times a week won't ensure success. All businesses operate in a dynamic environment and general management must continually exercise all five freedoms.

The five are not independent from each other, nor are they equal in their impact on success. From the perspective of creating positive results, the single most important freedom is Freedom #1: Choosing the Right Business. It is the most important because your choice of business creates the context in which you must exercise your other four freedoms. The better the business, the greater the latitude you will have in exercising your other four freedoms.

The second most important is Freedom #2: Creating the Right Strategy. The business' strategy positions it in its complex environment and, given the growth, profit, and diversification potential of the business, allows the general management team the best chance at success. A truly brilliant strategy may even rescue the shareholders in a lousy business.

The remaining three freedoms, Developing the Right Systems, Designing the Right Organization Structure, and Getting the Right People, are also critical to success. Failure to exercise these freedoms effectively will lead to failure in the business. Unfortunately, even the brilliant exercise of these freedoms will not save the shareholders' wealth in a lousy business with a mediocre strategy.

Because much less is known about the effective exercise of the processes you can use to choose the right business and create the right strategy, I will devote a significantly larger portion of this book to them than to the last three freedoms. In my discussions of the last three, I will emphasize those unique processes that I have found to be particularly powerful.

FREEDOM #1:
Choosing the Right Business

"How good is your business?"

"What do you mean, how good is my business?"

"How much growth, profit, and diversification potential does it have?"

"That's a good question. I don't usually think about my business that way."

The quality of your business is fundamental to your success. It's a lot easier to be successful in a great business than a lousy one. Wouldn't you rather be in a business that has growth, profit, and diversification potential?

For some reason, many managers do not assess the quality of their businesses. Examining the quality of your business can be frightening. There are more lousy businesses than great ones. There are more mediocre businesses than good ones. That is just the nature of the population of businesses.

When I give a talk on the five freedoms, I warn the audience that what I am about to tell them can cause sleepless nights, brilliant in-

11

sights, or both. After all, what do you do if you learn that the business to which you have devoted your life is a lousy business?

Even when they are confronted with the facts, some managers still believe in the greatest management myth of all time. You've heard the one I mean. It's the one promoted by some business schools and magazines. That's right. It's the "Great Man" (or "Great Woman") theory of management:

> *"The right manager can make any business successful."*

Baloney!

Growth, profit, and diversification potential largely drive the creation of shareholder wealth. How else could Microsoft, a $1.8 billion company at the end of 1991, have a market value in January of 1992 greater than General Motors, a $123 billion company?[1]

By January of 1993, Microsoft's market value even exceeded that of IBM. While Microsoft was perceived positively, IBM was viewed as a company in decline.

Unless you have an accurate assessment of your business' potential, you cannot exercise your other four management freedoms effectively. If you don't know what the business' potential is, it is difficult to take advantage of it.

The process of learning about a business' potential—whether the answer is that it's great, lousy, or something in between—is always a stimulus for creativity in a management team.

Yes, sometimes the news is bad. But it usually doesn't get any better by ignoring reality. If you are in a lousy business, you have four options for action:

- The first, and most commonly exercised option, is to enter a state of denial. You can deceive yourself into thinking you are not in a lousy business and things will get better soon.
- Your second option is to wrest as much in the way of results from your business as its potential will allow. The best way to do this is to maximize the exercise of your other four freedoms.
- Third, assuming your business has some shred of diversification potential, you can evolve a bad business into the next, better business.
- Finally, you could sell the business (to someone without Business Sense) and invest in a better one. There is almost always a market, even for lousy businesses. Someone always thinks

he is a better manager than you are and can turn around any situation.

If you are fortunate enough—or smart enough—to be in a great business, hang on. It's going to be a wild ride:

- Customers will want more of your products and services than you can supply right away.
- Investors will want to give you money to help you grow your company.
- Great people will come to you wanting to work for your organization.
- The business press will ask to interview you about your brilliant management style.
- If you are also an owner in the business, you will probably even get rich.

It's a tough life in a great business, but somebody has to live it.

Most businesses fall somewhere between the extremes of lousy and great. Knowing how attractive your business is will give you a realistic starting point from which to choose your future.

Before we can assess how attractive a business is, we need to know exactly how to define one.

Chapter 2
What Is a Business?

"What business are you in?"

"I'm in the computer business."

"What customer needs do you meet?"

"We meet their needs for, you know, computing."

Perhaps the single most powerful question ever asked in business has been, "What is your business?"

This question has generated more soul searching and caused more consternation among managers than any other single question. "What business *am* I in anyway?"

Why is it so important to know what business you are in?

Because without a clear, crisp definition you will not properly understand who your customers are, much less what they need. You will not monitor the most important technologies or battle all the right competitors. And worst of all, you will not be able to see what effect your decisions and actions have on your results. You will be operating in a fog.

With a clear definition of your business you can assess its potential, develop an effective strategy, and take action.

Defining your business is probably the most important challenge I am offering you in this book. When you crack the code of business definition, the rest of what I suggest you do will be easy.

The question of business definitions was popularized almost forty years ago by the world's most famous management consultant, Peter Drucker. In the sixth chapter of his classic book, *The Practice of Management*,[1] Drucker discussed the challenge created by the question:

> Nothing may seem simpler or more obvious than to answer what a company's business is. A steel mill makes steel, a railroad runs trains to carry freight and passengers, an insurance company underwrites fire risks. Indeed, the question looks so simple that it is seldom raised. The answer seems so obvious that it is seldom given.
>
> Actually "what is our business" is almost always a difficult question which can be answered only after hard thinking and studying. And the right answer is usually anything but obvious.[2]

Unfortunately, the challenge of defining a business has been made even greater by the confusion surrounding the definition of the boundaries of a business. For some reason, many people believe that *transportation* is a business.

In searching for the source of this confusion, I have learned that much of it stems from a single example published in an article in the *Harvard Business Review*. How can a single example be responsible for so much confusion?

It's easy when that particular article has been one of the best selling reprints from the *Harvard Business Review* for over thirty years! I am referring, of course, to Theodore Levitt's classic 1960 article "Marketing Myopia,"[3] and the example of the railroads.

> The railroads did not stop growing because the need for passenger and freight transportation declined. That grew. The railroads are in trouble today not because the need was filled by others (cars, trucks, airplanes, even telephones), but because they assumed themselves to be in the railroad business rather than in the *transportation business* [italics added].[4]

Levitt's well intentioned but unfortunate choice of words has been the bane of many managers' mental machinations as they attempt to define their business. Let me illustrate the difficulty.

If I say to you, "You are now in the transportation business," what are you going to do?

The best answer I have ever gotten to that question is, "Move something!"

The problem is fundamental. Transportation is *not* a business. It is a sector of the economy that contains literally a hundred or more businesses.

To prove this point, all you have to do is visit your local metropolitan airport. Even if it is as small as Tew-Mac Airport in Tewksbury, Massachusetts, where I used to fly light planes when I lived near Boston, it is likely that you will find several businesses in operation. At Tew-Mac we had a student flight training business, an airplane rental business, an aircraft charter business, and a car rental business. All four operated out of a very small airport where the runway was 2500 feet long and about as wide as the typical suburban driveway. Imagine how many businesses in the transportation sector we could find at a major airport like London's Heathrow or Chicago's O'Hare.

Levitt's intent with his example of the railroads was a positive one:

> The reason they defined their industry wrong was because they were railroad-oriented instead of transportation-oriented; they were product-oriented instead of customer-oriented.[5]

Levitt's intent was to point out that the customer's needs must be a significant part of any business definition. The means of meeting those needs, however, may change over time.

Unfortunately, many readers of his article thought that businesses could be defined by customer-oriented terms like transportation, entertainment, security, defense, or telecommunications. In reality, each of these is a sector of the economy which contains large numbers of businesses. None of these terms adequately draws boundaries around an entity for which we could develop a strategy and take action that would yield tangible results.

Similarly, there are significant problems with the common product-driven definitions that some people use for businesses, such as computers, steel, automobiles, oil, and aircraft. These sectors also contain many individual businesses that need to be defined more completely in order to be useful.

Using transportation as an example, let's take a look at the difference between a sector and an industry. *Industries* are a collection of businesses that provide goods and services that are at least partial substitutes for each other. *Sectors* are collections of related industries. Figure 2–1 shows one way to conceptualize the relationship. Transportation is an appropriate definition of the sector that contains the air freight industry and the small package overnight delivery business.

Figure 2–1

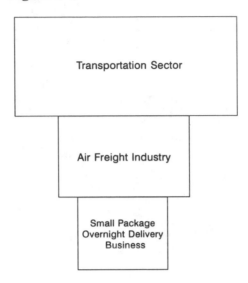

Using the refinements illustrated in Figure 2–1, notice the difference if I tell you, "You are now in the small package overnight delivery business." Can you take action?

Of course you can, because you have a well-defined business and you have models like Federal Express (FedEx) and United Parcel Service (UPS).

A business is a strategy unit. Each business must have its own strategy which can serve as a guide to action.

WHAT ARE THE MOST COMMON MISTAKES IN DEFINING A BUSINESS?

Managers without good Business Sense make two kinds of mistakes when defining their businesses. The first type of mistake occurs when managers *underdefine* their businesses. It is the most common type of mistake because it is driven by examples of business definitions like "transportation." The second type of mistake occurs when managers *overdefine* their businesses by focusing on individual product lines or fragmented organizational units.

Each mistake can and has caused business failures. But perhaps the most insidious problem caused by poor business definition comes in the

form of underperforming businesses. Without a clear, crisp definition of
the business, how can anyone develop a powerful, focused strategy for it?

Let's look at examples of each type of mistake.

Underdefining a Business

Underdefinition occurs when managers define a business at the level of
the industry or, more commonly, the sector. Examples abound.

A classic example is provided by Winnebago, one of the world's
leading producers of motor homes. In 1958, Winnebago was founded in
Forrest City, Iowa, to produce travel trailers. In 1966 the company
brought out its line of motor homes. By 1973, 91% of Winnebago's
sales were motor homes.[6] In 1976, the company discontinued travel
trailer operations, only to start them up in 1979 and discontinue them
again in 1981.[7]

Why did Winnebago fail in travel trailers? As with most business
situations, I am sure the reasons were complex. However, one contrib-
uting factor may have been the failure to recognize that motor homes
and travel trailers were different businesses, each requiring its own
strategy. By defining the combination of motor homes and travel trailers as a business called "recreational vehicles" it is possible to make
strategic decisions in such a way that either one business is favored over
the other, or many compromises are made.

An examination of motor homes and travel trailers shows that they
were sold to different people to fulfill different needs. Travel trailers
were vehicles that were towed behind large cars or small trucks and
parked at a site, usually for some period of time. They were sold to
younger people with children and lower incomes. They met customers'
needs for low cost, recreational shelter that was more comfortable than
a tent.

Motor homes were self-propelled, self-contained vehicles sold to
older, more affluent people. Sometimes characterized as "land
yachts," they provided a sophisticated "home away from home" for
weeks, months, or in some cases, years. With a number of different
systems like the engine and transmission, air conditioning, and appli-
ances, motor homes had extensive service requirements that needed
to be met by more sophisticated dealers than those needed for travel
trailers.

While there were some similarities in the technologies used to produce travel trailers and motor homes, there were also significant differences due to the motorized nature of the motor home.

Even the economic structures of the two businesses were different. Travel trailers was a lower margin business because it had low barriers to entry. Pricing was based on cost and was very competitive. This economic structure of the business led most producers to put their plants close to the markets because the cost of transporting travel trailers to the local markets could be a significant component of total cost. Doing all production in one centrally located plant might gain product efficiencies, but those were more than offset by the higher transportation costs incurred.

Motor homes, while a competitive business, had more room in their margins for premium pricing, particularly in the larger models that fit the "land yacht" label. Because of their higher price tag and self-propelled designs, transportation costs were a less significant component of total cost.

Trying to use one strategy to make both travel trailers and motor homes successful couldn't work. With significant differences in the products, the target customers, and to some extent the production technologies, significant differences in the development, marketing, and production strategies of the two businesses were needed.

Winnebago was fortunate. They only failed in one of their two businesses. I have seen other cases where failure to properly define the businesses has led both to fail because so many compromise strategies were developed that neither business could succeed.

Overdefining a Business

Businesses are overdefined in two common ways. The first is when managers equate business definitions with product lines. Every time they add a product line, they think they have a new business.

The second common overdefinition results when a company imposes an arbitrary rule about how big any single organizational unit can become. Some managers believe there is a limit to how many people one general manager can manage. Some companies set the number at 1000 while others believe the number should be 2000.

In one company engaged in a business in the medical electronics industry, the rule was to limit the size of a single division to 1000 people. The company had actually reached this limit twice. The first time, they split one division into two. When both of those divisions then grew to 1000 people at about the same time, they split both again. Then the company had four divisions, each thinking it was in a separate business.

One day I asked the four division general managers to bring their leading products from each division to our meeting. When I saw the products, they did indeed look different. They were different sizes, with different faceplates, and there were different model numbers on each. But when I asked what each one did and who it was sold to in order to perform that function, I got almost identical answers.

Then I asked a very simple question, "Who is your biggest, toughest, meanest competitor?"

They pointed at each other.

These four general managers thought they were in four businesses, but they were actually in one. With almost no differences in the technologies in their products, the products' features, or their customers, these four divisions were in the same business. As a result, they were their own worst enemies. Each division manager spent so much time trying to compete with his fellow division managers that he forgot about the other competitors.

By competing against each other, the divisions were wasting tremendous resources. For example, each division had its own marketing department which was spending a lot of time trying to differentiate its products from the other three divisions' products. This was a nearly impossible task that only contributed to increased customer confusion. There were no substantive differences among the products.

In the research and development area, each division had its own team. Because this company prided itself on being "customer-driven," each team was working on product enhancements that the customers wanted. Because the customers were the same for the four divisions, and wanted the same things, each R&D effort was essentially the same as the other three.

You might ask why the division managers didn't recognize these redundancies on their own. After all, they were part of the same company and located near each other geographically. The answer is simple: they were in competition. Each had his own fiefdom and fought the other three for every sale. In fact, when I told them they were in one business, not four, it created great concern among the four division general managers. They were afraid it meant that three of them would lose their jobs as general managers.

As it turned out, the rule about the maximum size that a division could be had become part and parcel of the parent company's culture. It couldn't be violated, so all four general managers' jobs were secure. What they had to do was develop a single business strategy and each of them could implement a piece of it. All they had to do was start talking to each other, stop competing and start cooperating. They had to behave as if they were part of the same company!

After some discussion, they decided that they could each take a part of the product line, centralize R&D, and segment the markets in such a way that their respective sales forces were not competing head-on.

The net result was the capture of 65% of the total market, and the highest profitability of any company in the business.

How do you avoid the problems inherent in an over- or underdefined business? You have to know how to define a business.

WHAT IS A PRACTICAL WAY TO DEFINE A BUSINESS?

What are the minimum conditions necessary for a business to exist?[8]

In its simplest form, a business exists at that point in time when a seller makes products and/or services available to a market. By doing so a seller establishes a potential economic relationship.

Does this mean that I am in the antique used car business if I make my 1929 Ford available to the market?

Absolutely!

It also means that I could exit that business by either selling the car or withdrawing it from the market. But, if I sold the Ford and then offered other antique used cars for sale, I could remain in the business. I am in a particular business as long as I continue to offer products and/or services, employing the same technologies in order to satisfy the same customer needs.

A business is defined by the combination of technologies, product/service features, and market needs that creates a potential or real economic relationship between buyers and sellers.

What would happen if I started offering maintenance services for antique automobiles? Would I be in one business or two? After all, many of the same people I would sell cars to would also want service, right? So they would be the same customer because they are the same person.

Wrong!

Each individual has many different needs. Each person is in many different markets with the potential to become many different customers. Besides, I would have changed the service I was offering from sales expertise to maintenance, and the technology used to produce that service from the "gift of gab" to tools, grease, and mechanical knowledge. So the markets, as defined by customer needs, the services offered, and the technologies used to produce the two services, are different. These differences would cause me to do significantly different things if I expected to be successful in each business.

WHAT ARE THE TESTS FOR DEFINING A BUSINESS PROPERLY?

There are three tests that help you define your business(es). They are the Direct Substitution, the Direct Competitor, and the Key Success Factor tests. These three tests have some interesting characteristics.

First, they are a combination of science and art. They are based on a combination of sound logic and common sense. You will probably need some practice before you can apply all three easily.

Second, the three tests vary in their discriminatory power. By that I mean that they vary in the likelihood of giving you the right answer if you apply just that one test. The most powerful of the three is the Direct Substitution test. The least powerful is the Key Success Factor test.

Finally, the three tests should give you the same answer from their three different, but related, perspectives. After all, they are looking at the same business definition situation.

Because each test gives a somewhat different perspective, I always perform all three. I have run these tests hundreds of times and in every situation in which the tests gave me different answers it was because I had not gotten enough data to run one or more of them thoroughly. Whenever you get contradictory results from the three tests, refine your data and run them again.

The Direct Substitution Test

Earlier, I defined a business as the combination of technologies, products/services, and market needs that creates a potential or real economic relationship between buyers and sellers.

Let's assume that you have two entities which you suspect might be two different businesses. If you treat them as one business and they are really two, you will make so many compromises in strategic decisions that you may cause one or both to fail. On the other hand, if they are really one business and you treat them as two, you might fragment your efforts too much and waste resources that you could use more effectively. Even worse, you might put them in direct competition with each other and lose sight of the real competition.

How do you tell if you have one business or two?

Using the definition of a business shown above, let's deal with the obvious, easy cases first.

To apply the Direct Substitution test you need to define your "possible businesses." You will be comparing them two at a time to see if they are really one business or two. If you are going to make an error here, overdefine your potential businesses by starting with your product lines. The Direct Substitution test is more effective at combining overdefined "possible businesses" than at splitting apart an underdefined business.

Once the "possible businesses" have been defined, you systematically compare like factors of the two "possible businesses" to determine the substitutability of one factor for another.

For example, if you identify the features in the products and services of "Possible Business 1," and compare them with the features in the products and services of "Possible Business 2," are they direct substitutes? In the simplest cases you get a "yes" or "no" answer to this question. For example, Coca-Cola and Pepsi are perceived by many people as direct substitutes for each other. A choice between the two is made on the marginal difference in taste. But for most people Coca-Cola and orange juice are not direct substitutes. There may be a few people who alternate between Coke and orange juice for breakfast, but I suspect they are a minority.

In addition to the substitutability of features you also want to know about the substitutability between the two businesses of the (1) technology in the products/services, (2) technology used to produce the product/service, and (3) the market needs served by the products/services. When you compare each factor between the two possible businesses, is the factor in one possible business substitutable for the same factor in the other?

One Business or Two?

Let's examine the two simplest possible results. In the first, you get "yes" answers to all four questions about substitutability. In this case, you obviously have one business, not two. All of the factors that create one possible business definition are the same as the factors that create the other. You need one business strategy, not two.

In the second case, you get "no" answers to all four questions. Obviously you have two businesses, because none of the factors are substitutable. Different business strategies are required for success.

Unfortunately, the easy cases don't cover all of the real situations.

In fact, since you are looking at definitions that have four possible dimensions, there are sixteen possible combinations that might exist. They are shown in Figure 2–2.

There is no exact science to determine whether you are looking at one business or two given the specifics of the sixteen cases shown in Figure 2–2. There are, however, some logical, useful rules of thumb:

1. Whenever three or more of the four factors are direct substitutes (i.e. "yes"), you are looking at one business.
2. Whenever three or more of the four factors are not direct substitutes (i.e. "no"), you are looking at two businesses.
3. All combinations of substitutability not covered in rules 1 and 2 indicate that the two possible businesses are in the "gray area" between being one business and two businesses.

Figure 2–2
Substitutability

Case / Substitutes ?	#1	#2	#3	#4	#5	#6	#7	#8	#9	#10	#11	#12	#13	#14	#15	#16
Technology In Product/Service	Y	N	Y	Y	Y	N	Y	Y	Y	N	N	N	Y	N	N	N
Technology Used To Manufacture	Y	Y	N	Y	Y	N	N	Y	N	Y	Y	N	N	Y	N	N
Features	Y	Y	Y	N	Y	Y	N	N	Y	N	Y	N	N	N	Y	N
Customers' Needs Met	Y	Y	Y	Y	N	Y	Y	N	N	Y	N	Y	N	N	N	N
Result	ONE BUSINESS					GRAY AREA						TWO BUSINESSES				

Y = YES   N = NO

Given these rules, cases #1 through #5 in Figure 2–2 would be situations in which you would have one business. Cases #12 through #16 would be two businesses. If you think about that for a minute, it makes sense. When three of the four basic factors that define a business are or are not direct substitutes for each other, that should be a good test of whether you are looking at one business or two.

For example, an airplane specifically designed for crop dusting may share a technology of manufacturing with a single-engine, four-place touring airplane, but the other three factors are significantly different. The crop duster has very different features based on somewhat different technology and is sold to a different customer. Thus with three of the four relevant factors being different, crop dusters and single-engine, four-place touring airplanes are products in different businesses.

The Gray Area

And then there is the third rule, the one that deals with the mysterious "gray area."

The "gray area" exists because businesses are constantly changing and evolving. Virtually no business is static.

When your two "possible businesses" are in the gray area it usually means that the two are either coming together to form one business or splitting apart to become two. When you ask the questions about substitutability of technologies, features, and customer needs, a clear signal that *convergence* or *divergence* of businesses is underway is when the two businesses are *partial* substitutes for each other.

Since substitutability is often partial, it is necessary to set some guidelines for when substitutability is and is not occurring. Based on experience, I have found a useful rule of thumb to be the "rule of thirds" (see Figure 2–3).

When comparing two possible businesses (PBs) on each of the four

Figure 2–3

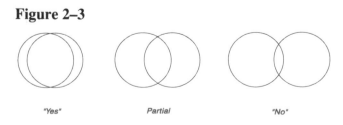

"Yes"   Partial   "No"

factors that define a business, a factor in one PB is a direct substitute for the same factor in the other PB if two-thirds of that factor are the same. That is, if two-thirds of the product features of the two PBs are the same, I treat them as direct substitutes (i.e., a "yes"). For example, while I might prefer a yellow legal pad to a white one, more than two-thirds of the features of the two kinds of pads are the same.

If less than a third of the defining factor is a direct substitute from one PB to another, then it is not a direct substitute (i.e., a "no"). For example, if less than a third of the technologies in the products from two possible businesses is the same, then they are not direct substitutes. If you look at dot matrix and laser printers, you will see that less than a third of the technologies in each product is the same.

If somewhere between one-third and two-thirds of the defining factor is substitutable, I label it a partial substitute. For example, the technology used to produce motor homes and travel trailers is a partial substitute.

Let's look at examples of divergence and convergence.

The Divergence of Businesses

In 1977 Debbie Fields opened her first chocolate chip cookie store on University Avenue in downtown Palo Alto, California.[9] Prior to that time, if a customer wanted to buy a freshly baked chocolate chip cookie, he or she would have to go to a full service bakery where all sorts of baked goods were available. Mrs. Fields created a separate business from just one product line in the full service bakery. In essence, she split out, or caused the divergence of, one business from another (see Figure 2–4).

Figure 2–4
Divergence of Businesses

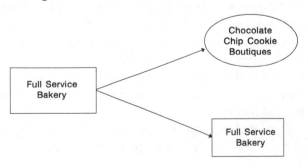

As with any retail enterprise, what was being sold at Mrs. Fields' stores was a combination of products and services. The product line was limited to a very few products. The cookie boutiques were located in high foot traffic areas like shopping malls. Even the ovens used to bake the products were specialized to their purpose. By limiting the product line and changing the service mix, Debbie Fields and other entrepreneurs (like Wally [Famous] Amos and David Liederman[10]) were able to create a new business.

Examples of businesses that have diverged from others are everywhere around us. They include such businesses as self service gas stations, fast oil-change shops, and one-hour photo developers.

The Convergence of Businesses

While some businesses in the "gray area" are in the process of diverging, others are in the process of converging to become one business. A good example is what has happened to electric typewriters, dedicated word processors, and microcomputers used as word processors. In the early 1980s these were three separate businesses. The products of these businesses met very different, although related needs. Electric typewriters provided the low-cost, high-quality method of producing written documents. Dedicated word processors had sophisticated programs for the editing and production of complex documents. They were, however, expensive. Early microcomputers had rudimentary word processing capabilities, but were limited in capability and could not produce high quality output because early printers were mostly of the dot matrix variety.

As microcomputers became more powerful with more sophisticated software, higher quality printers, and lower costs, the advantages of electric typewriters and dedicated word processors were subsumed in the microcomputer—or what we might call electronic writing systems. Subsequently, those systems have added capabilities that were only available through a commercial printer just a few years ago. A new business known as desktop publishing has emerged.

While all of the individual businesses shown in Figure 2–5 still exist as separate businesses, there are parts of several that have converged to create desktop publishing.

Monitoring and understanding the processes of convergence and divergence can be important in maintaining the flexibility to make the

Figure 2–5
Convergence of Businesses

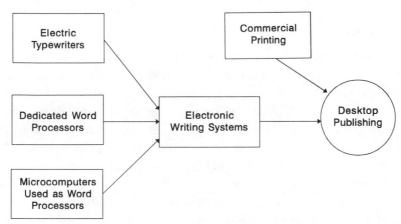

necessary changes in your business. As a result of the changes illustrated in Figure 2–5, IBM has sold its electric typewriter business. Another competitor, Wang Laboratories, one of the leading manufacturers of dedicated word processing systems in the 1970s and 1980s, has been unable to make the necessary transitions and has lost hundreds of millions of dollars.[11]

> . . . Arrogance is bad for business. And heaven knows, Wang Laboratories was one arrogant place after its great triumphs of the late 1970s and early 1980s. Its key product was its revolutionary word processor, a forerunner to the personal computer, a machine in such incredible demand that customers would wait months to get their hands on one. Unfortunately, Wang started to believe that its products were so good that customers would always wait months for them. In this it was mistaken. As for Mr. Wang, his arrogance took a somewhat different form.
>
> So convinced was he that his instincts were unerring that he simply refused the entreaties of his staff to develop a personal computer. It is quite possible that had Wang developed such a machine, it would have owned the PC market, since its word processor had given it a huge head start in penetrating the office market.[12]

Wang got into trouble because the company failed to see the convergence of its old business into a new business.

What causes the convergence or divergence of businesses? There are several factors, including economic, technological, political, legal, and social forces. All of these forces result in changes in the perceived value added of the business. (Chapter 7 shows how the "migration of value added" causes the convergence and divergence of businesses.)

The Direct Competitor Test

The Direct Competitor test is the second test of business definitions that I apply. If done properly, it should confirm your results from the Direct Substitution test.

To apply this test, it is once again necessary to define the two possible businesses that you want to compare. List the direct competitors for each PB. Direct competitors are those parts of other companies that compete most directly with your PB. For example, you would never list General Motors, Sony, or Siemens as direct competitors. You would list specific businesses within those huge companies as direct competitors.

Finer distinctions between businesses are usually more useful and accurate in applying this test. The way to make a mistake with this test is to list organizational units, such as divisions of competitors, as direct competitors. If that is the best you can do, however, it is probably an acceptable place to start.

Once the direct competitors of each possible business have been listed, I apply the "rule of thirds" noted earlier (see Figure 2–3).

1. If more than two-thirds of the direct competitors of the two possible businesses are the same, you are looking at one business.
2. If less than one-third of the direct competitors of the two possible businesses are the same, you are looking at two businesses.
3. If more than one-third, but less than two-thirds of the direct competitors are the same, then the two possible businesses are in the "gray area."

In general this test is quite straightforward and simple to use if you are careful about the direct competitor definitions.

The Key Success Factor Test

The third confirming, and sometimes the most enjoyable, test is the Key Success Factor test. In it you use as primary data exactly what the name implies—key success factors.

Its one requirement is that you must know something about how the possible businesses work, and what it takes to make them successful.

I prefer to apply this test with a team rather than individual managers because I tend to get better input. The assignment I give them is something like this:

> In front of you are two three-by-five cards and a pencil. I am going to give you ten minutes to write on the first card the five to nine things[13] that you must do to be successful in Possible Business 1. After you hand those cards in, I will give you another ten minutes to write down the five to nine things you must do to be successful in Possible Business 2.
>
> Just to make the exercise more realistic, I have chartered a jet to a remote Pacific island where you will be kept incommunicado for the next two years. In your absence, we will run these two businesses with what you write on these two cards. Your family's livelihood will depend on how well the businesses do while you are gone.

The results of this exercise are always interesting. Let's assume we have ten managers in the group, and each writes down seven keys to success for each possible business. The consistency of the keys to success for each possible business is usually amazing. In most instances, I have been able to sort the seventy items into a common ten or twelve for each business.

Once the lists are compiled, I apply the same "rule of thirds" mentioned above. If the keys to success for each possible business are two-thirds or more the same, they're one business. If the keys to success are less than one third the same, they're two businesses. Anything in between is in the "gray area."

WHAT ARE THE KEY SUMMARY POINTS ABOUT DEFINING A BUSINESS?

A business is the combination of technologies, products/services, and market needs that creates a potential or real economic relationship between buyers and sellers.

Many of the problems that managers find difficult to solve have their root causes in poor business definitions. Given that most people erroneously think "transportation" is a business, this is understandable. The most common problem is the underdefinition of businesses.

A business is a strategy unit. Each business must have its own strategy if it is to be managed effectively.

A business may or may not be an organizational unit. The design of an organization cannot define a business. On the contrary, the definition of the business and its relationships with other businesses in the corporation, if any, should play a key part in defining the organization structure.

When performed carefully, the Direct Substitution, Direct Competitor, and Key Success Factor tests will tell you whether you have one business or two. If run properly, they should give you consistent results and confirm each other. Once your business is clearly and crisply defined, or you know that you are dealing with a business in transition, you can proceed with identifying its growth, profit, and diversification potential.

The first thing you need to determine is your business' growth potential.

Chapter 3
How Much Growth Potential
Is There?

"How's business?"

"Business is great. Sales are down!"

"What? How can that be? Business can't be great if sales are down."

Of course, business could be great if sales are down and profits are up. The elimination of unprofitable revenues—the kind that bad customers generate—can be a good thing. But shrinking revenues is an approach with a limited future. At some point it's known as "going out of business."

Growth is the elixir of business. It is the single result that is most often used in defining business success.

Read the business press. In one way or another, most of the success stories relate to growth. The biggest success stories are about phenomenal growth in revenues and profits. Even the turnaround stories relate to stopping the losses, getting profitable, and then putting revenues back on the growth path. The themes of these stories are mostly about growth, growth, and more growth.

WHY IS GROWTH SO IMPORTANT?

Growth potential and actual growth are important because of their relationships with the creation of shareholder wealth, their importance in the development of business strategies, and the attention they draw to the business. Having an accurate assessment of your business' growth potential is crucial to your long-term success.

Increasing Shareholder Wealth

If you want to increase shareholder wealth, the surest formula is to create the expectation and then deliver sustained growth in revenues and profits.

Take Harte-Hanks Communications as an example. During the entire time this company was public, it had fifty straight quarters in which revenues and profits increased when compared to the same quarter during the previous year. Harte-Hanks' stock rose from its initial public offering (IPO) price of $2.63 [adjusted for subsequent stock splits] to $29.88 at the time that the company was taken private.[1] Shareholders who bought at the initial public offering price and held the stock saw their wealth increase more than eleven times in over twelve and a half years. That's one definition of increased shareholder wealth.

Harte-Hanks' increase in market value is not the exception, it's the rule. Let's look at a larger sample of well known companies and test a simple hypothesis. The hypothesis is this:

> If you grow revenues and profits over time, the market value (i.e., shareholder wealth) of your company will increase. Conversely, if your revenues and profits decline over time your market value will also decline.

Please realize that this is a very simple approach to value creation. It does not even take into account investors' expectations about the future.

To test the hypothesis, I asked my associates to analyze the Fortune 500 over a five year period. Using the Fortune 500 lists from 1992 and 1987 (1991 and 1986 year-end data), they determined that 352 companies appeared on both lists. Of those 352, complete data was available to sort 316 companies into one of four categories and determine whether their market values had increased or decreased. The breakdown into the four categories was:

		Revenues	
		Down	*Up*
Net Income	*Up*	12	164
	Down	28	112

Of the 164 companies that had increases in both revenues and profits, 141, or 86% also had increases in market value. Of the 23 companies that did not show increases in market value, 5 were aerospace/defense companies whose prospects for the future did not look promising because of expected cutbacks in defense spending in the United States. The remaining 18 were in varied industries, and would require additional analysis to determine why their market values did not increase.

Of the 28 companies that had decreases in both revenues and profits, 24, or 86%, also had decreases in market value. That is an interesting percentage. The fact that the percentages are identical in both cases is a coincidence, but the fact that there is a high correlation between increases and decreases in revenue, profits, and market value is not.

As you might suspect, in the other two categories where revenues and profits went in opposite directions, the changes in market value were mixed. Obviously, additional factors were important in the market's valuation of these companies and a more complex study would be needed to determine what drove their valuation.

Why is growth so important? Because it creates value. More specifically, the expectation of future growth creates value today.

Why are investors willing to risk losing their investments? Nobody invests to lose money. Everybody invests to grow. They invest because they have a positive expectation that the investment will be worth more in the future than it is today. When the business grows, the investment will grow.

Let's look at a classic example of value creation and loss: Compaq Computer Company. Until Conner Peripherals came along,[2] Compaq held the record for the largest first year revenues of any company. Compaq did $111 million in 1983, its first year in business. The company grew from zero to over a billion dollars in revenues in five years, also a record at the time.[3]

As sales grew to $3.6 billion in 1990 with a net income of $455 million the company's market value grew from $192 million to $5 billion, a twenty-six-fold increase between the first quarter of 1984 and the end of 1990. The market value of the company peaked in the first quarter of 1991 when it reached $5.9 billion dollars.

When the company reported a 19% drop in revenues and a 60% drop in profits at the end of the first quarter of 1991,[4] the company's stock took a nose dive. The ending stock price during the second quarter gave the company a market value of $2.75 billion, a 52% decline in market value in just one quarter. The market value decline continued throughout 1991 with the fourth quarter market value declining to $2.3 billion (see Figure 3–1).[5]

The message is clear. Growth is rewarded. Decline is punished.

Even the expectation of future growth alone, without much of a track record, can reap huge rewards. A recent phenomenon that illustrates this point is what has happened with biotechnology companies. At its IPO on October 10, 1980, Genentech had revenues of $3.4 million and a market value of $418 million. Similarly, Amgen, a Thousand Oaks, California, biotechnology firm had revenues of $1.5 million and a market value of $173 million at its IPO on June 17, 1983.[6] The purchasers of these stocks must have had some expectations of future growth in

Figure 3–1

Compaq Quarterly Financial History First Quarter 1984–Third Quarter 1992

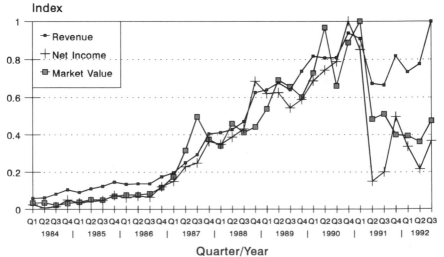

Note: Market Value calculated using the ending weekly stock price per quarter.
Source: Compaq Annual Reports and MicroQuote II, A CompuServe Service.

revenues and profits based on these companies' technologies. By 1991 Genentech had grown to $516 million in revenue and $44 million in net income.[7] Amgen had grown to $361 million in revenue and $34 million in net income.[8]

Matching Growth Potential and Business Strategies

Business strategies have to match the growth potential of the business. When the strategies and the real growth potential are inconsistent, trouble inevitably ensues.

Most managers want to believe their business has growth potential, even if it doesn't. Many have gone to great lengths to deny the realities of their markets. My experience with one client, a multibillion-dollar, single-business company, illustrates exactly how much managers want to believe they are in a growth business.

We plotted this company's revenue projections from their last five consecutive five-year plans, and the results looked like those in Figure 3–2.

When I showed the results to the top seventeen managers in a strat-

Figure 3–2
"We're not going to grow in the coming year, but after that, growth will really take off!"

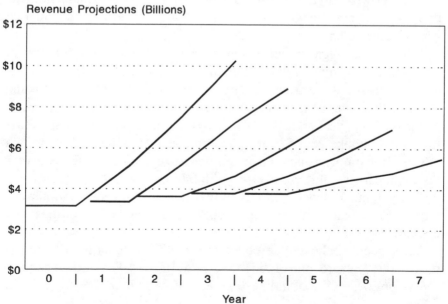

Revenue Projections (Billions)

egy session, some almost fell off their chairs. They couldn't believe they hadn't been in a growth business all these years. They had never taken the time to look at their historical projections.

When I then overlaid their actual revenues on the "hockey stick" projections, guess where they fell? Of course, they fell along the flat portion of each hockey stick.

The management team had believed for five years that their business was in a short-term slump and that revenue growth would resume soon. They had a business strategy in place that would position them for the expected upturn when it occurred. As a result they were carrying costs for excess capacity in people and plant and equipment that were destroying their bottom line. Once they realized that they were in a mature business, they made major changes in their business strategy to make it consistent with their business' growth potential. They cut excess capacity and people to size their business to match its market. They quickly improved service to retain their current customers. Profit margins improved.

Businesses eventually decline. Most managers do not like to be in declining businesses. A business that is getting smaller has less opportunity—unless, of course, you want to take advantage of the opportunity to learn how to lay people off and cut other expenses in order to preserve profitability. In one company that was experiencing the process of "downsizing," the standard joke among middle managers was that the new incentive system defined a "top performer" as someone who eliminated his own job.

While not enough growth potential can create strategy problems at one extreme, too much growth potential can be equally difficult to handle. One reason it's difficult to cope with a high growth market is the sheer mathematics of rapid growth. Let's assume your market is growing at 100% per year and all you want to do is maintain your share. How long would it take your $10 million company to reach a billion dollars in sales if it simply doubled its revenues each year? In its seventh year your company would actually do $1.28 billion.

Imagine the logistical nightmare that doubling sales every year entails. How would you find the people and build the facilities fast enough?

Some people believe that too much growth can actually kill companies. David Packard, one of the founders of Hewlett-Packard, once said, "More businesses die of indigestion than of starvation."[9]

Peter Senge, in his best-selling book *The Fifth Discipline,* highlights the problem of too rapid growth:

> For most American business people the best rate of growth is fast, faster, fastest. Yet, virtually all natural systems, from ecosystems to animals to organizations, have intrinsically optimal rates of growth. The optimal rate is far less than the fastest possible growth. When growth becomes excessive—as it does in cancer—the system itself will seek to compensate by slowing down; perhaps putting the organization's survival at risk in the process. . . . People Express airlines offers a good example of how faster can lead to slower—or even full stop—in the long run.[10]

Indeed, it is difficult for companies to develop strategies to maintain their rate of growth when their markets are growing rapidly.

For several years, *Business Week* has published a list of "The Best Small Companies."[11] These companies, all of which have less than $150 million in sales, are ranked according to their three-year results in sales growth, earnings growth, and returns on invested capital. A composite ranking is then calculated.[12]

A company's ability to stay on the list for any period of time is not very good. Of the 100 companies that appeared on the hot growth list in 1990, only about a third returned in 1991. Five companies outgrew the list (i.e., revenues became greater than $150 million). The rest just didn't make the grade. Staying on the list gets even harder as the years go by: "Just one tenth of . . . [the] 1988 class appear on this year's [1991] list."[13]

While there is no such thing as an ideal market growth rate for a business, growth in the 20–40% range is high enough to be interesting and low enough to be manageable.

Getting Attention

Expected and actual growth are also important because they attract attention. Potential growth attracts attention from investors, competitors, prospective employees, and even from customers. Everybody likes a success story and wants to participate in one way or another.

Investors want a piece of your action so they can increase their wealth. Their capital is often crucial to your company's ability to grow future revenues.

Competitors are looking for opportunities to grow and they try to take your business away if they can. This is the type of attention that you can do without, but the more successful you are, the more attention you get. The relative quality of your strategy and how well you implement it, in large measure, determines whether your competitors take your market share.

Prospective employees are looking for opportunity. If your business is growing, people come to you. Your challenge is to pick the best ones.

Even customers like to deal with a success. They know that there is usually a reason a company is growing, and often the reason is that the company provides value.

WHAT ARE THE SOURCES OF GROWTH POTENTIAL?

Whether the market is growing or not, almost every company *does* have growth potential. The exception is the company that has a monopoly in a dying market. All others can grow by growing with the market or by taking share from competitors.

The first and best type of growth potential comes from being in a growth market. A growth market is a wonderful thing to have. It means that demand exceeds supply. In the extreme, it means that you can avoid head-on, destructive competition. You and your competitors can develop win-win strategies that allow you to succeed and grow the market even more.

There are several lists published by the business press about fast-growing companies. Examine any one of these lists and you will find the same thing. Most fast-growing companies are in the fast-growth sectors of the economy. Take a recent Fortune "Fast 100" list. All of the companies on the 1992 list were public companies whose growth exceeded 50% per year for the most recent three to five years. Of the 100, 32 were in computers and electronics, 27 were in health care, and 16 were in businesses dealing with the environment and energy.[14] At least 75 of the "Fast 100" came from growth sectors of the economy.

The alternative source of growth is to take market share away from your competitors. You can do this by taking share from them in the marketplace or by acquiring them.

Taking market share from competitors is invariably a win-lose game. In the extreme, it can be a lose-lose game in which you and your competitors destroy not only each other, but the market as well. The latter case occurs when competitors are so desperate to take market share that all of them sell their products or services below cost.

The name of that game is "cutthroat competition" and the blood is green. It's called money. The winners of the battle are the competitors with the most blood and the strongest resolve. That is, if you define "winning" as gaining market share while losing a lot of money. But I suppose that's better than going out of business. The endgame is to get the other guy to go out of business so that you can readjust the industry's capacity down to, or preferably below, market demand. Then there's some potential for you to grow.

The airline industry illustrates the win-lose game. Competitors in that industry have engaged in cutthroat competitive practices for more than sixty years. In 1992, another round of cutthroat competition occurred.

By 1992 the seven largest air carriers in the United States controlled 91% of the market. Two of the seven were doing so poorly that they were operating in bankruptcy.[15] The other five were either losing money or were marginally profitable.

Competing in a high fixed cost business with large quantities of excess capacity is no picnic. Robert Crandall, chairman of American Airlines, noted:

> . . . This industry is always in the grip of its dumbest competitors. I was surprised when TWA cut fares. I don't understand TWA's strategy. It doesn't make any sense, and therefore I don't know what they will do to further lower fares. *All I know is that we have no choice but to match whatever low fare anybody puts out there* [italics added]. And so it will get as bad as they want it to get.[16]

In 1991, three major airlines went out of business in the United States. Eastern, Midway, and Pan Am all succumbed to the pressures of cutthroat competition. The growth potential for any of the remaining seven major players is tied directly to the failure of one or more of its competitors.

In this chapter I deal with assessing only the first type of growth potential, market growth. The second type, taking share away from the competition, is discussed in Chapter 9: "What Are the Alternative Strategies?" Without at least one of these two types of growth potential in your business, your ability to increase shareholder wealth is limited to what you can do to increase profits.

If you cannot grow revenues, the only other choice is to grow profits. Eliminating any possible inefficiency or waste to improve the bottom line is smart management.

In most businesses, short-term profitability can almost always be improved. But this approach can become dangerous if you reduce expenses too much.

Can a business be too profitable? Of course it can. If you cut expenses too much in areas that are developing the future of the business, such as R&D, or protecting the franchise the business has with current customers, like customer service, you may drain the business of its future.

The priorities are clear. If possible, choose a growth market. If a growth market is not an option, you have to get revenue growth by taking it from the competition. Finally, growing profits by improving the margins on flat or declining revenue can also be a source of increased shareholder wealth.

HOW DO WE DETERMINE THE GROWTH POTENTIAL OF A BUSINESS?

To assess the growth potential of your business, you can either buy the best market forecasts from prognosticators in the market research firms, or you can develop your own understanding of the forces that drive growth, or the lack of it, in your market. I recommend that you do both.

Since the market research firms that follow your business will find you, you don't need my help there. I can, however, give you a process for making your own assessment of your business' growth potential.

The three fundamental steps to understanding the growth potential of any business are:

1. Determine where your business is in its life cycle.
2. Assess how the three types of change—seasonal, cyclical, and structural—will affect the growth potential of your business.
3. Monitor the six meta-processes of change—economic, social, legal, natural, political, and technological—to be aware of their impact on the growth potential of your business.

If you take the above three steps, you will be well on your way to understanding the growth potential of your business and a lot more. You will in fact have a rudimentary understanding of the context in which your business operates now and in the future.

The Life Cycle

The fundamental driving force that makes understanding growth so important is the life cycle. People, products, and businesses all have life cycles. A business usually increases shareholder wealth the most when it is in the growth phase of its life cycle.

A typical life cycle of a business is illustrated by an S-curve with four contiguous phases (see Figure 3–3).

In the introduction phase, products are brought to market and a "new" business is created. Let's look at a specific example, motor homes.

The motor home business was created in the mid–1960s by a few entrepreneurs, like John K. Hanson of Winnebago, who felt that there would be a market for what amounted to a motorized travel trailer or a truck that had a house on it. Others soon entered and the business grew rapidly (see Figure 3–4).

With the exception of the rapid decline of sales in 1974 due to the Arab oil embargo and the subsequent gasoline shortages, the business exhibited a classic life cycle.

Rapid growth was evident until 1977 when sales flattened. The rapid decline in 1980 was due at least partially to another gasoline shortage. Although the shortage proved to be temporary, the sales of motor

Figure 3–3

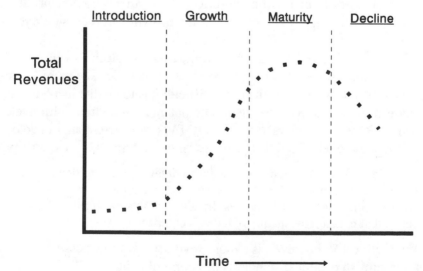

Figure 3–4

Motor Home Shipments, 1965–1991 (Includes Conventional, Type
B-1 Van Campers and Type C Chopped Vans)

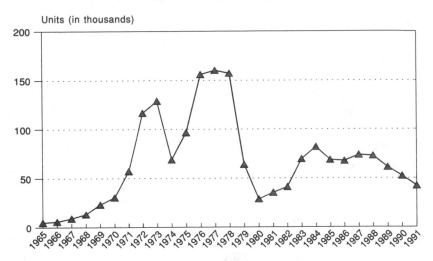

Based on data from the Recreational Vehicle Institute (1965–1971 data) and the Recreation
Vehicle Industry Association (1972–1991 data).

homes had only a modest recovery because the market had been satu-
rated. After a small growth spurt in 1984, sales of motor homes have
been relatively flat, with any year-to-year changes being highly correlated to changes in economic conditions. As a *discretionary* product,
motor homes are highly susceptible to the growth and recession cycles
in the economy.

While motor homes have clearly become a mature business with limited
growth for some time, other markets are less predictable. The more a business is truly a new business, the more difficult it is to predict its potential.

For example, it is easier to predict the potential of high-definition television (HDTV) than interactive TV. HDTV is an incremental development to standard television that provides better picture and sound quality.

High-definition television broadcasts an image twice as detailed as
today's television screens and comes close to matching the crispness and
wide-screen dimensions of movies. In addition, it is expected to deliver
sound that matches the quality of today's compact discs.[17]

Interactive TV, however, is a more revolutionary business which has
yet to establish technical standards or economic viability.[18]

By the end of 1992, interactive TV was only available in a few markets in the United States. The name was something of a misnomer because the interaction was not with the game shows or sporting events on the screen, but with other viewers who were also trying to outguess the game show contestants or predict the quarterback's next play. Whether this type of "interaction" would be as addictive as video games with progressive rewards was something to be determined.

It is possible to be either too early in a business or too late. In either case you miss the market.

Discovery Systems was too early an entrant into its business. Founded in 1985 by Jeff Wilkins after he left his earlier, very successful entrepreneurial venture, CompuServe, Discovery Systems was built on Jeff's dream to use the emerging CD-ROM (compact disc–read only memory) technology for economical mass distribution of information. Discovery Systems was very early to the marketplace. CD-ROM drives were expensive and were not selling rapidly. Because there was not a large enough installed base to supply information on CD-ROMs, Discovery Systems put the original dream on hold and took on the business of duplicating music CDs.

With huge excess capacity worldwide, the CD duplication business quickly became cutthroat. Discovery Systems went into Chapter 11, was reorganized by Jeff and eventually returned to a growth path as CD-ROM drive prices dropped and sales of the devices grew rapidly.

By 1993, some eight years after its founding, the company, with the new name Metatec Discovery Systems, was growing and profitable. It had finally realized the original dream by successfully producing and selling Nautilus, a monthly subscription service of information on CD-ROM.

At the other extreme of the life cycle, it seems that it doesn't matter how mature a market is or how cutthroat the current competition, someone wants to enter even the worst business. Can you believe that people are still trying to start airlines?

Since the beginning of 1991 over thirty attempts have been made to start new airlines. With used passenger jets in plentiful, inexpensive supply, a number of upstarts have put together business plans, given press releases, and sought funding. Only four have actually flown and two of them crashed—fortunately, only in the financial sense.[19] Two others, Kiwi International and Reno Air, have successfully started operations.

Without substantial changes in the growth potential of the market for passenger airline services, who would invest in these ventures?

Virtually all products and services go through a life cycle. If the cycle is very short, the business is called a "fad." (Remember Pet Rocks or Hula Hoops?) If it's very long, the business is called a "necessity."

The Three Types of Change

A human being's life cycle is driven primarily by the physiology of the aging process. The life cycle of a business is driven by three fundamental types of change.

If you can understand the seasonal, cyclical, and structural changes that are occurring in your business, you can predict its growth potential.

Seasonal change is both the easiest to predict and the easiest to survive, if you are prepared for it. Everyone is familiar with the impact of the seasons on such businesses as resorts and agriculture. But one of the most amazing seasonal businesses is the income tax preparation business. The perennial leader in this field is H&R Block. From a low of 960 year-round employees, H&R Block ramps up to over 77,000 employees during the tax season from January 1 to April 30 each year.[20] Just imagine the logistical challenge that process must present to Tom Bloch and his management team.

Almost every business is somewhat affected by the seasons. Whether it is the sales of personal computers or the amount of advertising placed in newspapers and magazines, the seasons usually have some effect.

Cyclical changes are driven by economic boom/bust cycles. Boom/bust cycles are driven primarily by global economic factors such as interest rates, the money supply, consumer confidence, government spending, and so on. These economic factors are particularly important in mature businesses with discretionary products.

Since the Arab oil embargo in 1974 there has been great consternation in the United States about the state of the U. S. auto industry. If you read the business or general press it sounds as if a growth industry is being taken over by manufacturers from other countries. In fact, the auto industry is mature in the United States. Sales of passenger cars and trucks are highly correlated with the country's economic cycle (see Figure 3–5).

The problem is that sales of imported cars have grown very slowly, but steadily, since 1970, and the domestic manufacturers have had to absorb virtually all of the fluctuations due to swings in the economy (see Figure 3–6).

Since there are very few scenarios that could return the auto industry

Figure 3–5

U.S. Motor Vehicle Sales 1970–1990

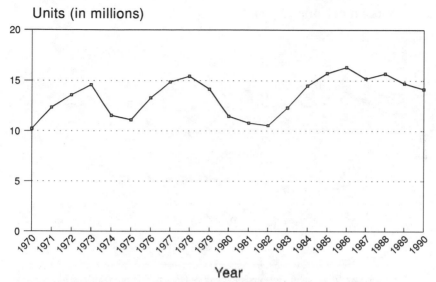

Includes domestic and imported new passenger cars and truck sales.
Source: Facts and Figures '91, Motor Vehicle Manufacturers Association of the United States, Inc.

to growth, the producers with marginal products will undoubtedly be the ones who continue to suffer the most in cyclical downturns.

Structural change occurs when one of the forces of change has such a large impact on the business that it permanently changes the structure of the business and in some cases eliminates the business altogether. For example, how many vacuum tube manufacturers are there today? How about full-service gas stations?

The sales of 1991 model automobiles in the United States were 12.5 million vehicles. This was "the first time since 1983 that sales fell below 13 million."[21] Most analysts attributed the decline to the recession occurring in the United States and, as noted above, the recession had a major impact. But other factors were also at work.

The automobile industry has made a major push to improve the quality of its products. In doing so, they have extended the useful life of the product. The average age of passenger cars in use in the United States has increased from 5.6 years in 1970 to 7.8 years in 1990. That is an increase of 39% in twenty years. The increase between 1980 and 1990 was 18%.[22] Customers do not need to replace their automobiles as often as they did. Thus, part of the decline in total demand has been due to

Figure 3–6
U.S. Motor Vehicle Sales 1970–1990

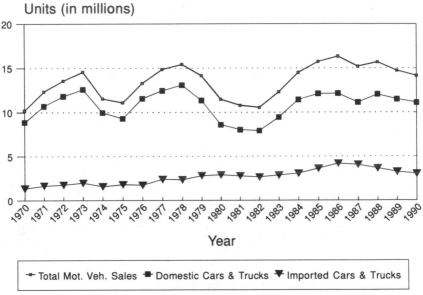

Source: Facts and Figures '91, Motor Vehicle Manufacturers Association of the United States, Inc.

changes in the products that give them longer product life cycles. This structural change in the business was caused by demands from customers for higher quality products that would last longer. The net result is a structurally smaller market because people do not need to replace their cars as often.

Deciding what type of change you are facing—and you're always facing at least one—is critical to continued success. Table 3–1 shows some of the mistakes you can make by an incorrect assessment of the type of change you must deal with in your business.

Monitoring the three types of change and assessing their effects on your business can be very interesting. It becomes even more interesting when you look at the impact of the six meta-processes on the three types of change.

The Six Meta-Processes

The six meta-processes create the external context in which your business must exist. They include economic, technological, political, legal, social, and natural processes (see Figure 3–7).

Table 3–1

		If you think it is . . .		
		Seasonal	Cyclical	Structural
And it's really . . .	Seasonal	Tune your strategy for the seasons	Good news: It will come back faster than you think	Way off base: May make needless changes
	Cyclical	Trouble: You'll need more resources than you think	Batten down the hatches and ride it out	May make unnecessary changes or sell too early
	Structural	Big trouble: this situation could kill you	Trouble: you'll try to ride out a changing situation	Change to meet the new requirements or get out!

Figure 3–7

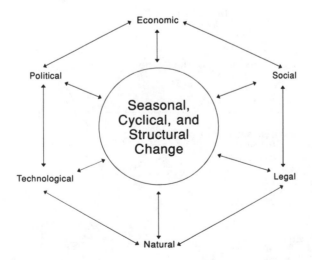

Every business exists in an *economy* that affects it. Whether it is the local economy of a Chinese village that affects today's rice price, or the global economy of the oil business that creates boom or bust cycles for tanker production, there is an economy that is relevant to every business.

Figure 3–8 shows the relationship to the economy of two types of products: a necessity and a discretionary product.

Knowing what type of product or service you have and where the economy is in its cycle is important in forecasting the growth potential of your business. For example, if you are facing an economic downturn with a mature discretionary product like motor homes, you can expect to see sales decline. On the other hand, if your products are in the early growth stage of their life cycle, there is a good chance that the economic downturn will have little or no effect on your sales. High growth businesses often experience little effect from the first economic downturn that they face. They are growth businesses because demand far exceeds supply. With all that excess demand, the real effect of the economic downturn is not visible to the business. Some potential customers may go away, but sales grow anyway because there is so much excess demand. This condition has led many managers to believe that their business is impervious to economic cycles, only to be clobbered by the second downturn they face when the excess demand is not so great.

Figure 3–8

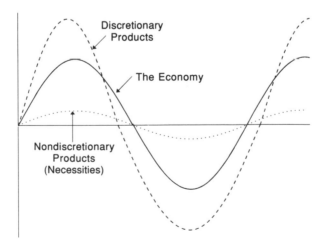

Such *political* factors as the Persian Gulf War, the reunification of Germany, and the decline of communism in the former USSR are harbingers of change that have or will provide growth opportunities for some businesses and sound the death knell for others.

Do you want to know a surefire formula for making money? Get the blue jeans franchise for Russia!

Businesses can be sustained by political actions even though they produce products that are not competitive. The twenty-six-horsepower Trabant, known as the "little stinker" for its noxious emissions that were at least five times worse than the emissions from any other car in West Germany, was produced in East Germany before the two Germanys were reunited. It was protected by the government in order to provide jobs.[23]

If you're in the handgun business, you undoubtedly have a fervent interest in gun control legislation. It could affect the growth potential and maybe even the existence of your business.

If you want to own a TV broadcasting business, you must obtain a license. You are limited to a total of seven stations, no more than five of which can be VHF-TV stations. These *legal* requirements strictly limit your growth potential, as does any licensing process.

If you are selling primarily to yuppies, your business may be in trouble. Yuppies are "out." Aging baby boomers are "in." Aging boomers have somewhat different tastes.

Another *social* trend that provides growth for some businesses is the growing number of families that are caring for aging parents while they still have children at home. This trend was created by improved medical care that enables people to live longer combined with many couples' decisions to delay childbearing into their thirties and forties.

The *natural* meta-processes include all of those forces of nature, such as the weather, that impact some businesses. If you want a successful fishing resort, you need to locate on or near a body of water and realize that certain seasons, such as summer, may offer more revenue opportunities than others.

Technology or, as Jacques Ellul called it in 1964, "the technological imperative,"[24] drives relentlessly onward. The list of businesses made obsolete by technology is endless. Transistors replaced vacuum tubes. Integrated circuits replaced transistors. Cable TV has largely replaced broadcast TV. Microcomputers that do word processing, adding machine, and other functions effectively replaced them in most offices.

The six meta-processes are continuously and dynamically changing in independent and interdependent ways to create the three types of change.

WHAT ARE THE KEY SUMMARY POINTS ABOUT GROWTH POTENTIAL?

No business grows rapidly, forever. All businesses experience a slowing of growth at some point. That is one reason you need to select the next business to jump to before your current business dies. At just the right time, you will want to jump to your next growth business.

Before looking for your next business, however, you need to assess the growth potential of your current one. You can do so by determining where your business is in its life cycle, and by developing an understanding of the seasonal, cyclical, and structural forces of change in your business. By understanding the six meta-processes of economic, social, legal, natural, political, and technological change, you can put your business and its growth potential in a larger context that gives you a greater understanding of its future.

Now that you have some assessment of your business' growth potential, you need to assess its profit potential.

Chapter 4
What Is the Profit Potential?

Conversation #1:

"How's business?"

"Business is great! We made a twenty-four-percent net profit this year."

Conversation #2:

"How's your business doing?"

"Business is great! We only lost a million dollars this year."

Is one of these people crazy? How can business be "great" for both of them?

What if the first person is in the software business and the second is a real estate developer, or a startup biotechnology business? Couldn't different businesses, or even the same business with two companies in different stages of their life cycles have different profit potentials?

In one sense all businesses are alike. Business is business.

But some have more, or different, profit potential than others.

Assessing the profit potential of any business should be simple. After all, in a business you typically buy something, like electronic components or a piece of land. You add value by assembling the electronic components to make a computer or building an office building on the land. Then you sell the computer or the developed land. Profit is the difference between the sale price of the products or services and what it cost you to create them. The profit formula for every business is to create value, sell it, and subtract the cost of creating the value. What's left is a profit or a loss.

Unfortunately, that is the way it works in only the simplest of businesses. A plethora of legal and accounting requirements make the assessment of profit potential a little more complex.

For example, have you ever wondered about the impact on different businesses that the requirement for a year-end financial statement imposes? Some businesses take longer than a year to produce and sell the value that they add. These businesses are automatically forced to show a loss on their income statements for some years.

What's magic about one year instead of two? Convention? And there is also the matter of the government wanting its tax dollars.

The paths to profit for a computer manufacturer and a real estate developer are somewhat different. You need to follow different maps when you examine their financial structures, or you might get lost.

Regardless of the type of business you are examining, there are three fundamental questions that you must answer in order to assess its profit potential.

1. How do you make a profit in the business?
2. How much profit can you make?
3. How will profitability change in the future?

HOW DO YOU MAKE A PROFIT?

Every business has two sources of profit potential. Profits can come from the ongoing operations of the business or from the ownership rights to the business (see Figure 4–1). In other words, profits can come from selling the *value the business creates* in the products or services it produces or from *owning the process* that creates the value.

In every case, and regardless of the legal structure of the company (i.e., sole proprietorship, partnership, corporation, etc.), profit potential must be assessed from the perspective of the owners of the business. The profits belong to the owners. They get to choose what to do with them.

From an owner's perspective there are four possible combinations of profit potential. The four cells of Figure 4–2 define the four primary

Figure 4–1
Sources of Profit Potential

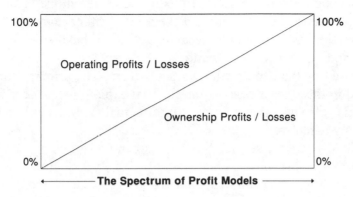

profit models. To accurately assess the profit potential of any business, you need to understand its profit model. If you misunderstand the profit model you will misunderstand *how* to make a profit in the business, and may miss a major opportunity.

The primary ways to make profits in a law firm and a real estate development company are significantly different. They are at opposite ends of the spectrum in Figure 4–1.

Figure 4–2

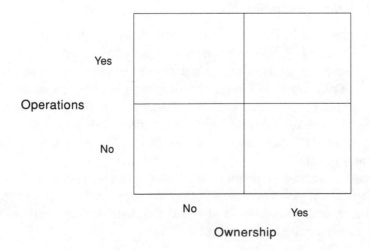

Profits from Operations

Many people-intensive service businesses make money solely from the operations of the business. Take a law firm or management consulting firm as examples. The assets of these businesses are not in plant and equipment or inventory. The assets are in the knowledge possessed by the people who work for them. The primary capital required in these businesses is intellectual capital. Money for working capital is also useful, but without intellectual capital these businesses are truly bankrupt.

People-intensive service businesses can be started by people who have intellectual capital, but little money. Usually these firms are set up as some form of partnership so that the owners can take the profits from operations out of the firm each year.[1] They rarely go public and if they do, they usually do not stay public as independent companies for very long.

Strategic Planning Associates (SPA), a strategy consulting firm; The Gartner Group, a market research firm; and Philip Crosby Associates, a quality consulting firm; all went public during the 1980s. SPA was acquired by Marsh & McLennan Companies, Crosby was acquired by Alexander Proudfoot, and Gartner returned to private ownership.

Little value resides in these types of companies because the company cannot capture and retain the value that is in its peoples' heads. The value remains in the people. If the ownership rights to the value cannot be captured by the company, then the company's ownership rights aren't worth much.

Profits from Ownership

At the other end of the spectrum shown in Figure 4–1 are those businesses whose profit potential is derived solely from ownership rights. If you buy raw land and hold it for a period of time hoping to sell it for a profit, the only profit potential your business has is in the appreciation of ownership rights. Since you added no value to the land, you depend entirely on market improvements (i.e., increased demand) to create your profits. There are no operations in this business from which to make any profit.

Because the vast majority of the value of a real estate development company at any point in time is in the ownership rights to the properties that the company controls, and those fluctuate widely, most of these companies are privately, not publicly, held.

Catellus Development Corporation, one of the largest publicly held real estate companies in the United States, illustrates the difficulty of consistent performance. Between 1989 and 1991 Catellus' revenues dropped from $255 million to $152 million during the nationwide real estate recession. Virtually all of the lost revenues came from reduced sales of properties, not commercial and industrial rentals, which actually increased. The impact on net income was devastating, dropping it from $104 million in 1989 to just $5 million in 1991.[2]

It is very difficult to assess the real profit potential inherent in a company like Catellus because the value lies primarily in the properties that the firm controls and not in its ongoing rental operations.

If you run a business that derives its profits from ownership rights, you worry much less about annual operating profits and much more about cash flow. Do you have the cash to make it to the time when you sell the property and realize your profit?

Businesses that derive their profits only from ownership rights are businesses in which some tangible asset is controlled by the owners. If it is owned by one set of owners, others cannot also own it. The asset must somehow be exclusive if it is to have much value.

Profits from Operations and Ownership

Most businesses fall between the two extreme profit models and have the potential to generate profits from both operations and ownership rights. In a typical business people with money and people with intellectual capital come together to form a company. The intellectual capital and the money are brought together to create a process for developing, producing, and selling products and/or services. The processes for creating value become the property of the company. The people may leave, but the value resides in the company.

When the company is first started, the ownership is divided among those with intellectual capital—that is—those who know how to create, produce, and sell the products and services of the business, and those with financial capital. The division of ownership is negotiated among the parties based upon the perceived relative importance of the intellectual and financial capital to the success of the venture. For example, in a biotechnology startup the owners of the intellectual capital, the technology, are extremely important. Without their unique knowledge there is no business. In a retail banking startup, however, the owners of the financial capital get most of the ownership. The knowledge required to run a retail bank is readily available from a number of sources.

In exchange for their contributions, owners get pieces of paper called stock. These pieces of paper are inherently worthless, unless they some-how come to represent control over some value. Value, of course, is always in the eye of the beholder.

The challenge for the owners is how to extract financial value from the company. Other than also being an employee and taking a salary and possibly a bonus, there are only two ways for an owner to extract financial value from a company. The first is to take cash directly out of the business as dividends. The second is to sell his or her ownership rights by selling the representation of those rights, the stock.

Whether or not a business pays dividends to its owners is a decision that is made by the board of directors. Period.

Whether the business is making or losing money doesn't determine the payout of a dividend. Dividends are a matter of policy.

During the 1970s, when many utilities were losing money, some maintained their dividends even though they had to be paid out of capital instead of earnings.

In 1977 and 1979, Portland General Electric had earnings per share of $1.09 and $1.06, respectively. In each of those years the company declared dividends of $1.70 per share.[3]

The logic of many utilities was that changing the company's historic dividend policy would do more to damage its ability to raise capital in the future than paying out some capital as dividends would do in the short term. Because utilities are capital-intensive businesses, the ability to raise capital at a reasonable cost is essential to long-term success.

Sometimes businesses that are very late in their life cycles, with too many competitors, are not able to generate profits from operations. In this case, the board may decide that the greatest value to the owners is to pay the accumulated capital to them as dividends.

There is a limit to how long a company with a negative cash flow can pay dividends. The limit is the amount of capital that remains at any point in time. Some businesses have been completely "harvested" by paying all of their capital to the owners as dividends.

In general, a wise board of directors does not declare a dividend un-less the business is generating a cash flow in excess of that which is needed to operate and grow the business. Thus, most high-growth busi-nesses do not pay dividends. They need their cash flows to support their growth. Besides, their owners usually have a greater opportunity to make money on the appreciation of their ownership rights.

What are ownership rights?

Practically speaking, if you own stock in a company, you own a proportional share of the net assets of the company. Net assets are those left after all superior claims, like any form of secured debt, have been satisfied. Thus if the company were to stop operating today, you would get your proportional share of what was left after the liabilities had been paid.

Unfortunately, when companies stop operating suddenly, it's usually because there aren't enough assets to pay all of the creditors.

The only practical right that stock ownership gives you is the right to elect the board of directors, who in turn are responsible for hiring and firing management.

That's it.

Ownership does *not* give you the right to a profit, special deals on the company's products, use of the company's technology, or even a ride in the company jet. If you don't like the way things are going in the business, you have only two practical choices. You can either vote for different directors, in the hope that they will change management, or you can sell your stock, if there is a market.

Capitalist economic systems depend heavily on the creation and maintenance of public stock markets where the owners of capital can buy and sell ownership rights in various companies. Without a broad public market that lets the owners of companies trade ownership rights in relatively small quantities, it is doubtful that a capitalist system could survive. The number of private transactions required to make the system work would simply be too large. Owners would not have a method of becoming liquid, and liquidity is a requirement for a vibrant investment climate.

As discussed in Chapter 3, the greater the perceived growth and profit potential of a business, the more investors will pay for the stock. They want the rights to the value creation system that is the business.

Unlike a car, a boat, an airplane, or a house, a stock has little intrinsic value. It won't do anything for you except to serve as a currency that can fluctuate wildly depending on what others believe it's worth. When a stock market crashes, billions of dollars of value disappear without a dollar of it ever changing hands between two people. That's because perceived value can disappear in an instant.

In general, the perceived value of any stock is directly proportional to the expected growth of the business' revenue and profits, and the consistency of the business' performance. Value is easier to perceive when performance is predictable.

Profits from Neither Operations Nor Ownership

If a business doesn't have the potential to make a profit from either operations or ownership, it is truly a lousy business.

If you want to make a small fortune in the airline business, start with a big one.

Sometimes a business is attractive because of the activity it involves. People will pay to be allowed to participate in the activity full time. For example, racing cars, boats or airplanes can be a lot of fun, but they are tough businesses in which to make a profit. If you are wealthy enough to be in this type of business, please enjoy yourself. But realize that it doesn't have much profit potential unless you become one of the superstars in your business.

Some businesses consistently lose money, and have little hope of ever making a profit. Eventually, after all of the shareholder value is drained from these companies and their internal cash flow cannot sustain them as going businesses, they are liquidated. This often happens when a business is in its declining stage.

One of my favorite businesses of all time is fast disappearing from the scene, at least in the part of California where I live. Independent hardware stores, where you can actually buy bolts, nuts, and washers in the quantity you want instead of packaged quantities from the factory, are being put out of business by the large discount chains. One after another, they are running out of cash, and the remaining inventory is being liquidated. They cannot compete with the discount chains' pricing which is based on huge volume purchases.

Those businesses that require more than a dollar's worth of incremental assets to generate an incremental dollar's worth of sales are very expensive to grow. The only strategy that makes sense is to "milk" or "harvest" them in such a way as to maximize the returns to shareholders or use the cash flows to invest in a new business.

If you acquire assets through the issuance of debt to grow a business whose profitability is less than its cost of capital, you actually hurt the profitability of the business. If you assume that the asset-to-sales ratio stays constant as the company increases revenue, marginal profitability will decline. You may be saying, "Of course I wouldn't do this, what rational manager would?" Let's look at an example.

By looking at the Fortune 500 lists in 1987 and 1992 (which contain fiscal 1986 and 1991 data, respectively) and calculating a standard cost of capital[4] for 1986 and 1991, it is possible to determine that in 1986, 266 of the 477 companies for whom adequate data was available earned a return on their assets that was less than their cost of capital. In 1991 the number had grown to 313 of 473 companies that did not earn a return on assets greater than their cost of capital.[5]

Of the 352 companies that were on the Fortune 500 lists in both 1987 and 1992, there was data available on 272 to determine how many had grown revenues in that time period and what their earnings were in 1986 and 1991.

Of the 272 companies who grew their revenues between 1986 and 1991, the following breakdowns occurred.

		Earnings Exceeded Cost of Capital in 1986?	
		Yes	*No*
Earnings Exceeded Cost of Capital in 1991?	*Yes*	82	21
	No	74	95

Ninety-five of the 272 companies did not earn returns on their assets greater than their cost of capital in either 1986 or 1991. If they performed the same way in 1987–1990 and used debt to finance their growth, these companies were systematically reducing their rate of profitability.

In businesses that earn less than their cost of capital, growth can be stymied because the sources of capital, debt and equity, will migrate elsewhere. You might, however, find some "stupid investors" who are willing to take lower than market rate returns because they love your business so much. Obviously, given the above data on the Fortune 500, a potential source of these types of investors are the major corporations who, assuming that they are using debt to fund growth, are continuing to invest in poorly performing businesses.

While this continued investment is sometimes done because management either does not have appropriate information or does not understand the situation, it is more often a case of fear. The fear is driven by two potential losses. The first is the loss the company will have to declare if it sells the business for less than its value on the company's books. The negative impact on earnings could damage the company's stock price. The second fear is that of losing a management bonus based on earnings. Given that most senior managers have bonuses tied, at least in part, to earnings, the write-down could also impact management's compensation at year end.

WHAT ARE FINANCIAL STRUCTURES?

Within each profit model, there are a variety of financial structures that are created by the opposing forces of the owners' desire for a return on their investment and competitors' attempts to capture business. In general, owners want to maximize the return on their investment. They can do so when the business prices its products at the point that generates the maximum total dollars of profit. Competitors will price their products to do the same for their owners. Competitors will use whatever weapons they have in order to extract the maximum profits from the market. The more directly substitutable the products are and the more that supply exceeds demand, the greater the tendency of your competitors to resort to the price weapon to take business. The more price is used as a weapon, the less profitability remains in your business.

Because the relative strengths of the ownership and competitive forces constantly change over time, the financial structure of a business is dynamic. You need to assess it both at a point in time and into the future.

Let's examine two companies operating under the same model, but in different businesses, to get a better understanding of how dissimilar financial structures can be. Table 4–1 compares the fiscal 1991 income statements of two real companies which I will call Company M and Company W for the time being. Spend a minute on Table 4–1. Which company has the higher profit potential?

Clearly, Company M has a higher rate of profitability when you look at the profits generated from operations. But Company W is making more absolute dollars of profit.

Does the absolute dollar amount of profits make a difference when you are assessing profit potential?

Table 4–1

Financial Structures ($ in Millions)

	Company M		Company W	
	$	%	$	%
Revenues	1,843.4	100.0	32,863.4	100.0
Cost of Revenues	362.6	19.7	25,499.8	77.6
Gross Profit	1,480.8	80.3	7,363.6	22.4
Research & Development	235.4	12.8	N/A	
Sales & Marketing	533.6	28.9	N/A	
General & Administrative			N/A	3.4
Total Operating Expense	831.0	45.1	5,152.2	15.7
Operating Profit	649.8	35.3	2,211.4	6.7
Interest Expense (Inc.)	(37.3)	(2.0)	168.6	0.5
Non-Operating Expense	16.5	0.9	0.0	0.0
Income Before Tax	670.6	36.4	2,042.8	6.2
Provision for Inc. Taxes	207.9	11.3	751.7	2.3
Net Income	462.7	25.1	1,291.1	3.9

Source: Company M 1991 Annual Report and Company W 1991 Annual Report.

Absolutely!

The number of dollars can have a major impact on the choices the owners have to make with regard to those dollars. The owners of a business generating $1.3 billion in profits each year have more choices than the owners of a business generating only $463 million!

Have you figured out who the two companies are?

Company M is Microsoft and Company W is Wal-Mart. The financial statements are taken from their fiscal 1991 annual reports. In 1991, Wal-Mart was the world's largest retailer and Microsoft was the world's largest software company. Each company's founder, Sam Walton and Bill Gates respectively, became a billionaire.

There are a number of important things which need your attention in Table 4–1. First, Wal-Mart's revenues are almost eighteen times as large as Microsoft's, but its profits are only 2.8 times as big. Given the financial structure of Microsoft's business, it would only have to have a little over $5 billion in sales in order to earn the same dollars of profit that Wal-Mart earned on $33 billion.

The differences in financial structure continue as we move down the income statement. Wal-Mart is a retailer. It buys finished goods and resells them. Therefore, a large proportion of its costs are in buying those goods for resale. Microsoft, on the other hand, creates software. This is "knowledge work" that requires little in the way of raw materials or components. That's why their gross margin exceeds 80%!

Conversely, Microsoft's operating expenses per dollar of sales revenue is three times as high as Wal-Mart's. A much bigger component of their value added comes from R&D and Marketing.

Operating profit margins also vary significantly. Wal-Mart has only a 6.7% operating profit margin, while Microsoft is much higher at 35.3%.

Wal-Mart's net income after tax is only 3.9% of revenues, while Microsoft's is 25.1%. On the surface, this might appear to show that Microsoft is in a better business with higher returns. But profit margins on operations are not the only ways to measure profitability. They are certainly not the only ways investors measure their returns. Investors are more interested in the return the business is generating on their investment. Table 4–2 shows some different measures.

When you examine the returns on stockholders' equity you see that both are very good companies. Wal-Mart is earning 27.7% and Microsoft is earning 40.8%. While a stockholder takes the highest return he/she can get, most would be very happy with a consistent 27% return. If you invest just $10,000 and compound it at 27% per year for ten years, your investment would be worth $109,153. That kind of growth should outpace inflation!

Table 4–2

	Company	
	M	**W**
Return on Equity[1]	40.8%	27.7%
Return on Assets[2]	33.7%	13.2%
Return on Invested Capital[3]	57.3%	28.2%

[1] Average equity
[2] Average assets
[3] Earnings before taxes, interest, and dividends divided by common and preferred stock equity plus long-term funded debt.

Over time most companies in the same business develop similar financial structures, but not every company that competes in a business experiences the same financial results. In fact, in most businesses one or two companies usually outperform the others consistently. Look at Boeing in jetliners, Wal-Mart in retailing, or Microsoft in software.

But even the high performers experience results that are related to the realities of the business. Wal-Mart's results are a lot more like other retailers' than like Microsoft's.

The opposing forces of the owners' desire for a return on their investment and competitors' attempts to capture business will continue to do battle over time. To continue to participate, investors will need some minimum return on their investment. Competitors will need a certain minimum amount of profitable business, or they will leave the fray.

WHAT CAUSES PROFITABILITY TO CHANGE?

The profit potential of a business over time is directly related to:

1. The magnitude of the growth potential in the business.
2. The ability of the participants in the business to keep competition out by building barriers to entry.
3. The ability of any competitor to build barriers to success against others.

I discussed the first topic in Chapter 3 so let's move on to look at barriers to entry and success.

Pick an industry that has been around for a while and look at its history. How many of the companies that created the industry are still around?

Where is Bowmar in calculators? What about IMSAI in personal computers? Where is Pierce Arrow in automobiles, or Munson in television sets? Where is Univac in computers, Norton in motorcycles, or Pan American in airlines?

Let me give you an absolute, ironclad guarantee. If you create a good business, one that has growth, profit, and diversification potential, but you fail to build significant *barriers to entry,* someone will come along and try to take that business away from you. If you can't build barriers to entry strong enough to keep competitors out, you must build *barriers to success* that will keep them from taking your fair share. If you don't, they will put you out of business. That's the free enterprise system!

Barriers to Entry

Many things can serve as barriers to entry. Some of the key barriers can be strong enough to make potential competitors decide not to compete with you.

The ultimate use of barriers to entry is to make them so strong that you have a monopoly in the business. While pure, unregulated monopolies may be difficult to create, there are many examples of "near monopolies." If you own the only daily newspaper in a town of 150,000 people, or the only supermarket in a town of 5,000 people, you own a near monopoly.

Any time you can so dominate a market that the entry of a second competitor would create large amounts of excess capacity, you have a near monopoly. Creating a near monopoly is a great strategy as long as your potential competitors are intelligent and rational. Once in a while you will run into a potential competitor who is either stupid or crazy.

Capital

The first barrier that most people encounter when entering a business is the capital requirement. Capital requirements come in two forms.

The first is *startup* capital. It is the amount of capital you need to invest if you have no related businesses. It is also the amount of capital you need if you are starting a new company to be in a particular business.

The second type of capital is *incremental* capital. If you are entering a business for which you already have the necessary technology, or perhaps plant capacity that can be used to enter the business, then you do not need to spend the same amount of capital as someone who has neither of these assets. Therefore, if you are in the motor home business and want to enter the travel trailer business, you may be able to do so with an incremental capital investment.

Capital is, of course, used to create the infrastructure of the business. It is used to purchase assets and fund the growth of the business.

A certain, minimal amount of capital is required to enter any business. If you want to start a local delicatessen, the amount of capital required is much less than if you want to build a new line of light airplanes. The capital required simply to construct the airplane and get a four-passenger single-engine airplane certified by the government is in excess of $10 million.[6]

Brand Identification/Reputation

The second barrier to entry is the positive association of a particular brand of product or, in the case of a service business, reputation, with one and only one competitor. The names Coca-Cola, Bayer, Boeing, and McKinsey & Co. all have a particular ring that is associated with quality and leadership.

At the flight operations desk in Wichita for the Beechcraft Aircraft Company there used to be a sign that said, "Beechcraft on aircraft is like sterling on silver." Beechcraft airplanes are well known for their durability and luxury.

Brand identification can be an effective barrier to entry, but it takes time and a leadership position to create it.

Technology

Technology is one of the most important barriers to entry at the end of the twentieth century. The rapid pace of technological development creates and kills businesses in faster and faster cycles.

Technology, when used as a barrier to entry, comes in two flavors, patented and proprietary.

Patented technology is that which a government of a country has granted protection for some specified period of time. The advantage to patented technology is that there is legal recourse against anyone who violates the patent. The disadvantage to patented technology is that it becomes public in detail. Others then have an opportunity to try to work around the patent by doing something in a slightly different and therefore legal way.

Proprietary technology has the opposite set of advantages and disadvantages. Because a technology is proprietary, the key to using it as a barrier to entry is keeping it secret. If it is discovered by a competitor, it can be used. The original discoverer of the technology has no legal recourse.

When IBM introduced its Personal Computer in 1981 it adopted, for the first time in any of its computers, an "open" system architecture. By moving away from its historic approach of maintaining its systems as proprietary, IBM did two things. First, they assured rapid, early success in the marketplace. At the time, the leading microcomputer was the Apple II, which also had an open architecture. The rules of the game had been set by Apple, and IBM complied.

The second thing that was certain was that other manufacturers would copy or "clone" the IBM machine. With IBM's traditional pricing strategy, they created a price umbrella under which the clone manufacturers could operate and take business from IBM. Becuase IBM lowered the barrier to entry, competition in the PC market became intense.

Meanwhile, Apple introduced its Macintosh computer with a proprietary operating system, creating a barrier to the use of that system.

Control of Scarce Resources

Not all resources are equally available to all competitors. The lack of raw materials, people with specialized skills, or facilities can each be barriers to entry to a particular business. In the area of raw materials, aluminum has been on allocation in many countries around the world at various times over the last thirty years. If you cannot get the raw material, it is pretty difficult to make the finished product.

There are not enough trained people in some technical fields to meet the needs of all of the competitors. For example, when compact disc technology for music CDs came on the scene there were very few people in the world who knew how to manufacture them effectively. Control over the scarce resource represented by those people was a powerful weapon for the leading manufacturers.

Scarce facilities can also be a barrier to entry. Independent filmmakers cannot afford to build the expensive sound stages and the "back lots" that larger movie production companies own. Unless they can somehow lease such facilities, they are barred from making their movies.

Legal/Regulatory

Many businesses have legal barriers to entry. If you want to practice medicine, psychiatry, or home building, you must get a license to do so. The requirements for the license may be stringent or minor, but they do provide some barriers to entry.

Some businesses can build barriers to entry because they are *exempted* from certain laws. Major league baseball is an example of a business that has been allowed to create barriers to entry because it has been largely exempted from meeting the requirements of the antitrust laws. Each league is a legal cartel which strictly limits the number of franchises that are available. If you want to own a major league baseball team, you cannot simply put together a group of investors, hire players, coaches, and managers, and be in business. None of the current teams will play against you. In order to start a baseball team, you would have to create an entire league!

Distribution (Channel Clout)

In some businesses, barriers can be created by limiting the competitors' access to distribution channels. One way to do this is to acquire the distribution channels so that you control them.

Whenever retail distribution is involved, shelf space becomes important. Only so many products will fit on the shelves. Once the channel is full, a new product must create some compelling reason—for example, customer demand—or the retailers won't switch.

Barriers to Exit

Anything that can be a barrier to entry can also be a barrier to exit.

High barriers to exit can impact profit potential by creating lousy businesses.

All those things you have to do to prevent others from taking your business away can also be things that force you to stay in the business longer than you should. Perhaps the most common example of this is the barrier to exit created by capital. When a business is worth less than its book value, a company must take a write-down against profits when it exits the business. This is a huge barrier that prevents many management teams from exiting businesses that no longer have growth, profit, or diversification potential. Thus, many companies stay in a business much longer than they should because of the barrier to exit created by capital.

Another common barrier to exit is the damage exiting could do to a company's reputation. A company that has been successful in a business simply cannot leave that business without losing the faith of its customers.

When Kodak first entered the copier business against Xerox, Kodak could not compete successfully. They withdrew their products from the market with a promise to return. Because Kodak was not perceived as a copier company and Xerox was known to be a formidable competitor, Kodak's barriers to exit were low. Eventually, Kodak did successfully reenter the copier market with a high quality line.

However, when Kodak was in a cutthroat competitive battle with

Polaroid in instant photography in the late 1970s, Kodak could not exit the business voluntarily. Any admission of defeat in instant photography could seriously damage Kodak's reputation and hurt its core business of conventional photography. Even though it was losing money, Kodak had to stay and fight to protect its name and its customers' confidence in the future of the company.

Eventually, Kodak was forced to exit the instant photography business in 1986 when it lost a patent suit filed by Polaroid in 1976.[7] Given how much money they had lost in the business, I'll bet that there was a huge sigh of relief at Kodak's headquarters.

Barriers to Success

Because the process of building barriers to success is the art and science of creating an effective business strategy, the bulk of that discussion is found under Freedom 2 later in this book. Let me just introduce the topic here.

If you have competition in your business, and almost everyone does, the barriers to entry were not strong enough to keep others out. It's now up to you to develop and implement a business strategy that will keep the competition from taking your business away.

As you will see in Chapter 6, there are many elements to a business strategy. Any and all of them can be used to create barriers to your competitors' success. Two of the most powerful competitive weapons you can use are the product's or service's features and price. They can be combined and analyzed with a tool called "The Chess Game" (Figure 4–3).

The Chess Game helps you assess whether your current combination of features and pricing will be a winner or loser in the marketplace. To apply The Chess Game, you need to know what features the customers want and in what priority. You can then determine the relative merits of your offering's features against each of your competitor's offerings. Do you have more features, the same features, or fewer features that the customers want?

Once you have assessed the features, you can do the same for the price that the customers pay for the features. Is your price perceived as higher, lower, or the same as each of your competitors?

When Lexus entered the luxury car market in the United States in 1989, it sold approximately 18,000 cars compared to approximately 77,000 cars sold by Mercedes. By 1991, just two years later, Lexus sold

Figure 4–3
The Chess Game

FEATURES

		Fewer	Same	More
	Lower	80/20 features that meet "must" requirements. Price battle, must be LCP.*	Price battle, must be LCP*	Differentiated big winner
PRICE	**Same**	Loser	Execution is key	Differentiated winner
	Higher	Big loser	Loser	Must have the features people will pay for.

*LCP = Low cost producer.

71,206 cars and Mercedes sold only 58,868 cars.[8] Why? Lexus had the same or better features at a substantially lower price.

If Lexus can sustain its position in the Chess Game, they have a winning strategy that will build a barrier to success for Mercedes.

The Chess Game can also be used to predict a competitor's behavior. The managers at Mercedes are anything but stupid. What are they likely to do?

They will probably either move to bring out products that will compete head-on with Lexus in features and price, or find those features that customers will pay a premium for. If they only go for the "head-on" strategy, the winner will be the company that best executes the details of its strategy.

WHAT ARE THE KEY SUMMARY POINTS ABOUT PROFIT POTENTIAL?

Profits in a business come from either operations or ownership rights. The exact source and mix of profits defines a business' *profit model*.

Within each profit model there are a variety of financial structures that are created by the opposing forces of the owners' desire for a return on their investment and competitors' attempts to capture business. Owners will try to maximize profits while competitors will cut margins in an attempt to gain business at a reasonable return.

The primary weapons used by competitors to keep other players out of a business and maximize their profits are *barriers to entry*. Examples of barriers include (a) capital, (b) brand identification/reputation, (c) technology, (d) control of scarce resources, (e) laws and regulations, and (f) distribution (channel clout). The ultimate use of barriers to entry is to create a legal, unregulated monopoly.

The risk to building barriers to entry is that everything that can be a barrier to another competitor's entry into your business can become a barrier to your exit. It is possible to get stuck in a business.

Once others have entered your business, it is your job to create a business strategy which incorporates such powerful *barriers to success* that it prevents, or at least limits, your competitors' success to something less than your own. The Chess Game is one tool you can use to test the quality of your strategy against your competition.

No matter how good you are at building barriers to entry and success, no business lasts forever. You need to know what your next business will be while the first one is still doing well. That's why you need to understand diversification potential.

Chapter 5
Where Is the Diversification Potential?

"What's your next business?"

"What do you mean, 'next business'? I'm too busy running this one to think about the next one!"

"Don't you know that the best time to pursue diversification is before you have to?"

"Then let's get started!"

Diversification potential is the third characteristic of a great business. Although it is important, it is less crucial to success than growth and profit potential.

If you have a business with excellent growth and profit potential, but no diversification potential, you need a clear, clean exit strategy from the business. As long as you can exit because the barriers are not too high, a business with only growth and profit potential can be a very good business.

Diversification potential makes the marginal difference between a very good business and a great one.

The purpose of this chapter is to show where to look for the diversification potential inherent in one business to create or enter another, preferably better business. When choosing a business to be in, one with high diversification potential is preferable to one without potential.

All businesses go through the life cycle introduced in Chapter 3. Whether a business' life cycle lasts a few months or a hundred years depends on the nature of the business and how the forces of change affect it.

As your business' growth begins to slow, you have some choices to make. You may want to begin an exit strategy by changing the method of increasing your shareholders' wealth by paying dividends if you haven't paid them in the past, or increasing them if you have. After all, you won't need as much cash flow for future growth.

Or you may want to diversify your business in such a way that you move on gradually to the life cycle (see Figure 5–1) of your next business.

There are only two ways that you can diversify your company. You can either start a new business or acquire one. There are some variations on these two methods depending on whether you do either of these things alone or with another company.

There may be many different reasons that you want to diversify your company. As mentioned above, growth in revenue and profits may have slowed and you need to regain that growth in order to continue to increase shareholder wealth. There may be opportunities to serve additional needs in your customer base. You may see how you can use your

Figure 5–1

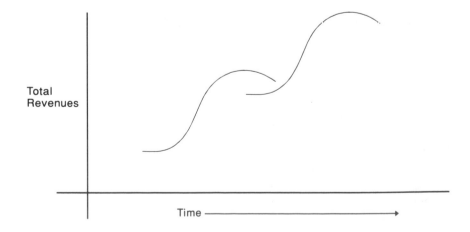

current technologies to serve different customers. Other technologies may be developing in such a way that they will encroach upon your products and take away your current customers. Or perhaps you have accumulated too much cash on your balance sheet and are worried about someone making a hostile takeover bid and buying you with your own money.

There are also many different logics that can be used to build a diversified company. That logic, or *set of criteria that determine what businesses you will and will not be in and how you will allocate resources among them,* is your *corporate strategy.* As soon as your company enters more than one business, you have a corporate strategy. As you will see in Chapter 6, a corporate strategy is very different from a *business strategy.*

This chapter is not about the best way to build a multiple-business company. That topic requires another entire book. (I think I'll call it "Corporate Sense, The Rarest Form of Common Sense!") The processes necessary to build and sustain success in multiple business corporations are related to, but significantly different from, the processes for creating and sustaining success in a single business.

Let's start with a premise.

The only valid reason to take a company into multiple businesses is to enhance shareholder wealth.

Any other reason for taking a company into multiple businesses should be done in a different company, probably with different shareholders.

Please notice that I did not say increase shareholder wealth. I said *enhance* it. Increasing shareholder wealth is clearly enhancing it. So is protecting shareholder wealth from erosion.

WHAT IS DIVERSIFICATION POTENTIAL?

A business has diversification potential if you can use specific knowledge gained in that business to enhance the probability of success in a second business. In most cases the specific knowledge that is valuable in diversification is knowledge about the customers, the products, or the technologies in the business. It is valuable because it often provides you with a competitive advantage over others.

Please note that I did not define diversification potential as the ability to use the resources of one business in the second business. "Resources" could include money and money is an undifferentiated resource which has no knowledge content. Having money to invest may improve your chances of success in a business, but money, other than perhaps in amount, does not provide a differentiating impact in any particular business. It is equally useful in all businesses. Anybody's money is equally as good as yours in creating odds in favor of success. If a business is a good business, there will be plenty of investors, many of whom have more money than you do, who will be willing to invest.

General knowledge about business, such as how accounting works or what alternatives there are for pricing products, is not very useful in diversification. With the large number of MBA programs available that teach the subject matter, general knowledge about business is a near-commodity.

The key to looking for diversification potential is to understand how *what you have learned from being in one business gives you an advantage in another business*. To understand how you acquire such an advantage you need to know the difference between data, information, and knowledge.

Data is simply randomly organized facts or opinions. For example, a list of customers and what each has bought over time is data. Data becomes *information* when it is organized in some logical format. For example, if you take the same list of customers and organize them into market segments based on some common set of characteristics, you have information. If you analyze the information to extract value from it—for example, which segments have bought the largest quantities of your products—you have *knowledge*. It is knowledge that you can use to make decisions that will give you an advantage in the business.

WHERE DO YOU LOOK
FOR DIVERSIFICATION POTENTIAL?

Think back to when you first started in your current business. How much knowledge did you have about your business then? How much do you have now? How much better is your judgment now than it was when you started?

As you gain more specific knowledge about a business, you are able to make finer distinctions about what decisions and actions do and do not work in the business. As your mental data base grows, you learn the paths through the data that yield the most value in any situation.

The three primary sources of knowledge that provide diversification potential from one business to other businesses are (1) the customers, (2) the technologies in the products and the technologies used to produce the products and/or services, and (3) the products and/or services. Using a series of specific questions, let's explore the types of diversification potential created by each of the three.

Customers

When your business has customers, it has something that can be even more valuable than the revenue dollars those customers spend. If you have a customer, you have a *relationship*. If managed properly, that relationship can provide data which you can turn into knowledge that can be used to advantage in another business.

How else could you meet your customers' current, or closely related, needs?

Weight Watchers, the internationally known diet clinic business, found that many of its customers were interested in staying on the Weight Watchers diet, but wanted more convenient food preparation. Weight Watchers solved this problem by diversifying into another business: diet foods. This was their way of meeting their customers' current and closely related needs with a new business.

What other products or services could you sell to your current customers?

H&R Block answered this question by entering the legal clinic business. Using Joel Hyatt and his concept for a legal firm that would sell services to people who currently do not use law firms, H&R Block entered a business that provided service to customers with a similar demographic profile as those who used their tax preparation services.

How could you provide products or services that are consistent with current buyer behavior?

One company that noticed how to do this was ARCO, the oil company. ARCO noticed that the people who used self-service, convenience outlets for their gasoline products also stopped at convenience stores like 7-Eleven. ARCO was able to combine the features of both and create the AM-PM Mini-Mart business. While self-service gasoline and convenience food stores are clearly different businesses, they have been combined at a single location as a way to meet the needs driven by similar customer behaviors.

How could you use the same distribution channel or method to sell products from multiple businesses?

Hewlett-Packard uses a single sales force to sell instrument products from its highly varied instrument businesses. This is because the large corporations that the HP sales force calls on need multiple products from multiple businesses. The efficiency created by a single sales force gives Hewlett-Packard a competitive advantage over other smaller competitors who have to support a sales force with many fewer products.

A second example is the chain of Disney retail stores that opened in recent years. These retail stores use a single channel and the Disney name to sell multiple products from highly varied businesses. Within these retail outlets you will find a range of products which includes movie videos, games, clothing, and toys.

How can you use your brand identification to cross-sell products and/or services?

A classic example is the Gillette Company. You can buy Gillette Right Guard Deodorant or Gillette Good News Razors. Razors and deodorant are very different businesses, but they are sold through similar distribution channels and the Gillette name provides a barrier to entry against others in both businesses. The barrier is a result of the relationship that Gillette has developed over many years in providing high quality, low cost products to its customers.

Technology

How could you use the same science-based technology to produce new products or services for current or new customers?

A classic example is Texas Instruments' use of voice synthesis technology to produce voice-synthesized cockpits in military airplanes and a children's toy, Speak & Spell. While the technology was certainly related, I hope the technology in the fighter aircraft was better than that in the toy!

How could you use the same production process technology to produce new products and/or services?

An example is the families of products produced in an oil refining plant. The same polymer cracking technology is used to produce widely varied products for different businesses. The businesses might be as different as heating oil and refined lubricants for special use in certain applications. The customers and the use of the products may be different, but the process technology used to produce them is very closely related.

Products and/or Services

How could you move backward or forward along the product flow chain to provide additional products to current or new customers?

When Silicon Graphics announced its proposed acquisition of MIPS, it was both protecting a source of supply of one of its key semiconductor suppliers, and proposing to enter the business to supply MIPS's chips to others.

When International Nickel (INCO) integrated from copper and other metals forward into batteries, the company was moving forward along the product flow chain toward the customers.

In other cases, companies have acquired their distribution channels as a method to capture more control over a channel. The history of Hewlett-Packard is replete with activities like this. For many years some divisions, for example, the Neeley Division, were still named for the original distribution companies.

How could you scale the product up or down in size and capability as a way to create a new business?

Personal computers are an excellent example. If you scale a personal computer upward in capability, it becomes a workstation. Workstations are particularly useful in heavy processing applications such as computer-aided design and engineering.

If you scale a personal computer down, it becomes a home computer. If you scale it down in size, it may become a notebook, or if reduced even further, a "palm top" computer.

WHEN IS THE BEST TIME TO DIVERSIFY?

Diversification is a difficult game. Studies show that more companies fail than succeed at diversifying. Depending on what studies you read, acquisitions fail somewhere between 50% and 90% of the time.[1] Entrepreneurial startups are even less likely to succeed. Most reports indicate that only one in ten will survive to the five-year point.

The probability of successful diversification from one business to another is directly proportional to how tightly linked the two businesses are by the number of defining factors (markets, technologies, product features) they share. The tighter the linkage, the greater the potential to share knowledge between the two businesses and therefore the higher the probability of success.

If two businesses are tightly linked and the first business is declining, it is possible that the second business will have limited profit and growth potential because it is in related products, markets and/or technologies to the first. This point emphasizes the importance of your search for a new business while your current business is still growing. The best time to diversify is before you are forced into it by a declining current business.

WHAT ARE THE KEY SUMMARY POINTS ABOUT DIVERSIFICATION POTENTIAL?

Diversification potential is the marginal difference between a good business and a great one. A good business has growth and profit potential. A great business also has diversification potential.

Diversification potential is desirable because no business keeps growing forever. When your current business declines, you need the next business to move to in order to continue to enhance shareholder wealth.

The three primary sources of diversification potential are the various aspects of the business' current customers, products, and technologies. The knowledge you have gained about these elements of your current businesses can be used to build linkages to new, better businesses.

The growth, profit, and diversification potential of your business are critical pieces of information to know as you start thinking about creating the right strategy.

FREEDOM #2:
Creating the Right Strategy

"Okay, so how much growth, profit, and diversification potential does your business have?"

"Unfortunately, not much. And I can't get out of my business easily."

"Well, you know what you have to do first, don't you?"

"No, what's that?"

"You have to create a brilliant strategy!"

Even in mature or declining businesses, it is usually possible to find at least one company that is profitable and continues to enhance its shareholders' wealth. What is it that makes the difference between these special companies and the rest of the competitors in the business?

In virtually every case, it's a brilliant business strategy.

I've already mentioned how Sam Walton used a powerful strategy to become successful in discount retailing when that business was already overpopulated and very competitive. Let's look at an even worse business to find an example of a company that has used a brilliant strategy to be succcessful.

You'll remember that I mentioned the airlines once before. In the early 1990s there were few businesses of any size that were worse businesses to be in than the domestic passenger airline business in the United States. Of the seven major carriers, American, Delta, Northwest,

United, TWA, Continental, and USAir, two were operating under the protection of Chapter 11 and a couple more were on the brink of bankruptcy. There was clearly too much capacity trying to serve the available demand, and too many competitors who were willing to "buy" revenues with fares that were below cost. During a fifteen-month period in 1991–1992, the U.S. airlines lost $6 billion dollars. This loss was greater than the sum of all the profits in the sixty-seven-year history of the industry.[1]

Within the industry, there is one competitor, Southwest Airlines, that has consistently made money since 1973. The company boasts an excellent balance sheet and consistently reports one of the highest, and often *the* highest return on stockholder equity.[2] How has the company's management done it?

The total formula is complex, but some of the key components include an avoidance of head-on, across-the-board competition with the major airlines by flying only the high-frequency short-haul routes; a low-fare no-frills service which attracts high passenger loads; one type of airplane (Boeing 737) to simplify training and service; and flexible work rules for unionized employees. The result is the lowest cost structure in the airline industry. Southwest has proven that even in a business as lousy as the domestic passenger airline business, it is possible to grow a billion dollar company, be profitable, and increase shareholder wealth over a long period of time.

If you want to develop the best possible strategy for your business, you need to complete the six steps in Freedom #2: Creating the Right Strategy (see Figure F–1) by answering six basic questions.

1. What Is the Current Business Strategy?

Few words in the English language are more overworked or less understood than "strategy." Ask any ten high-level managers what a business strategy is and see what you get in reply. I predict ten somewhat-to-significantly different answers with a potential theme.

The theme? "It's where you want to go and how you're going to get there."

Wonderful!

Now send those same ten managers out to look at a business and identify its current strategy. Guess how many significantly different answers you'll get?

I predict ten!

Figure F–1
Freedom #2

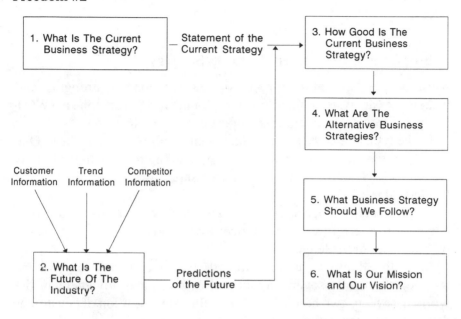

In order to answer this question it is imperative that you have a practical, operational definition of a business strategy that can be used to run the business. It should also yield a consistent picture of reality when several different people use the concept to identify a specific business' strategy (see Chapter 6).

2. What Is the Future of the Industry?

Many people think they need a crystal ball or the skills of a futurist to predict the future of an industry.

I have a surprise for you. In most businesses the future is highly predictable. To predict it you have to use some tools of industry structural analysis (see Chapter 7). If you do this analysis properly you can be 80–90% correct in predicting the future of an industry, where "correct" is defined as predicting both what will happen and when.

Furthermore, when you miss a prediction, it will most often be because you predict things will happen faster than they actually do. Although the pace of change is rapid and accelerating, most managers err in their predictions by predicting key events will happen even more rapidly than they actually do. Strategically, this is the better mistake to make because you will be prepared for key events when they do occur.

3. How Good Is the Current Business Strategy?

Most people have at one point or another done a strengths and weaknesses analysis on their business. (Some have even done a SWOT analysis: strengths, weaknesses, opportunities, and threats.)

In the typical analysis, the management team makes two lists. One list gives their opinion of the strategy's strengths and the other its weaknesses. Sometimes the results are useful. More often they are of limited value.

The typical result of a strengths and weaknesses analysis is that, after a few hours of effort, someone notices that the items listed are the same on both sides of the ledger.

Marketing thinks it's a great strength that the company can produce its widgets in forty-seven flavors and deliver them anywhere in the world in seventy-two hours. That's the ultimate definition of "customer driven"— whatever they want, whenever they want it!

Manufacturing thinks this same situation is a nightmare. How can the company possibly produce forty-seven different flavors of widgets at a reasonable cost on any rational production schedule?

And Finance isn't too happy with all the inventory that strategy requires, either.

The typical strengths and weaknesses analysis yields the traditional conflicts that exist among functions in every business. How many businesses can you name in which marketing and production aren't at odds? There are a few, but not many.

If you really want to learn the strengths and weaknesses of a given business strategy you must apply nine specific tests (see Chapter 8). Each test will tell you something different about your strategy by exposing different facets of it.

4. What Are the Alternative Business Strategies?

Once the advantages and disadvantages of the current strategy are thoroughly exposed it is possible to take on the creative challenge of formulating alternative business strategies.

Is this task easier in successful or troubled businesses?

It's easier in businesses that are in trouble. Change is clearly necessary in troubled businesses.

People in a successful business develop blinders. The business can be facing massive change which will render their strategy obsolete, but past success has conditioned them to continue to take the same course of action.

There are several methods through which I get people to explore the "performance envelope" of alternative strategies (see Chapter 9). Creativity is essential here.

5. What Business Strategy Should We Follow?

This turns out to be the simplest step, once you set the criteria. The process of setting the criteria, however, contains some interesting challenges.

I said earlier that the definition of a good business is one that increases shareholder wealth. That's exactly right, but there are several ways to increase shareholder wealth.

The objectives that you set in order to increase shareholder wealth may be different in different types of companies. For example, objectives may be significantly different in a private company and a public company. The private company has many more options for the ways it can increase its shareholders' wealth.

The objectives may be different in a growth company and a mature company. In a growth company shareholder wealth may be improved through consistent increases in revenues and profits that drive stock prices up. In a mature company shareholder wealth may be best enhanced through high dividend payouts.

The objectives in a real estate development firm may be different from a high technology startup. The endgame in the former may be capital appreciation on the developed properties. In the latter the venture capitalists/owners may simply be looking forward to an ongoing public market for their stock.

The desired result is increased shareholder wealth. The objectives that will yield increased shareholder wealth may vary across businesses and over time. In fact, objectives have a funny characteristic. There is no such thing as an "objective" set of objectives. All objectives are subjective (see Chapter 10).

6. What Is Our Mission and Our Vision?

Mission and vision statements are the management rage of the 1990s. It seems that every company has to have one. Unfortunately, once you read a couple dozen of them, they all start to sound alike. Most start to look like a generic vision statement, that goes something like this:

> *Our company will ethically provide a complete line of products and services to meet the dynamically changing needs of our corporate, group, and individual customers by innovatively developing new approaches, using new technologies while simultaneously enhancing our employees' lives, and providing superior returns to our stockholders.*

Sound good? Can you envision the future of this company?
Of course not.

The problem with generic mission and vision statements is that people inside and outside the company have "hot air detectors." They recognize meaningless statements when they hear them. They won't be inspired by or attracted to a company that holds forth such corporate pabulum.

Perhaps the biggest problem that managers have when they try to create mission and vision statements is that they try to do too much with them. They want one simple statement that will excite customers, motivate employees, interest investors, and frighten competitors. That's a big order for a few words or a sentence.

To be meaningful, a mission has to go somewhere and a vision has to be visionary. Your mission is what you do. Your vision is what you will become if you successfully and repeatedly accomplish your mission.

Both the mission and vision statements must be derived from your strategy. Too many managers believe that you can start your strategic thinking by creating, out of thin air, an awe-inspiring vision of the future. It doesn't work that way. Your mission and vision statements are key links between your strategy and its implementation (see Chapter 11).

Let's go to work. The first thing we have to do is figure out our starting point by asking what a business strategy is.

Chapter 6
What Is a Business Strategy?

"Do you have a business strategy?"

"Of course I have a business strategy. Do you think I would be crazy enough to operate without one?"

"Great, then you can tell me what one is. What is a business strategy, anyway?"

"Well, um . . . uh . . . it's . . . uh.."

I learned about business strategy the hard way.

During the early 1970s when I was still a business school professor, I received many calls from companies wanting help with their strategic planning efforts. I thought this was terrific. After all, I had a Ph.D. in business and was teaching in the field of strategic management. Besides, I had read the books and it didn't look too difficult.

I would hop on an airplane—because a consultant is someone from out of town—and go to work with a team of managers running a business. From my training I knew that the first thing we needed to do together was set the objectives for the business.

So I would ask the team to set their objectives.

But, something wasn't right. The process wasn't working. I wasn't getting productive responses. In fact, about half of the time I tried this, I couldn't get any response. The team would refuse to set its objectives before they figured out what they realistically could do.

Figure 6–1
"We grew 25% this year, so let's keep it going next year."

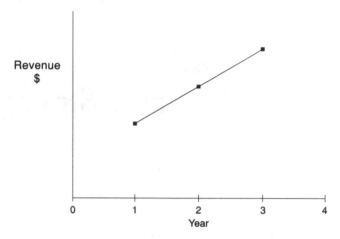

In those cases in which I could get them to set their objectives, I would get one of two responses. The first response would occur when recent results had been good. It was simply an extension of last year's results (see Figure 6–1).

The second response would occur when recent results had not been very good (see Figure 6–2).

Figure 6–2
"We're not doing very well right now, but trust us, things will get better soon."

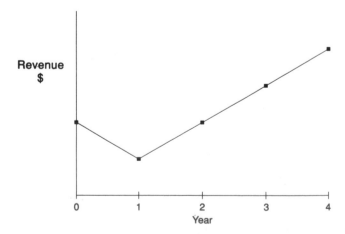

Anyone who has looked at a few strategic plans has probably seen at least one that is full of "hockey sticks."

It didn't take me very long to figure out that trying to start a strategy development process by setting objectives, literally in a vacuum, was not going to be very effective.

So, where should we start?

If a company is in business, it must have a strategy. The strategy may have been developed consciously or unconsciously. It may be a good strategy or a bad strategy, but the company must have one if it's in business. Even if the situation is an entrepreneurial one in which the business has not been started yet, the team must have some ideas about what they are going to do. After all, if you are going to go someplace in the future, you and your management team need to agree on the direction.

Great! Let's start the process by simply identifying the current strategy.

So I went back to the books to find a practical definition of a business strategy. I had two requirements. First, once the strategy was identified, it had to be practical enough that it could be used to run the business. It had to contain enough information so that a good general management team could use it to actually run the business. Second, the definition had to be one that would pass a simple test of "replicability." By that I mean that if I assign a dozen knowledgeable business people the task of identifying the strategy of business X, the definitions they would develop would be the same.

The definitions in the textbooks were relatively useless. In one text I learned that the word strategy is derived from the Greek word "strategos," which is the art of the general.[1] How practical is that?

In my search for a definition that would meet my two requirements, I learned that the term "strategy" must be one of the most overused and least understood words in our business vocabularies. Its great appeal must lie in the belief that anyone who has a strategy must know what he or she is doing. One result is that everyone thinks he knows what a strategy is. Unfortunately, few really do.

A second result is that "strategic" has become a synonym for "important." Anything that is important is labeled "strategic." Thus, we have terms like "strategic investing," and "strategic life planning." One day in a Denver bookstore I even saw a book on "strategic gardening."

Since the expert authors on the subject were of little help, I next turned to practicing managers. I asked them to define "strategy." The typical response was, "It's where you want to go and how you are going to get there." While that is a definition, it is not very helpful. Using it, different managers looking at the same business would define its strategy differently.

As I observed managers in what they called "strategic planning sessions," I learned that there was widespread confusion about business strategy. One day, I sat in a meeting for two hours and observed managers in one of America's "best run" companies argue over whether the topic of discussion was a "strategy" or a "tactic." What I noticed is that this discussion is usually about whose job it is. If you work for me, what I do is strategic. What you do is tactical.

I sat in other meetings and watched high level managers in leading companies argue about the difference between a goal, a mission, and an objective. Obviously, these managers had been reading the textbook definitions that I had already discarded.

As I asked questions about the definition of a business strategy in many different companies, it became apparent that confusion was rampant. A simplified approach was needed.

WHAT IS A PRACTICAL DEFINITION OF BUSINESS STRATEGY?

In working with a number of companies, I developed an approach to strategy identification that appears to eliminate most of the confusion. It is also consistent with the language used by most managers.

Two basic definitions are the foundations of this approach. They are that a *strategy* is a *means,* and an *objective* is an *end.*

Note that I do not try to define any differences among an objective, a goal, or a target. Nor am I concerned about whether we are talking about a strategy or a tactic. The differences are neither important nor meaningful. One person's strategy is another's tactic. In those situations where managers have tried to make fine distinctions among these terms, they generally have caused more confusion, not less.

Instead, I use practical business terminology where the important word is the adjective that modifies the words "strategy" or "objective." I will talk about a production strategy or a financial objective.

A business strategy is that set of dynamic, integrated decisions which you must make in order to position your business in its complex environment.

An examination of Figure 6–3 (p. 92) will help to clarify this definition.

But first, there are some key words in the definition of a business strategy that I need to emphasize.

A business strategy is made up of a set of *decisions*. The purpose of the decisions is to *position* the business in its environment to meet the potentially conflicting needs of its stakeholders. The decisions must, for example, position the business to serve customer needs, beat the competition, meet regulatory requirements, satisfy employees, and pay creditors while providing a return to shareholders. While thousands of decisions are made in any business, the decisions that comprise the business strategy are the ones that *must* be made in order to position the business. They must be made if you are going to be in the business.

The decisions that comprise the strategy are an *integrated* set. If you move one strand of a spider's web, you move all the strands. If you change one decision in the business strategy you will affect, and may need to change, several others.

Because these integrated decisions are also *dynamic*, the strategy can be changing rapidly, or slowly, depending on the needs of the business. A static business strategy in a dynamic environment is a recipe for failure.

A business strategy is typically composed of decisions in the areas of marketing, production, finance, and research and development. Other decision areas are occasionally important, such as a legal strategy.

Within each area, certain decisions need to be made for that function to fulfill its purpose in positioning the business. Those decisions are illustrated by the arrows shown within each area in Figure 6–3. Although each business is somewhat different, the strategy for your business can be identified if you just isolate the decisions that must be made in order to position the business in its environment.

Note that there is a significant difference between the *decisions* that comprise the business strategy and the *action processes* that are used to implement the strategy. Figure 6–4 illustrates the difference.

The business strategy is a set of decisions. What we want from the business, however, are results. We get results by converting decisions into action through the three action processes of (1) developing the right systems, (2) designing the right organization structure, and (3) getting the right people. The sections in this book on Freedoms 3, 4, and 5 discuss each of these three action processes.

Although every action is preceded by a decision of some sort, these decisions are about what action to take or how to take it. They are the

Figure 6–3

Examples of Key Elements of a Product Business Strategy

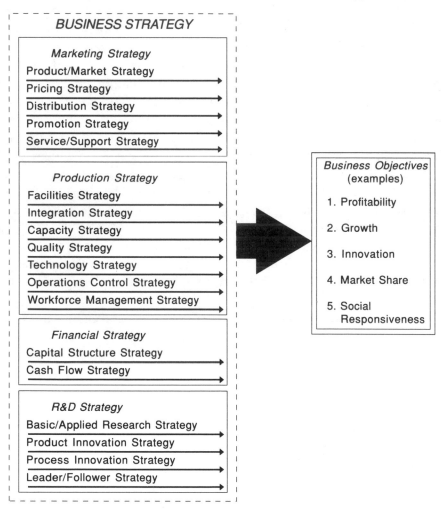

decisions that precede the actions that will implement the strategy. They are not the decisions that position the business in its complex environment. For example, a decision on how to organize the business, or what systems are needed to run it, rarely does anything to position the business.

Given the above definitions, it is now possible to identify the components of a business strategy and see how the business is positioned in its environment. One of the most interesting aspects of business strategy is the

Figure 6-4

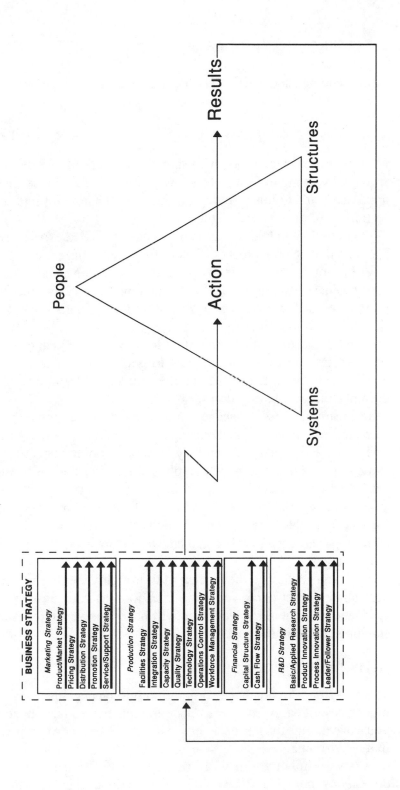

infinite combination of decisions that can be made. Business strategy is fascinating because of the creativity that is employed by its practitioners.

WHY IDENTIFY THE CURRENT BUSINESS STRATEGY?

Most managers would prefer to start the process of creating the right strategy by trying to formulate a new strategy. This "Ready, fire, aim!" approach leads to lousy strategies. Socrates' "Know thyself" can here be translated to "Know thy strategy."

On literally hundreds of occasions, I have watched experienced managers go through the process of identifying their current business strategy. In almost every case, they learned something significant about their business that they did not understand previously. For the first time, they developed an adequate understanding of the answer to the question: "What is our business strategy?"

Another reason that it is important for the management team to identify the current business strategy is to get *agreement* on the strategy. Most management teams believe they understand and agree on their current strategy, but they don't.

In a team of a dozen managers in a business in a large aerospace company, the average tenure in the company and in the business was twenty-five years. They each believed they knew everything about their current strategy and did not want to complete the strategy identification process. I asked them to do it so that I and my team could understand the strategy better. Before lunch on what was to be an all-day meeting, voices were raised, tables were pounded upon, and names were called. It became apparent very quickly that there was not total agreement on the current strategy!

After you go through the process of thoroughly identifying your business strategy just once, you will never look at your business or your competitors in the same way. You will have a powerful tool for understanding any business better.

HOW DO WE PROCEED?

The first step is to break the corporation into businesses using the techniques described in Chapter 2. Once the businesses have been defined you can examine the key decisions that have been made to position each in its environment.

It is very important that you concentrate on what is actually being done *today*, not what you would *like* to see done. It is also important to postpone judgment on whether what is being done is *good* or *bad*. Your job is to identify what that strategy is, not whether it is good or bad. Leave evaluation for later or you will shortchange the creative part of the strategy development process.

You can ask a series of questions which aid in the identification of your business strategy. Examples of these questions will be discussed in the remainder of this chapter. Please note that these questions are not intended to be exhaustive or to fit every business. Additional and/or different questions must be asked depending on the business. Figure 6–5, for example, shows some different elements of business strategy for a service business.

Figure 6–5
Examples of Key Elements of a Service Business Strategy

Identifying the Marketing Strategy

Your marketing strategy is what makes the connection between the value your business can produce and your customers. The quality of your strategy determines the quality of the connection. A brilliant marketing strategy will yield a strong connection. Without this connection between value and potential buyers you don't have a business.

How does your business make the connection?

Table 6–1 shows a series of questions that might be asked in the process of identifying your current marketing strategy.

Table 6–1
Marketing Strategy

Product (or Service) / Market Strategy

- *What products/services are offered?*
- *How are the markets segmented?*
- *What customer needs or wants do the products/ services fullfil?*

Pricing Strategy

- *Is the price higher, lower, or equal to competition?*
- *Is the business a price leader or follower?*
- *Is the price value-based or cost based?*

Promotion Strategy

- *What attributes of the products/services are promoted?*
- *Where are the products or services promoted?*
- *How big is the promotion effort?*

Distribution Strategy

- *How are the products or services distributed to the end-user?*
- *How many steps are there in the channel?*
- *Are the distribution channels independent or owned?*

Service / Support Strategy

- *Are the product / service warranties the same, less, or greater than the competition?*
- *How are the products or servces repaired or replaced when defective?*
- *How are customer needs for information about products / services met?*

Product or Service/Market Strategy

If one element of a business strategy can be said to be more important than the others, it is product/market strategy. The choice of products and markets largely drives the remaining elements of the business strategy. This is not surprising when the business is defined by *the combination of technologies, product and/or service features, and market needs that creates a potential or real economic relationship between buyers and sellers.*

The identification of your current product/market strategy can start with some simple lists. What are the products or services offered? What features does each have? Who are the customers? What needs are they seeking to satisfy with the products and/or services of your business?

These questions should be answered in as much detail as possible. The more specific you are in identifying the products and markets, the easier it will be to answer the remaining questions.

If the three keys to success in real estate are "Location, Location, and Location," then the three keys to success in marketing are "Segment, Segment, and Segment." Find a group of potential customers with common needs or wants and sell to them.

As far as I know, there are only three ways to segment a market. You may want to remember these as the "DAB" method of market segmentation: (1) demographics, (2) attitudes, (3) behaviors. Figure 6–6 shows examples of these three segmentation methods. They work equally well

Figure 6–6
The DAB Method of Market Segmentation

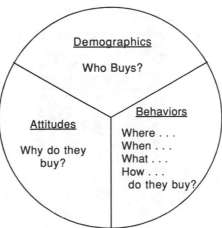

for consumer and commercial products, although the exact terms are slightly different.

The major difference between the segmentation processes in consumer and commercial markets is in the demographics of each. In consumer markets the demographics of interest are often geographic location, age, income, sex, and education. In commercial markets the demographics of interest are type of business, size, ownership, profitability, growth rate, age, and location.

In both markets, an assessment of "who buys" should include both the user and the purchaser of the product or service. They may be different.

The development of packaged software for microcomputers illustrates market segmentation during the growth of an industry. At the start of the microcomputer revolution, the customers or "early adopters" tended to be people who had scientific or technical backgrounds. These people wrote their own programs using computer languages. Microcomputer sales did not take off until generic programs were developed that met the fundamental needs of a large number of customers. VisiCalc, a spreadsheet program, was one of the early generic packages. It was followed quickly by packages for word processing, data-base management, and accounting.

Generic or horizontal markets are usually attacked first as new industries develop. They are almost always larger and require less customer specific knowledge than vertical markets (see Figure 6–7).

Once the large generic market needs were met, the software developers tackled vertical markets. Commonly, vertical markets are defined by industry, and that is what happened in microcomputer software. Ver-

Figure 6–7
Horizontal and Vertical Markets

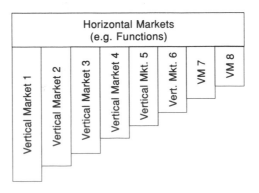

tical market packages were developed to meet the specific needs of dentists, lawyers, doctors, farmers, and so on. This process of further specifying the market segments by adding additional variables usually continues until the market segment is so small that it cannot be economically served. For example, writing a software package for the unique needs of the seventh sons of seventh sons of Irishmen—who are reputed to have the ability to heal serious injuries by touch—is probably not a viable market.

One specific part of the market segmentation analysis deserves additional discussion. Why do they buy?

The need to answer the "Why do they buy?" question carefully was brought home to me when I was the subject of a telephone market research effort. I have been very fortunate in being able to own sports cars most of my adult life. Although I respond to very few mail surveys, I did take the time to fill out one on my latest "investment," a bright red, turbocharged number from a leading manufacturer. As a result of the survey I mailed in, I received a follow-up call. When asked why I bought the car I, of course, gave all the rational reasons:

"Well, I've done my homework and I think this is one of the finest cars ever built. It goes from zero to sixty in under six seconds, has perfect weight distribution, ABS brakes, an integrated roll bar, . . ."

I clearly demonstrated what a rational customer I was. But when I hung up the phone, it hit me that the researcher had failed to ask the right question. I didn't buy the car because of its technical specifications, I bought it because of the way it made me *feel* when I took it for a test drive. The second I tromped on that accelerator and the car's rapid response threw me back in the seat, I felt like I was nineteen again. That car had to be mine! The rest was just rationalization.

Does anybody buy a sports car solely for transportation? Of course not. There are specific *features* of the car that must meet the needs of the prospective customer if he or she is to become a real customer. It is only when the customer experiences the features which generate *benefits,* and the benefits generate positive *feelings,* that the customer's needs are satisfied (see Figure 6–8).[2] Ultimately, customers make buying decisions based on their feelings.

Think about the process you went through the last time you made a significant purchase like a car or a house. Once you narrowed your choices to the realistic alternatives, I'll bet the key difference between what you did and did not buy was what "felt" best.

Figure 6–8

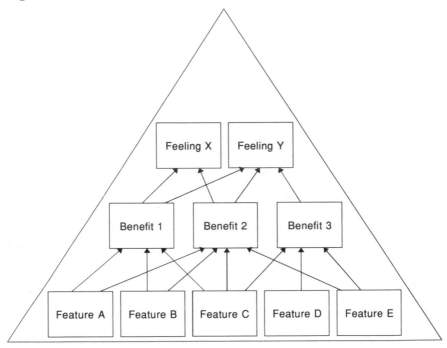

When you identify *why* your customers buy, you want to identify all of the features they find important, the benefits they derive from each, and the feelings that those benefits elicit in them. You may be surprised to learn how your customers feel about your products or services. I have seen cases where customers buy a product because it is the only alternative that comes close to meeting their needs. It wasn't what they wanted and it was too expensive, but they had no choice. A product like that is extremely vulnerable to competition that provides a better solution.

Another analysis concerns the question "How do they buy?" It is often useful to break the buying process into several steps and put a time frame on it. Your customers' buying processes can vary from those that are impulse purchases and happen in an instant to those that are deliberated and can take years. The purchaser of a package of chewing gum may make his decision in an instant at the checkout stand. When a country's air force purchases a new fighter aircraft, the purchase is usually carefully deliberated and often takes years.

Figure 6–9 shows, in the format of a sales funnel, one way to concep-

Figure 6–9
The Deliberative
Purchase Process

Awareness

Learn/Investigate

Shop/Compare

Select

Purchase

tualize the buying process. This model probably works best for more deliberated purchases.

There are several questions implied by the sales funnel. For example, how do customers become aware of the product? How do they get more information about it? What is the final decision-making process? What is the deciding factor that gets the customer to choose one product over another? Breaking down the buying process in this way will give you much more specific information about your actual product/market relationship.

Pricing Strategy

Are the products or services priced higher, lower, or equal to the competition? Relative price positioning is a competitive weapon that is used in almost every business. It is a particularly potent weapon when the products or services are undifferentiated. Occasionally it leads to "cutthroat competition" in which competitors price below cost in an attempt to drive each other out of business. As mentioned in Chapter 4, the airline industry has a history of this type of competition. So do "clone" manufacturers in the personal computer business.

On the other end of the price scale, some businesses price their products so high that their premium price intentionally limits the market, while greatly increasing profits per unit. Rolex watches come to mind as one such product. Fila sportswear is another.

Are the prices value-based or cost-based? A *cost-based price* is developed by adding up the cost of producing and selling the product and adding a profit margin on top. In some industries conventions have developed around pricing. For example, some high technology firms use the rule of thumb that the product should sell for five times its direct manufacturing cost. In other companies product costs are totaled and profit margins are added to yield certain standard operating and net income figures.

A *value-based price* is one that treats the product's cost as irrelevant. The value that the product has in the marketplace is much higher than its cost. Computer software is often a value-priced product. Once the initial software is developed, the incremental cost of another floppy disk or tape is very small. Thus, the value of the software is measured by the problems it will solve.

Tax consulting is a value-based service. The price of this service is usually set so the client can see that he saved more in taxes than the service cost. The actual cost to produce the service is irrelevant to both the client and the consultant.

Value-based prices are dependent on the customer's perception of value. An oil company was going to open a chain of fast tune-up shops in the Midwest. They first did a study of the market. The cost-based price for the service was set at $29.95 plus parts. When surveyed, potential customers said they would not buy the service. Upon further investigation, the oil company learned that the potential customers did not believe they could get a good tune-up for $29.95. The price was too *low*! When the study was redone at $39.95 a large market was discovered.

Is the strategy to be a price leader or follower? Some businesses have enough power in the marketplace to set the prices for the industry. Others must follow the prices set by the industry leader.

Price leadership is usually based on market share or technological leadership in the market. IBM is the price leader in most of the computer markets in which it competes. That does not mean that IBM is necessarily the lowest priced competitor in the market. Clearly, the clone manufacturers have lower priced personal computers. It does mean that all those in competition with IBM pay close attention to IBM's prices. When IBM moves, they usually do too.

Promotion Strategy

What attributes of the product or service are promoted? The product's function, characteristics, price, or availability are just a few of the attributes that might be promoted.

Typically, a business will promote something about the product or service that differentiates it from the competition's product. Wendy's "Where's the Beef?" advertising campaign was an example of this type of promotion. Wendy's, unlike the competition, used a square beef patty in a round bun. The corners extended beyond the edge of the bun, giving an appearance of abundance. Meanwhile, the competitors were hiding their round beef patties inside their round buns.

Where are the products or services promoted? There are almost an infinite number of media that can be used in your promotion strategy. I am using the term "media" here very broadly. It includes any method you use to get your message across. Obviously, you may use radio, television, newspapers, magazines, trade shows, conventions, brochures, and/or a direct sales force. Every product or service can be promoted in many different ways. The medium is only limited by imagination. For example, Pepsi-Cola has a skywriter that promotes Pepsi at airshows.

Your choice of promotional media is usually dictated by the target audience. A promotion strategy can be aimed at the end users of a product or service, or at some intermediate point in the distribution chain, such as dealers, distributors, or retailers. It can be aimed at new customers or previous customers.

If aimed at previous customers, it is often done to reduce "post-purchase dissonance," also known as "buyer's remorse," that many customers experience after making a major purchase. For years, auto manufacturers targeted a portion of their advertising at people who had recently purchased their cars. This advertising was used to reduce doubts about the decision that their customers had made and reinforce their decision as the correct one.

How big is the promotion effort? The most common ways to measure the magnitude of the promotion effort are to look at its absolute cost in dollars and as a percentage of sales. However, other costs, such as management time and effort, should be included also. In some businesses the management time spent on promotion costs more than the formal promotion campaign.

Distribution Strategy

How are the products or services distributed to the end user? It is often useful to draw a diagram to illustrate the channels that the product or service can go through to get to the end user. You may own your distribution versus others who go through independent representatives.

IBM made a change from its historical direct-sales only approach when it entered the microcomputer business with its Personal Computer. This product was distributed through computer retailers. Support and service were provided by the independent retailers.

In the early 1990s, computer retail stores were being challenged by computer "superstores" that were the discount retailers of the microcomputer industry. Channels are businesses and they are often in a state of change as much as the businesses who supply the products they sell. As the structure of the channels changes, the distribution strategy of various suppliers is also likely to change.

Still another method of distribution is represented by the direct sales organizations such as Amway, Mary Kay Cosmetics, Shaklee, and Tupperware. These companies primarily use independent contractors, structured in a multilevel sales organization, to sell their products. While a few of these independent contractors are able to attract others to work for them and sell large dollar volumes, many of the salespeople have been known to buy only for their own use and that of their friends. Some even pass on the company discount to their friends and make no profit on the sale! These sales methods are an interesting, low-cost method of distribution.

Service/Support Strategy

As customer service has become more important in a highly technological world with extensive communications capabilities, entire strategies have been built by some companies that differentiate themselves primarily on customer support. Are the product warranties the same, more extensive, or less so than the competition?

One company making a computer peripheral product had adopted a warranty equal to its competition. While testing the competitor's product they discovered that it failed, in most cases, shortly after its warranty expired. Their own product had an average life three times as long as the competitor's product. The company doubled its warranty and rapidly took market share. The competitor could not respond in the short run because its warranty costs would be intolerable. By the time the competitor redesigned its product for longer life, the battle was essentially over. The competitor never regained a significant position in the market because its products were perceived as unreliable.

How are products/services repaired or replaced when defective? Strategies vary widely on this dimension, from "they aren't, you just throw it away and buy another" to very sophisticated, fast systems. The advent of overnight delivery services has allowed many businesses to adopt twenty-four or forty-eight hour replacement of defective products.

How are customers' needs for product/service information met?

Catalog retailers, for example, can handle almost any customer order or concern quickly and easily by phone or fax.

Dell Computer built a several hundred million dollar business on its ability to sell and support its products largely by phone.

IDENTIFYING THE PRODUCTION STRATEGY

Your production strategy is like the engine and transmission in your car. It drives the creation of the products and services you sell. The more efficient and flexible it is, the more options you have.

New emphasis is being placed on production processes in virtually every business. Whether it is the emphasis on quality from such processes as total quality control (TQC) or total quality management (TQM) or the push toward improved processes like continuous flow manufacturing (CFM), the advent of a true global economy has pushed companies to get quality up and costs down.

With greater information content inherent to many products and services, the customer's desire to have those products customized has also increased. The old way of thinking about the ideal production process was as a means to produce larger volumes of identical products in a long production run. Modern production strategies are aiming more at producing the highest quality products at the lowest cost in a customized quantity of one.

Production strategy can go by several different names, including "manufacturing strategy" and "operations strategy." I have chosen the term production strategy because it applies equally to product and service businesses. Please note, however, that you may have to modify the questions in Table 6–2 to fit the production process in your particular type of business.

Until the last dozen years or so, production strategy has not been given nearly as much emphasis as marketing. Over the last twenty years, however, the Japanese have taught the world many lessons in competition through their effective and efficient production strategies in several industries. The automobile, motorcycle, and semiconductor industries have gone through major restructurings due to successful Japanese inroads.

Table 6–2
Production Strategy

Facilities Strategy

- *How many production facilities are there?*
- *Where are the production facilities located?*
- *What type of facilities are used?*

Integration Strategy

- *How vertically integrated are the facilities?*
- *Are facilities single- or multi-purpose?*

Capacity Strategy

- *Do you add capacity ahead of or behind demand?*
- *How fast can the capacity be expanded or contracted?*

Quality Strategy

- *What level of quality has been selected for the product?*

Technology Strategy

- *What specific technology does the production process use?*
- *Does the production system use state-of-the-art technology?*

Operations Control Strategy

- *Is the product/service made to order or inventory?*
- *How is production scheduled?*

Workforce Management Strategy

- *Is the workforce union or non-union?*
- *What are employees paid relative to the competition and the local market?*
- *What is the skill level of the workforce?*
- *What is the productivity level of the workforce?*

New emphasis is being given to production strategies in virtually every business. The questions discussed in this section should give you some insights into your production strategy.

Facilities Strategy

What type of facilities are used and where are they located? How many are there? Facilities can be single-purpose or multipurpose. They can be located near the sources of raw materials or near the end-user. They may be located near cheap sources of labor or near good transportation.

Some businesses have a large number of small production facilities and others have a few large facilities. The choice is often dictated by the economics of the business and the product/market strategy. In fact, the same product can be produced in two different ways because of the differences in product/market strategy.

French bread is an example. Colombo Baking Company produces French bread at a centralized plant in Oakland, California, and distributes it by truck throughout the San Francisco Bay Area to retail grocers. Another company, La Baguette, has put small bakeries in shopping malls. The bread is baked on the premises and sold off the racks where it cools. In the latter case, the concept of selling fresh, warm bread requires the bakery to be on the premises. (Note that part of the promotion strategy here is to make sure that the aroma of freshly baked bread wafts throughout the mall. This draws customers like fish being reeled in on a line.)

A similar example is the advent of one-hour photo-processing businesses. By taking the processing out of a central lab and to the local shop, the processor is able to reduce total turnaround time to the customer. This meets some customers' needs for convenience and speed in getting their pictures developed.

A different kind of convenience is provided by mail order companies. By allowing you to shop from a catalog in your home, these companies are able to have large, centralized facilities that provide merchandise quickly and efficiently. L.L. Bean, for example, still has only one primary retail location in Freeport, Maine, but they have an international customer base from their catalog business.[3]

In the food and beverage industry it is not uncommon to locate the container manufacturing plant next to the processing plant. There are several places where the aluminum can plant is next door to the brewery and a conveyor belt goes from the can maker into the brewery. Now that's getting close to your customer!

The specific location of production facilities is often a critical strategic decision. Large companies spend millions of dollars each year on location studies. These studies weigh economic, legal, social, and political factors to determine the best location for production facilities.

When General Motors started searching for a site for the location of its $1.9 billion Saturn manufacturing and assembly facility, thirty-eight states submitted bids. A major study was completed on several competing sites. Springhill, Tennessee, was chosen for its:

- central location (within 600 miles of 65 percent of the nation's population)
- utilities, including water, sewer, electricity, and natural gas
- available land
- favorable business climate, including tax packages
- favorable work climate
- available services for employees
- variety of lifestyles
- physical conditions[4]

Other companies locate production facilities by happenstance. It may be where the company founder wants to live.

Integration Strategy

How vertically integrated are the facilities? In many product businesses, it is important to understand how far forward and backward the manufacturing facilities are integrated. Backward integration means the movement back toward the sources of raw materials, often by acquiring the capability to manufacture previously purchased components. Forward integration is the acquisition of a downstream manufacturer or of parts of the distribution channel so that they become owned instead of independent.

One trend in forward and backward integration is to make equity investments in suppliers or distributors.

In 1988 AT&T agreed to buy 20% of Sun Microsystems over a three-year period. AT&T was developing Unix software for Sun's proprietary microprocessors and the investment would allegedly forge a stronger alliance between the two.[5]

Although the alliance fell apart in 1991 when Sun began competing more vigorously in some AT&T markets,[6] the three-year effort is an illustration of a strategy being employed to develop "strategic alliances" instead of complete forward or backward integration by one company.

Integration can even be important in professional service businesses. Some companies, such as the so-called "beltway bandits" around Washington, D.C., are using techniques that allow them to get a government contract and hire independent contract consultants on a job-by-job basis. Thus, they do not have full-time employees, but instead have independent subcontractors who are paid on a temporary, project basis. This dis-integrated approach allows the parent firm to have a highly flexible capacity strategy. Because the beltway bandits do not have a large overhead structure to support, this strategy has provided a competitive advantage in obtaining government contracts that are particularly price-sensitive.

Capacity Strategy

Do you add capacity ahead of or behind demand? Some businesses always have excess capacity and are set up to meet peak load demand. Others find ways to add temporary capacity to meet peak demands. Still others have ways to encourage reductions in demand. For example, Pacific Gas & Electric has a major program to encourage co-generation and energy efficient retrofitting of buildings by its customers.

Virtually every electric utility has a strategy for meeting peak load demand. This demand often occurs in the summer months, when the demand for electricity to run air conditioners is the highest. The specific strategies, however, vary widely. Some utilities maintain excess plant capacity that they can fire up when needed. Some buy electricity from others in their region. Others have policies that give priority to some customers in times of shortage.

You should also identify how flexible the capacity is. How fast can it be expanded or contracted?

Technology Strategy

What specific technology does the business use? Although technologies vary quite a bit, each business typically employs an identifiable technology in producing a product or service.

Fundamentally, production technologies can be classified as job shop, batch, mass production, or process flow. *Job shop* technologies are employed where the products or services are customized or produced in small quantities. An auto repair shop or tool and die company is an example. *Batch* production technologies are used where small quantities of similar products are produced. Most cookie stores use batch processes. *Mass production* is typified by the automobile assembly line. *Process* or *continuous flow* is the technology used by the oil companies to produce various products based on crude oil as the raw material.

Within the general category of production technology, it is also important to determine the specific technology, if any, used to produce the products or services. These technologies are usually based on a scientific field relevant to the industry.

Does the production system use state-of-the-art technology? In some businesses, this would include the use of computer aided design (CAD), computer aided manufacturing (CAM) and/or computer aided engineering (CAE) systems.

On a trip to Germany a few years ago I had the pleasure of touring the Mercedes Benz and Porsche automobile plants on successive days. The contrast in the technology strategy of the two firms was striking.

At the Mercedes plant in Zindelfingen, the cars were produced in a highly automated factory. Several car bodies were placed in huge jigs and moved automatically down the line. As they were moved, robot welding arms came snaking out to weld the bodies. Even the painting process was automated.

Approximately thirty kilometers away in Stuttgart, Porsche produced the classic 911 sports car, now called the Carrera. The basic car bodies were placed on dollies—small tables with wheels. Every ten minutes the dollies were moved to a new station and a German auto worker bolted on some additional parts. The car was virtually handmade. When I asked my guide if Porsche planned to automate in the near future, I was told no, ". . . because the only way to build a fine car is to build it by hand." Undoubtedly the managers at Mercedes would have disagreed.

Quality Strategy

Quality can be both a strategy (i.e., a decision) and an implementation process. As an implementation process, such as the aforementioned TQC or TQM, a quality process is a method of improving anything that can be viewed as a process. Since virtually all management and implementation activities can be viewed as processes, approaches like TQC and TQM can be applied virtually everywhere in a business.

Quality strategy, however, is the decision about what level of quality is set for the products and services of a business. Arguably, quality strategy could just as easily be categorized as a marketing strategy or a production strategy. It is certainly a key feature of any product or service.

I don't care what category you put it in, as long as you identify the level of quality that you have selected for your products or services. What is your quality relative to customer requirements? What is it relative to your competitors' offerings?

Operations Control Strategy

Is the product or service made to order or inventoried? Typically, products that are standardized can be inventoried. Those that are customized must be made to order. Most modern manufacturing theories emphasize the elimination of inventories, especially work-in-process inventories, wherever possible. The ideal situation is to have an instantly customizable product or service that can be produced as rapidly as possible. That way the customer can have whatever he or she wants, whenever he or she wants it.

How is production scheduled? What is the process for deciding how much of a product or service to produce? Professional service firms often use "backlog" as their production scheduling tool. Some manufacturers schedule to forecast, others schedule only against orders.

By examining McDonald's and Wendy's, two competing companies in the fast food business, you can observe some interesting differences in operations control strategies.

McDonald's runs a batch production process, in which the specific products (e.g., Big Macs, Quarter Pounders) are produced in batches and stored in hot bins as inventory. Clerks fill orders from the hot bins. When the number of a certain type of burger falls below a specified level, the manager orders another batch.

At Wendy's the burgers are never batched. They are produced one at a time. Instead of multiple order lines that pull burgers from hot bins, there is only one order point. The "chef" watches the length of the line approaching the order point and begins cooking an appropriate number of burgers. As each customized order is announced to the production team, the chef's assistant prepares the bun with appropriate condiments. A third person bags the French fries and pours the drinks. The burger is then placed on the bun and is delivered "hot and juicy" to the customer. Although there are many other elements to the strategy, Wendy's production strategy has been a key differentiator in its approach to the business.

Work Force Management Strategy

Work force management strategy has received a great deal of attention in recent years. Several books have compared work force management strategies among companies and cultures. Some practices may be better for low-cost production while others appear to enhance innovation. Still others may be better for customer service.

One question you want to ask is whether the work force is union or nonunion. This obviously impacts the relationship that you can have with that work force. A unionized work force has specific legal, and often cultural, requirements that must be met. In some cases, the existence of a union creates an adversarial relationship with management. In others, the situation is more cooperative.

What is the skill level of the work force relative to competition? You will want to know whether your workers are more highly skilled, about the same, or less skilled. A highly skilled work force can be a competitive advantage in some industries. In the computer sector there has been a long-standing competitive battle for engineers and software developers.

What are employees paid relative to competition and the local market? Occasionally, because of a specific location strategy, you may be able to get your labor force at a rate that is less than that of your competitors.

One example of the use of pay as a way to attract a skilled labor force occurred while I was on the faculty of the Harvard Business School. During the mid–1970s a young, rapidly growing consulting firm needed to attract top MBA graduates in order to meet their growth objectives. Unfortunately, they were not meeting their targets because they could not attract enough of the best MBAs. After seeking advice from some professors at the school, the firm raised its starting salaries by approximately 33% over the average.

Two results followed. First, the firm was able to hire top graduates from Harvard quite easily. That much additional money made an impression on the typical twenty-six to twenty-eight-year-old graduate student, even if he or she really wanted to do something other than consulting.

Second, it made the recruiters from other companies very angry. They would return to their companies and complain to their chief executive officers (CEOs) about how this upstart consulting firm was "ruining the market" and "stealing all the brightest MBAs." Even this, however, worked in the firm's favor. When that same CEO ran into a problem and wanted to hire the best consulting firm around, he would naturally think of the firm that had hired the top of the class each year from Harvard and Stanford.

What is the skill level of the work force? Obviously, it is related to the specific production technology employed in the business.

What is the productivity level of the workforce? One of the forces that has caused the explosion in sales of fax machines and cellular phones is the drive to increase the productivity of so-called knowledge workers. The ability to communicate instantly, in written or verbal form, anywhere in the world at any time is a key element in increasing the knowledge workers' productivity. It's also increasing the hours we work each week.

As we progress through the "restructuring" and "right-sizing" era of the 1990s, some very interesting changes are taking place. Major company turnarounds are being based on fundamental changes in relationships between managers and workers. Unions are making concessions that would have been unimaginable a decade ago.

In many instances, the workers became owners through leveraged buyouts (LBOs). Both Harley Davidson and Avis Rent-A-Car have been acquired with heavy employee participation in ownership.[7]

One example of a company with a unique work force management strategy was People Express. A nonunion company, People Express had its employees carefully screen potential hires. Specific technical skills were important, but since there were only two job titles—Customer Service Manager and Flight Manager—personal "fit" (i.e., "our kind of people") was very important. When hired, each employee had to buy one hundred shares of stock. All employees were cross-trained to do more than one job. A pilot, for example, might also do crew scheduling when not flying. The chief financial officer even flew as a flight attendant on occasion. The work force management approach contributed to

People's high productivity and low cost per seat mile. (Purchasing used airplanes at bargain prices from other airlines and increasing the number of seats by 25% or so didn't hurt either!) Unfortunately, People Express' rapid expansion outdistanced its cash flow and the airline is no more.

Identifying the Financial Strategy

Your financial strategy is the way in which you balance and allocate the resources of your business through a common currency called money. Your ability to make effective choices that keep your business in balance will be greatly enhanced with effective financial strategies.

All businesses have a financial strategy. Although businesses that are part of a larger corporation have a financial strategy, they may not control it. Finance is often the first function to be centralized by large corporations. Many operate on the historical General Motors model that allows for decentralized marketing, production, and to some extent R&D, but a centralized financial strategy. The corporate managers have control over resources, and carefully measure the success and failure of each business in the one measure that is common to all—money. By controlling the purse strings, they often feel that they control the businesses and their managers.

Even in the case of the large corporation, it is important to identify the financial strategy of the business. In almost every case there are some elements of financial strategy that the individual business does control. Table 6–3 shows some of the key questions you may want to ask about financial strategy.

Table 6–3
Financial Strategy

Cash Flow Strategy

- *Where are cash flows from the business going?*

Capital Structure Strategy

- *What is the ratio of debt to equity?*
- *What is the working capital position?*
- *What is the specific composition of assets and liabilities?*

Cash Flow Strategy

In Silicon Valley, home of many high tech startups, I have often seen T-shirts with the statement "Happiness Is a Positive Cash Flow!" When a young company first reaches positive cash flow, it is cause for a celebration. It means that the company has a chance to be self-supporting.

Negative cash flow, on the other hand, reduces capital. Once all the capital has been expended, additional equity or debt must be obtained in order to continue in the business. If no additional capital can be located, the business will fail.

Where are the cash flows from the business going? Cash flow can be used in one of four ways: (1) to pay dividends to stockholders, (2) to "invest" in other businesses, (3) to buy back stock, or (4) to "invest" back in the same business.

Some might argue that a fifth category is to pay taxes. However, that choice is mandated by law and only occurs if there is a profit. As all good managers know, profit is a management decision. It is quite possible to have very positive cash flows while losing money and, therefore, paying no taxes. Many LBOs have been structured in this manner.

The fundamental structure of a leveraged buyout is to take a company private using very little in the way of equity funds. Instead, borrowed funds pay most of the purchase price. Often this borrowing is through "junk bonds" which have no collateral or call on the company's assets. Because this type of debt is very risky, the creditors demand high interest rates. The LBO specialists are willing to pay these high rates in exchange for the capital to buy the company. Because the company is now private, virtually all the cash flow from the business can be used to pay off the debt. Once the debt is paid down, the company can be taken public or sold to another company. The equity holders have, in effect, used a company to buy itself and then received full market value for the company.

Some companies choose to pay out some portion of their earnings to stockholders as dividends. The dividend policy should be identified as part of the financial strategy. Obviously, a company that chooses to pay out none of its earnings in dividends is choosing to follow one of the other three paths noted previously. A company that pays out 100% of its earnings in dividends can only "invest" cash flows from sources other than earnings, such as depreciation.

There are two kinds of "investments" one can make when using cash flows from the current business to invest in other businesses. The first is an expense investment and the second is a capital investment.

An expense "investment" is any expense from a second business that ends up on the income statement of the first business. For example, when a company is entering a new business it may pay for the R&D expenses out of the budget for the old business.

Capital investments in another business require capital formation to take place. Capital formation occurs when profits are earned and all taxes and dividends are paid. The remainder is newly formed capital. When you run a business, the problem of capital formation is rapidly brought home. To form one dollar of new capital, you must generate revenues, pay expenses, generate earnings before tax, and pay all applicable taxes. With a tax rate of 34%, $1.50 of earnings before tax are typically required to generate one dollar of new capital.

The pattern of capital investments can be determined by looking at changes in the balance sheet. Given the fundamental balance sheet relationship that total assets equals total liabilities plus stockholders' equity, we can easily determine where the cash flows are being invested. Changes in current or long-term assets must be offset by changes in current or long-term liabilities or stockholders' equity.

The third thing you can do with cash flows from a business is use those cash flows to buy back stock. Often this strategy is followed by companies that believe their stock is undervalued on the market. It is also done by private companies who are buying out some portion of their stockholders.

The fourth thing you can do with cash flows is to invest them back into the same business. The choices under this option are the same as if you are investing cash flows from another business (i.e., "expense" or capital investments), but now the source of the cash flow is the business in which you are investing. By making this choice you are continuing to bet on the wisdom of your original business selection.

Capital Structure Strategy

Capital structure is the ratio of debt to equity in the business. Some companies can take much more financial risk than others because they are in businesses that are extremely stable. Creditors are willing to let them become highly leveraged. Other companies in less stable, more risky businesses do not have this luxury.

What is the working capital position of the business? Working capital is defined as current assets minus current liabilities and it can be either positive or negative. Maintaining a large positive working capital position is a strategy to stay liquid and flexible.

In addition to looking at the ratio of debt to equity you will want to examine the composition of assets. Some businesses require heavy investments in fixed assets, while others are placing their dollars in current assets. Even within these two categories it is important to look at the composition of the assets. What is the asset strategy? Is it to be highly liquid in cash, carry large accounts receivable, have high inventory, or heavily invest in plant and equipment? Each of these is a choice that is made to position the business. Each will have some impact on the flexibility of that business to change and compete.

What is the composition of liabilities? The mixture of current and long-term liabilities is important. More than one company has gotten into serious trouble by funding long-term needs with short-term liabilities. The level of expensive, short-term debt eventually becomes so high that the business fails.

The composition of stockholders equity can also be of interest. The mix of paid-in capital and retained earnings tells you how much of the business' equity is invested by stockholders versus being generated by the business.

Identifying the Research and Development Strategy

Your R&D strategy holds the future of your business. New products and services will be needed as old ones mature and die (see Table 6–4). Without an R&D strategy, your business has no future.

Most businesses do research and development, but not all businesses call it that. Some professional service firms, for example, do not have an overt R&D strategy but they do develop their knowledge while working with clients. This knowledge, or "intellectual capital" as it is sometimes called, is the basis on which the firm builds its new services.

Basic/Applied R&D Strategy

Are you doing basic or applied research, or both, in your business? Not all companies do basic research. For others it is their lifeblood. For example, makers of prescription drugs make large bets that they can develop the best drug for a particular need. Basic research is conducted in

Table 6–4
Research & Development Strategy

Basic / Applied R&D Strategy

- *What basic research is being conducted?*
- *What applied research is being conducted?*

Product / Service Innovation Strategy

- *How does the business develop new products or services?*
- *How much of its resources does it devote to this task?*

Process Innovation Strategy

- *How does the business develop new processes for getting quality up, costs down, or both?*
- *How much of its resources does it devote to this task?*

Leader / Follower Strategy

- *Is the business an intentional leader or follower in developing new products and/or processes?*
- *What is the amount of lead or lag (e.g. innovator, fast second, late entry)?*

laboratories by these companies in an effort to develop the science that will eventually lead to the development of specific drugs. Similarly, in the computer industry, fundamental research is conducted in areas such as superconductivity in order eventually to produce advances in semi-conductor design. These companies must advance the state of the art if they are to be successful in rapidly changing technological environments.

Applied research takes findings from basic research and tackles a specific customer problem. When a biotechnology firm takes the results of its basic research and develops a medication for a specific condition or disease, it is doing applied research. What does applied research mean in your business, and how is it being done?

The fundamental differences between basic and applied research can be illustrated by the work currently being done in the field of biotechnology. The original research done in this area was theoretical work to restructure DNA. This successful basic research has led to the development of literally hundreds of products aimed at specific problems. The development of Interferon to use in curing some forms of cancer is just one example.

Product/Service Innovation Strategy

What is your business' strategy for developing new products or services? Are the customers routinely asked about their needs? Do your R&D managers go to the field to determine what may be needed?

For years at Hewlett-Packard, there was a product innovation strategy in instrument businesses known as the "next bench syndrome." An engineer would be working on a problem and have an idea for a product. He would take that idea to the engineer working on the "next bench" and ask him if it would help solve his problems as well. When he got enough people on nearby benches to think he had a good idea, the product was developed. By developing products for its own use, HP was able to develop products that could be used by customers.

In addition to the method used to develop new products, you also want to identify the level of resource commitment. In many high technology firms, there is a rule of thumb that approximately 10% of revenues should be reinvested in R&D. It is interesting how many of the high technology firms fall between 9% and 11% of revenues spent on R&D.

Process Innovation Strategy

How do you do process innovation in your business? Process innovation is the development of ways to get quality up, costs down, or both.

In the section on quality strategy I mentioned some of the tools used for process innovation, including TQC, TQM, and CFM. There are others, including "value engineering" and quality function deployment (QFD). (Yes, the alphabet soup does get a little thick, doesn't it?)

Using these processes is a way to create development, marketing, or production processes that do not have unnecessary steps in them or produce results that are not valuable to customers.

Coleman, the camping equipment manufacturer, used techniques of process innovation to reduce its inventories from two months to one week's supply while simultaneously increasing the number of models of ice coolers it offered from 20 to 140. The company reduced inventories by $10 million and raised productivity by 35%.[8]

Process innovation is a very important element of strategy. It occurs in both product and service businesses and is a primary tool for productivity improvement. It is particularly important in those businesses where price is a major consideration.

Leader/Follower Strategy

The position that the business takes with respect to being a leader or follower in the development of new products can also be an important element of the strategy. Some companies like to be a fast second and not spend the resources required to be the leader. This is a particularly smart strategy when the first innovation is very expensive to develop and easily copied.

In other industries, particularly those in which the technology can be protected, being the leader is essential. It is not possible to save resources by being a fast second. One example is the pharmaceutical industry. To be successful in the proprietary drug business, a company must be first in the development of a particular drug.

WHAT ARE BUSINESS OBJECTIVES?

To have all the information you need to proceed further, you must also identify your business' objectives. Although there has been an academic debate for many years over whether the objectives should be included as part of the definition of strategy, I don't think it matters. If you are trying to understand a business strategy, you must also understand the business' objectives.

The objectives are the ends you are trying to achieve with the strategy. In most companies there are two kinds of objectives—stated and unstated. The stated objectives often include such things as market share, growth rate, and profitability.

Unstated objectives are those ends that the business is moving toward, but that have not been explicitly stated. More than one family business has been created and continued for the welfare of the family, including jobs for family members.

All objectives are subjectively set. They simply reflect the ends that the strategy is trying to achieve. Be careful to identify both the stated and unstated objectives.

Only with a thorough understanding of the current business strategy and objectives can you tackle the question: "What *should* be our strategy?"

WHAT ARE THE KEY SUMMARY POINTS ABOUT IDENTIFYING THE CURRENT BUSINESS STRATEGY?

Your business strategy is probably unique to your company and your business. It is the dynamic, integrated set of decisions that you have made in order to position your business in its complex environment. These decisions are the means that you use to achieve the ends called objectives. Typically, decisions are made in marketing, finance, production and R&D in order to position the business to meet the sometimes conflicting demands of various stakeholders.

The process of identifying your current strategy is almost always enlightening. You may be surprised at what you are currently doing in your business. The process can be completed by answering the questions discussed in this chapter.

Identifying the current business strategy is a crucial part of the process of creating a new strategy for two reasons. First, the current strategy is the starting point from which any future strategy must evolve. Knowing where you are starting from is essential if you are setting a new course. Second, the process of creating a new strategy is a change process. For that process to be successful, the management team must be in agreement about the starting strategy.

Your strategy may be a brilliant strategy or a doomed one. You won't know that until you complete the work in Chapters 7 through 9.

Now that you know what the current strategy of the business is, you can ask the challenging and enlightening question, "What is the future of the industry?"

Chapter 7
What Is the Future
of the Industry?

"What's the future of your industry?"

"What do you mean? Do you think I have a crystal ball? How should I know what the future is going to be?"

"If you don't know with some degree of certainty what the future is going to be, how can you develop a strategy for your business?"

"Oh . . ."

Managers who can make better predictions have more options to take actions that will allow them to create and sustain success. Few companies that only react to events around them stay in business for very long.

Managers who make good predictions about the future have an opportunity to influence that future. Without a thorough understanding of what is likely to happen, the possibility of influence is lost.

"Predicting the future" sounds like wizardry, but it's not. While 100% accurate prediction of all events and their timing is unlikely, predictability of 80–90% is highly likely. How do I know this? Because I've reviewed work that I've done with clients over the last twenty years. The client management teams have been able to predict almost all of the key events in their industries. When they made mistakes or missed predictions it was because they predicted that events would happen sooner than they actually did. This, of course, was the right mistake to make if they had to make one. By predicting something would happen sooner than it actually did they were at least prepared when the event did occur. Not making the prediction, or predicting that it would happen later than it actually did, would have been more difficult mistakes to handle.

The secret to handling the timing of key predictions is to put in place a process for monitoring the trigger events that surround the prediction. When the trigger events happen, you can then take appropriate action.

Predicting the future of an industry is a lot like predicting the behavior of people you know extremely well. If you know someone's history, past behavior, and way of thinking, you can usually predict how that person is likely to behave. This is particularly true if the characteristics of the situation are known and have been experienced before.

Trend analysis is not enough. I once was amazed by a general management team that thought they had done a very thorough analysis of their industry. They handed me a notebook that contained a list of 137 trends in their industry—137! I didn't know how to respond. What do you do with a list of 137 trends?

Worse, there was neither an implication for the business of any single trend, nor any prioritization of the importance of the trends.

Trend analysis is an important step, but what you should be doing first is a structural analysis of your industry. By examining the structure of the industry, and the relationships among the various players, you can develop a more thorough understanding of likely future behavior.[1] It is in the context of that future that you will develop a strategy that will position your business.

To predict the future of your industry, you need to ask four fundamental questions:

1. What is the scope of the industry?
2. How are the players participating in the industry?
3. What are the relationships among the players in the industry?
4. How will the future unfold?

WHAT IS THE SCOPE OF THE INDUSTRY?

The process of scoping the industry is a process of putting some boundaries around the industry and a structure within those boundaries. It also includes an identification of the key players. The scope of the industry will define the limits of the future you are going to predict.

Defining the Industry

An industry is typically defined as consisting of all of those businesses selling substitutable products or services. You will immediately recognize that we have the same question of substitutability that we discussed in Chapter 2. Exactly how substitutable do the products and/or services need to be?

The answer is up to you. If you define the industry quite narrowly, you deal with only those businesses selling direct substitutes. In this case you only deal with one business. If you choose to add partial substitutes, I suggest you add those businesses that are in the gray area next. You remember the gray area. That's where two or more of the four factors that define a business are partial substitutes, and the two businesses are either converging or diverging.

The broadest definition of the industry includes all of those businesses whose products or services have any substitutability whatsoever. For example, a vacation in Disneyland could be perceived as a partial substitute for a fishing and waterskiing trip to the lake. While I would discourage you from expanding your definition to include this third category, it does have the advantage of thoroughness.

You can make two types of mistakes when defining the industry. If you define the industry too narrowly you are likely to miss businesses converging or diverging from your business that may change it in the future (see Chapter 2).

On the other hand, if you define the industry too broadly, you may find the analytical task to be so huge that it becomes an activity trap rather than a useful analysis.

My own preference is to deal with the direct substitutes and those in the gray area that have significant substitutability for your business.

My recommendation on defining your industry depends heavily on your experience. If this is your first industry analysis, I recommend strongly that you only deal with direct substitutes. Once you have completed that analysis you can add partial substitutes. Some day, if you have a lot of time on your hands, you can add to your industry definition everything that could possibly be a partial substitute. I doubt you'll ever get around to it!

Drawing the Product/Service Flow Diagram

To analyze the structure of an industry, you need a picture of it. Since the creation of a product or service is a process, that process is what you will illustrate with your picture. You want to understand several differ-

Figure 7–1
Generic Product Flow Diagram

ent flows in the picture or diagram, so that you can understand the relationship between the parts of the industry diagram.

I use two methods to create a product/service flow diagram. The first is to start with nothing, build the product or service, and sell it to the customer. A simple, generic product flow diagram is shown in Figure 7–1. You might start with raw materials which are converted into components. Components are assembled by manufacturers who sell them through various distribution channels to customers. Remember that customers include not only purchasers but end-users as well.

A second generic diagram is shown in Figure 7–2. This diagram is a useful starting point when you are dealing with a mediating service industry. Mediating services, such as real estate and financial services, bring buyers and sellers together and provide a service between the two.

Each of these diagrams is inadequate for effective structural analysis, but each is an effective place to start in order to build a more specific diagram for a particular industry. These are just two generic examples among many you could create to describe different fundamental types of industries.

As I mentioned above, one easy way to start to draw a product/service flow diagram is to start with nothing, build the product or service, and sell it to the end customer. A second way to create an industry structure diagram is to look at all of the ways there are to be in businesses related to the fundamental industry definition. From whatever business you use as the starting point to define the industry, you can look backward toward sources of supply and determine all of the different busi-

Figure 7–2
Generic Diagram for a Mediating Services Industry

nesses that lie between you and the raw materials. You can also look toward the customer and see what downstream manufacturers and channels of distribution are available. Once you have identified all of the ways to be in business and the customers who buy the end products, you have a good industry structure diagram.

Each industry, and therefore each product/service flow diagram, is somewhat different. Some are extremely complex, and others are quite simple. An example of a relatively straightforward industry diagram is shown in Figure 7–3. It depicts the "door hardware industry," created from the perspective of a wholesaler. You can see that the key players are shown and their relationship to each other is mapped.

Because it is a much more complex industry, a diagram of the microcomputer industry, especially if you include personal computer systems and peripherals, could cover a large wall.

I have found that managers can fairly quickly draw the product/service flow diagram for their industry, given a little practice. This step is important because it is the foundation upon which the remainder of the analysis is built.

Figure 7–3
Door Hardware Industry Diagram

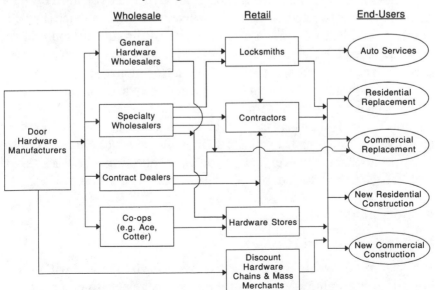

Source: "Door & Security Industry Note," by FOCUS: The Management Process Company. © 1992, p. 3. Reprinted with permission.

Identifying the Players

For each cell in your industry diagram that contains competing companies, you next need to identify exactly who the current players are. You should also identify likely entrants who may join the industry in the near future.

If your industry is like most, you will probably find that your list of competitors, and possibly customers, is fairly long. You may need to prioritize your lists and only deal with the most important ones the first time through. You can also choose to do the full analysis described below on some competitors and customers and a partial analysis on others.

Identification of the competitors is important. You would probably make different predictions about an industry populated by competitors like Joe's While-U-Wait Semiconductors than you would for an industry containing Intel and Motorola. Knowing the size and type of companies you are dealing with is an important step toward understanding the competition in each cell.

In addition to the competitors in the industry, the customers are also key players. You will want to analyze them very carefully in the future. Be careful to identify everyone's customers, not just yours.

HOW ARE THE PLAYERS PARTICIPATING?

In order to understand the functioning of the industry you must examine each of the parts as represented by the cells on a product/service flow diagram. Using Figure 7–1 as an example, you need to understand how the component manufacturers function in this industry. In order to do so you need to answer a series of questions that enable you to develop a comprehensive understanding of the functioning of these players in the industry.

Let's take a look at the series of questions I usually ask when doing an industry analysis. There is some, albeit limited, logic to the order of the questions, so I suggest that you ask them in the sequence presented. What is most important, however, is that you cover all of the questions as you look at each part of the industry. First, let's examine the competitors.

Competitors

How Many Companies Compete?

Whether the answer to this question is two or two thousand will make a big difference in how one part of the industry relates to other parts. If there are a thousand component suppliers you can expect vigorous competition among them. They will have little power over their customers, the product manufacturers. On the other hand, if there are only two sources of components for the manufacturers, competition may not be as intense between the two and they may have a good deal of power over the manufacturers.

The number of competitors in any part of the industry tells you how fragmented that part of the industry is. Fragmentation can have both advantages and disadvantages. In general, a fragmented part of an industry is usually unstable. The higher the degree of fragmentation, the higher the probability of consolidation in that part of the industry at some point. Whether or not that consolidation ever takes place depends on what is causing the fragmentation.

Do the Competitors Break Into Any Logical Groups?

Particularly when the answer to the first question is a large number, you want to ask whether or not the competitors break into any logical groups. If they do, you may want to expand your diagram to separate the various component manufacturers into different logical groups.

Taking the example of the motor home industry, the component suppliers break into several groups, as illustrated in Figure 7–4. There are small suppliers and large suppliers. There are companies that supply only the motor home industry, and suppliers that supply to the motor home and other industries. These two dimensions of size and target market for the component suppliers give you a four-cell matrix that could be four logical groups in this industry.

You are concerned with logical groupings because you want to examine the behavior of each closely related group. For example, in the "large suppliers to motor home plus other industries" cell in Figure 7–4 you would find such companies as Dodge and Coleman. These companies probably behave differently than the mom and pop companies you would find in the cell for small companies supplying only the motor home industry. Therefore you want to identify the two types of component manufacturers on your overall industry diagram and ask the remaining questions about each of these cells independently.

Note that this question is a test of your overall diagram and its effectiveness for the industry analysis process. You want a diagram that has a cell for each logical grouping of companies along the product/service flow chain so that you can ask the appropriate questions about each cell.

Figure 7–4
Motor Home Component Suppliers Logical
Groups

	Small	Large
Supply Only the Motor Home Industry		
Supply the Motor Home Plus Other Industries		

Michael L. Lovdal, "Winnebago Industries Inc. and the Recreational Vehicle Industry," Harvard Business School, Case #9–
375–092, 1974, p. 5.

What Is Each Competitor's Business Strategy?

Using the process of strategy identification described in detail in Chapter 6, you can identify each significant competitor's strategy.

Yes, a major effort is required to identify even a few competitors'
strategies. Doing it, however, makes the difference between the success
and failure of your industry analysis.

While I prefer not to take shortcuts, they are sometimes necessary. A
couple of tricks of the trade may be useful to you here.

For your direct competitors, the ones that are after your business, I
strongly recommend that you do individual strategy identifications.
You need to know the details to compete effectively.

For suppliers, any downstream manufacturers, and the distribution
channels, you may be able to do composite strategy identifications for
several key players if they follow one or two similar strategies. For example, if the component suppliers break into high-quality/high-price
versus low-quality/low-price suppliers, the participants may follow
similar strategies within those categories. If so, you can do a composite
strategy identification for that "class" of competitor.

Even when you do composite strategy identifications, be sure to note
any major differences in the individual players you have grouped together.

Why Is Each Competitor Here?

The motivation that brings a competitor to compete in the industry is
one of the most important forces that determines the future of the indus-

try. While many competitors enter the industry to increase shareholder wealth, some may not.

Sometimes an industry is attractive because of the activity it involves. In general aviation there is a business known as the fixed based operator (FBO) business. An FBO is someone who sells gas, rents airplanes, gives lessons, and sometimes services the airplanes. There are thousands of FBOs in the United States. You can find at least one in almost every airport in the country. I have seen people go into this business, work twelve to fourteen hours a day, seven days a week, and put everything they owned into the business. Eventually, because there is such cutthroat competition to participate in the business, they fail. Why would anyone do this?

It's simple. They love airplanes. They want to be around airplanes and aviation.

The official, academic name for a someone who enters business for noneconomic reasons is "stupid competitor." Does this mean that the individual is stupid? No, it certainly doesn't. It means that there is some reason, other than economics, for their entry into the business.

Perhaps the most prominent motivation of stupid competitors is the one mentioned above, a love of a particular activity. There are many examples, including sailboat manufacturing, thoroughbred racing, and restaurants.

There are other ways to be a stupid competitor. I have seen companies enter a business simply to build a relationship with a customer base. Once the relationship is built, the company aggressively takes market share and begins to make money.

In other cases I have seen companies enter a business simply to learn and develop a particular technology. The companies involved thought that the technology was essential to their future, and that they could not stay out of the market, despite losing millions of dollars each year on the business.

Sometimes companies stay in businesses much longer than they should because of an executive's ego. It is very difficult for some CEOs to divest businesses that they have purchased earlier in their careers. Even though the company can no longer compete, the CEO is sometimes unwilling to admit that the business is no longer viable.

Understanding a competitor's motivation tells you how hard that competitor will fight to participate in the industry. It may also tell you what weapons the competitor is willing to use in the battle.

If the competitor's motivation is other than economic, the competitor may be willing to give up economic returns for other, noneconomic returns. They may take their "return on investment" in emotional rather than monetary terms. From the standpoint of a rational, economic player, this can be disastrous. People who do not play by economic rules may cause cutthroat competition.

How Do They Compete?

In order to understand competitive dynamics you need to understand four basic concepts: competitive arenas, weapons, signals (see Figure 7–5), and levels (see Figure 7–6).

Figure 7–5

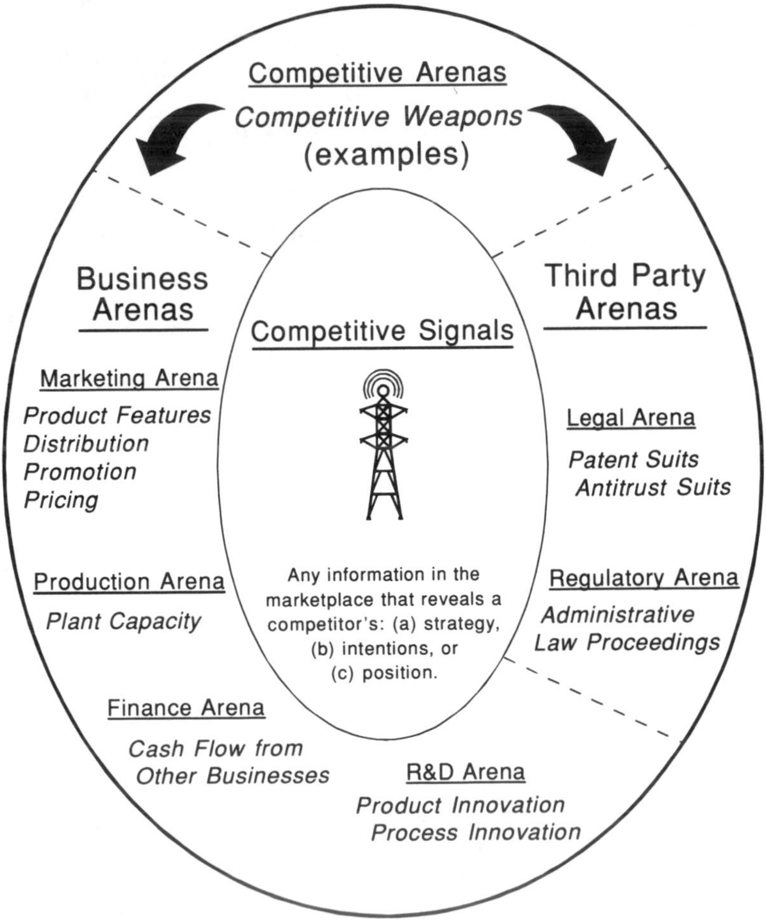

Competitive Arenas
Competitive Weapons
(examples)

**Business
Arenas**

Competitive Signals

**Third Party
Arenas**

Marketing Arena

*Product Features
Distribution
Promotion
Pricing*

Legal Arena

*Patent Suits
Antitrust Suits*

Production Arena

Plant Capacity

Any information in the marketplace that reveals a competitor's: (a) strategy, (b) intentions, or (c) position.

Regulatory Arena

*Administrative
Law Proceedings*

Finance Arena

*Cash Flow from
Other Businesses*

R&D Arena

*Product Innovation
Process Innovation*

Figure 7–6
The Four Levels of Competition

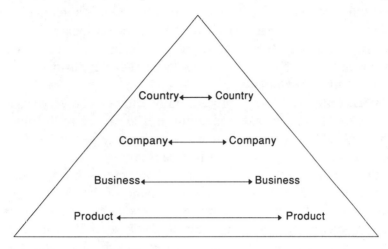

COMPETITIVE ARENAS. The competitive arena is where the battle takes place. There are two types of arenas. First are the business arenas, including marketing, production, finance, and R&D. Obviously, competitors will try to get the battle fought in the arena in which they are the strongest.

The second type of arena is the third party arena. Third party arenas include the legal and regulatory arenas. They are where you go to get the battle adjudicated. In essence, when the battle is being fought in a third party arena the competitors are asking some third party to determine the rules of the game of competition.

COMPETITIVE WEAPONS. Within each arena there are usually a number of competitive weapons that can be used by various competitors to try to win the battle. Within marketing, typical weapons include product characteristics, pricing, distribution, and promotional efforts. For example, using a new combination of product characteristics, Chrysler took market share from other auto manufacturers when it introduced the minivan.

When Burger King advertises that you can "have it your way!" they are using a promotional weapon against McDonald's, which has standardized products. Frito-Lay uses its strong distribution channels as a way to counter other, more local snack food manufacturers.

Within the production arena, plant capacity is often a weapon. Someone with excess plant capacity can easily use it to marginally price incremental capacity and drive prices down in the marketplace. Companies at full capacity have difficulty responding to this approach.

In the financial arena, cash flow from other businesses is used by large corporations to fund a new, growing business. A company that does not have another source of funds from other businesses has to source its funding externally.

In R&D both product and process innovation can be very important weapons to use against the competition. The ability to develop new products rapidly and accompany them with processes that get quality up, cost down, or both, are very effective weapons.

In the legal arena it is common to see competitors use weapons like patent suits and antitrust suits. The first round of a major competitive battle was settled in early 1992 when Apple's patent infringement suit against Microsoft and Hewlett-Packard was essentially thrown out of court. Apple had been using this suit to try to keep Microsoft and HP from producing and selling products that had the "look and feel" of its Macintosh operating system.

Antitrust suits are another weapon that can be used against a competitor. They are useful when one competitor is pricing its products below cost in an attempt to capture market share. In 1992 Nintendo was accused of such behavior and the potential for an antitrust suit was a weapon being considered by some competitors.[2]

In the regulatory arena, competition among industries for the rights to participate have been dealt with in administrative law proceedings. Starting in 1966 and continuing until 1980, the Federal Communications Commission held a series of hearings on the boundaries between communications and computing. The outcome of the two "computer inquiries" was the definition of "basic" and "enhanced" network services. Basic services remained regulated while enhanced services became deregulated.

At the third computer inquiry in 1986, the FCC stipulated that Regional Bell Holding Companies (RBHCs) must offer basic and enhanced telecommunications services through separate business operations.[3] By 1991, the FCC stipulated that the RBHCs could offer unregulated enhanced services and regulated telephone services through the same business units.[4] Thus, over time the boundaries of computing and communications have been blurred as competitors have fought in the regulatory arena.

COMPETITIVE SIGNALS. The concept of a competitive signal can lead you to think of a sailor on the deck of a ship sending semaphore code to another ship within sight. Although sending a signal sounds like a deliberate act on the part of a competitor, it is not necessarily so. *A competitive signal is any information in the marketplace that reveals a competitor's strategy, intentions, or position.*

A "signal" can be sent intentionally or unintentionally. Some happen by accident. Whenever a company announces its quarterly revenues and profits, it is inadvertently sending a signal about its performance to its competitors.

When one of my clients announced a price reduction in its major product line, the industry press heralded the move as a signal of a price war. While my client had no intention of starting a price war, the press articles led the competitors to match my client's price reduction very quickly. Because of the press' interpretation, the competitors *perceived* the situation as the start of a price war. Fortunately, through my client's diligent use of appropriate signals, the pricing actions halted before cutthroat competition started.

Signals can be true or false. In the latter case they're called "bluffs." Competitors have been known to signal that they are going after a particular market and then not actually make the move. What they sometimes want is their competition to spend a lot of money chasing an unprofitable segment and lose money.

Finally, signals can be aimed at various interested stakeholders. They might be aimed at competitors, the financial community, stockholders, distributors, or customers. The target of a signal's message can influence its content. For each signal, you should attempt to discern the target audience.

If you want to see some exciting signaling, watch the airline industry during its annual fare wars in the spring and summer. The airlines say and do outrageous things with pricing.

Some industries have very sophisticated processes for signaling. Others are quite routine and, perhaps, not very interesting. Regardless of how exciting they are, you need to monitor the signals in the marketplace in order to have the maximum information about the competitors' strategy, position, and intentions.

COMPETITIVE LEVELS. There is a common misconception that competition only takes place on the product-against-product level. This is certainly one area where competition does take place but, as shown in Figure 7–6, competition really occurs on four levels.

The four levels of competition operate in a manner similar to Maslow's hierarchy of needs. You have to meet the "must requirements" at the lowest level of competition before you can participate effectively in the next level. For example, you have to meet the "must" level of competition at the product-against-product level before participating at the business-against-business level. Then you have to meet the business-against-business "must requirements" before you can participate in the company-against-company level. If you haven't met the "must requirements" of a level, moving up is a waste of resources.

Let's take a look at how this works by looking at the characteristics of each level.

At the product level of competition you are looking predominantly at a features battle. These features provide certain benefits to various segments of the market, and those benefits generate certain feelings. This process is shown in Figure 7–7 as product/service positioning.

Figure 7–7
Product/Service Positioning

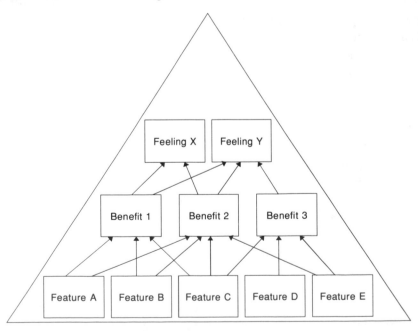

Although one product may be superior to another if you just compare the two product's lists of features, as long as the two competitors' products both meet the "must" criteria, the battle will move to the next higher level. A customer doesn't care very much about the features a product has that are not on his or her "must" list.

I once chided a client in a high-technology business for building a "doomsday box." This piece of electronic test equipment could have withstood most nuclear attacks. The product was massively over-engineered, with entirely too many features that the customers did not want. It was, however, the best in the business—if you had to have everything. Few customers did.

IBM traditionally has been a company that has been extremely good at meeting the "must requirements" and moving the competitive battle up to higher levels. In the mid-1980s many observers agreed that the Macintosh from Apple was a better product than IBM's PC. The Mac was easier to learn and use. IBM's PC, however, was adequate for most customer needs.

Once the "must requirements" are met, the competition in the customer's mind moves to the next higher level. It is at this level that one business strategy competes against another business strategy. We are no longer talking about just product characteristics, but all of the other elements of the business strategy in the battle. While one company may have a better product to offer than another, the company with the best business strategy wins at this level. For example, it may be that one competitor provides financing or faster delivery than the other that makes the difference in the customer's decision to buy.

Those competitors who meet the "must requirements" for business strategy against business strategy can move to the company against company level. Two battles in major sectors of the economy illustrate that battle extremely well.

AT&T's fight against MCI, Sprint, and other service providers in the long distance telephone business illustrates the company-against-company battle. AT&T is well known for its reliability and service. When the other companies entered the business they had some reliability problems. AT&T exploited the competitors' initial problems with their "Ma Bell" image and assurance of service and quality. AT&T even advertised that they cost the same, or slightly more, than the competition, but they kept pushing quality.

For years IBM has been identified with phrases such as "IBM Means

Service" and "Nobody Ever Got Fired for Buying IBM." These messages of security were very powerful company-against-company weapons that IBM used against other competitors. Unfortunately, IBM's difficulties in 1992 and 1993 may have damaged some part of its great reputation.

When Steve Jobs was running Apple Computer, he intentionally positioned Apple against IBM. Remember the Super Bowl ad with people all dressed alike and acting like lemmings as they walked off a cliff? Jobs' positioning was great to get early adopters, who are also often rebels, to try his products. It didn't communicate a lot of security to the corporate world, however, and Apple failed several times in its large account efforts under Jobs' leadership.

The highest and last level of competition is country-against-country competition. This battle can be seen in its rapidly changing dynamics during the 1990s. Countries are vying for leadership positions in various global industries.

Countries play a very important role in setting the rules of the game in various industries. Their ability to restrict or encourage imports and exports is an important factor in world markets. For example, the reformulation of the Common Market into the European Economic Community was an obvious move by the European countries to gain competitive power in the world markets. The previous organization was unable to compete against the economic powerhouses of the United States and Japan.

To understand the four levels of competition, there are two important generalizations. The first is, as mentioned above, that you have to meet the "must requirements" before you are able to participate effectively in the next level of competition. Meeting more than the "must requirements" does little good. Why would you want to provide more value, and therefore more cost to you, than the customer is willing to pay for?

The second generalization is that the company that is able to compete on the highest level usually wins. I say "usually" because customers are not always rational. They sometimes pick maverick competitors simply because they like mavericks.

What Strategic Groups Have Formed?

A strategic group is a set of companies in an industry that is following similar strategies in an attempt to set the rules of the competitive game[5].

As industries develop and grow, the battle over rules of the game often becomes quite important. These battles can be over such things as technological standards or the "must requirements" for a particular product. There are a number of classic strategic groups that serve as examples of the concept.

THE AUTOMOBILE SECTOR. From 1946 until at least 1974 there was a group in the automobile industry known as the Big Three: General Motors, Ford, and Chrysler. The Big Three set the rules of the game for the automobile industry, at least in the United States and perhaps in other major markets. The rules of the competitive game were based on a fundamental concept promoted by the Big Three. This concept was "planned obsolescence." What that meant was that the car you bought from one of the Big Three had a limited life. It would become obsolete within a few years.

For the sake of this example, let's assume that at around 40,000 miles a car would start to become obsolete in several ways. Its style would become obsolete because one rule of the game was that each of the Big Three made annual, significant style changes. Second, the car would start to have significant mechanical problems. Third, since gas was inexpensive, big, powerful cars were more desirable than small cars, so as a young person, you would start out with a small car, and trade up throughout your lifetime as you became more successful. Cars and status were equated.

By maintaining the rules of the game, the Big Three were able to dominate the U.S. domestic and worldwide automobile markets from the post-World War II era through at least 1974. In 1974 a major discontinuity hit the auto industry. The Arab oil embargo occurred, changing forever the way we think about gasoline. Virtually overnight, a luxury car became a gas guzzler and people who drove them were socially irresponsible wastrels.

With gasoline costing more than $1 a gallon in the United States in 1974, and four times that in many European markets, the economics of operating an automobile changed dramatically. As the economics of ownership changed, so did the requirement for a quality product. Forty thousand miles was no longer enough life for something that cost so much. Planned obsolescence was history; quality was the new byword.

The Arab oil embargo allowed a new strategic group, the combination of Japanese and German economy car manufacturers, to penetrate the huge U.S. and European markets. This group successfully promoted new and different rules of the game, where standardized, high-quality, low-cost, economical products were sold against the gas-guzzling, planned obsolescence products of the Big Three.

THE COMPUTER SECTOR. In the computer sector the dominant worldwide strategic group has been one company: IBM, also known as Big Blue. There have been several other strategic groups in the industry, and they continue to develop and evolve as the industry moves forward. The first significant strategic group was known as the BUNCH, which was an acronym for Burroughs, Univac (Sperry Rand Corp.), NCR, Control Data, and Honeywell. The BUNCH was the other strategic group that competed heavily against Big Blue in the computer sector.

Over the years, the BUNCH lost its punch. Burroughs and Sperry merged to form Unisys Corp., a company that had significant profitability problems for several years. NCR was acquired by AT&T as an attempt to compete in the computer sector. (Previous attempts by AT&T had met with limited success, so an acquisition was made.) Control Data basically exited the computer industry by selling off all except a few peripheral products. Finally, Honeywell left the industry by selling its computer operations to the French company Honeywell Bull.

The disintegration of the BUNCH points out the first fundamental law in understanding strategic groups: to be successful you must be in a winning strategic group. If your group is unsuccessful in getting its rules of the game adopted, it is unlikely that you can be successful as an individual competitor.

The second law of strategic groups is: to be successful you must be a winner within a strategic group. Many of the companies that made IBM-compatible equipment learned the vagaries of competition against an aggressive player like IBM. Many left the business because they couldn't keep up with the development of technology and continually declining costs.

There are other strategic groups in the computer sector. For example, the minicomputer manufacturers follow similar strategies in an attempt to compete against Big Blue. Hewlett-Packard, Digital Equipment, and Data General have all, over the years, made Big Blue a primary target.

Some strategic groups have formed what are called strategic alliances as a way to formalize their relationship. In 1992 two previously mortal enemies, Apple and IBM, formed Taligent, a strategic alliance in the microcomputer industry. The purpose of the alliance was to develop an easier-to-use computer operating system. Doing so pit Taligent directly against Microsoft, which by 1991 provided the operating systems for 90% of the world's PCs.[6]

What Are the Barriers to Entry?

I discussed barriers to entry, success, and exit in Chapter 4. Here, you need to determine what the barriers are for each type of participant in your industry. What are the barriers for component suppliers? What about distributors?

How difficult would it be for some participants to move backward or forward along the product/service flow chain?

How easy is it for one player to dominate a particular portion of the industry because he has developed significant barriers to his competitors' success?

How difficult would it be for some competitors to leave the industry? What keeps the poor performers, if there are any, in the game?

Customers

It is a truism to say that without customers you don't have a business. And yet, many companies know very little about their customers.

One company knew how many units of their product they had sold, but had no idea who had bought them, or how much they liked the product. Another was betting that the market would prefer to buy entire systems rather than the pieces that made up the system, but hadn't tested their assumption on any customers. A third was literally betting the entire company's future on a complex software product that they hoped the market would buy, but they had not asked any potential customers what they wanted in such a product.

Customers are not aliens. They normally speak some intelligent language, and are usually more than happy to tell you what they want. After all, it's their own needs they want fulfilled.

Good customer data is essential to doing an intelligent job of predicting the future.

How Is the Market Segmented?

As you know from Chapter 6, there are three primary ways to segment a market: demographics, attitudes, and behaviors. These elements are detailed in Figure 7–8. Note that with customers you must segment both the end users and the purchasers. They may or may not be the same people.

Figure 7–8
The DAB Method of Market Segmentation

What Is the Growth Rate of Each Segment?

Growth is a very important force in the dynamics of any industry. To understand what growth has been and will be, you need to get the best possible forecasts of growth, preferably for each market segment. You will also want to understand the forces causing the growth in each market.

Since growth potential is such a driving force in the development of any business, making the best possible forecasts of growth rates is well worth the time and effort. I discussed previously (see Chapter 3) the mistakes you can make by thinking you are in a growth market when you are not. Missing a growth market by projecting too low a growth rate is an equal sin.

When projecting growth rates, make sure that you have considered all possible channels for your products and services. In the minicartridge tape drive business in which cassette tapes are used as backup storage devices, a small company, Colorado Memory Systems, literally stole the market from the leaders. The company first penetrated lesser known independent dealers and slowly worked its way into the major chains. Using a low price and an adequate quality strategy, the company became the market leader with an estimated 40–45% share of the total market in 1992.

At the price Colorado Memory Systems was willing to sell its drives, there was significant latent demand for the product. Most market prognosticators had failed to perceive this demand because they had talked only to the major dealers and not the secondary channels.

WHAT ARE THE RELATIONSHIPS AMONG PLAYERS?

Now that you understand the relationships within groups of participants in the industry, you need to understand the relationships across the groups on your product/service flow diagram.

There are two forces that drive most of the dynamics in any industry. They are the economics of the industry and the trends/discontinuities created by the six meta-processes of the business' larger context.

Economics

To understand the economics of any industry it is necessary to look at four different perspectives. The first perspective is to examine the value added. The second is to look at the type and amount of profit available. Third, examine economies of scale. Finally, you want to know how the industry is related to the total economy.

Where Is the Value Added?

"Value added" is defined as what you can sell something for, minus what it cost you to purchase raw materials or components. It is the measure of total value that you add through whatever process you use to create your product or service. It is calculated by taking the difference between what the customer thinks your product or service is worth and therefore will pay for it, and what you have to pay to buy the components. A business with zero value added is a pure commodity. As Chiquita Banana and Idaho potatoes have proven, there are few true commodities.

Value added has both positive and negative aspects. High value added businesses tend to be those with high profit potential. Note that I said profit *potential*, not profitability. Companies can add a lot of value, but the cost of that value can be more than customers are willing to pay. This is true in a number of automobile businesses. Players in the automobile industry will tell you that their subcompact cars lose money. There is a large amount of value added, but they can't get the customers to pay for that value. They continue to produce these cars because regulations require them to have a fleet mix that meets certain gas mileage requirements. Without the subcompacts they could not do so.

The key to taking advantage of a high value added business is to drive the cost down to the point where profit is available.

High value added businesses tend to have more control over the events in their industries. Low value added businesses have little control. The reason is that who gets how much of the total value added in

Figure 7–9

an industry is a negotiated amount relative to the power that each player has in the industry.

Let's look at an example.

Two powerboat companies are selling their boats through dealers. A simple industry diagram would look like Figure 7–9.

The "Putt-Putt" boat company has an exclusive set of dealers who both sell and service only Putt-Putt boats. Putt-Putt has developed strong brand recognition through heavy national advertising. All its boats carry the Putt-Putt brand name. Putt-Putt has integrated backwards into component manufacturing to ensure quality components for its boats. Its products are low-cost, but reliable pleasure craft.

"Zoom Boats," on the other hand, has a line of boats known by their individual model names. These boats are sold through independent dealers who carry other lines in addition to Zoom. Zoom provides little support to its dealers and only occasionally does cooperative ads with them. Zoom boats are known for their sleek design and speed.

Putt-Putt and Zoom compete across the product line in price and performance.

To compare the two pleasure boat companies' economics of value added, you would look at how each dollar of sales is distributed along the product/service flow diagram.

Company	Manufacturer's Cost for Components	Dealer Cost	Sales Price
Putt-Putt	$0.45	$0.87	$1.00
Zoom	$0.50	$0.80	$1.00

While the two manufacturers have competing products, Putt-Putt captures more of the value added because of its backward integration into components and its greater power over its exclusive dealers.

Company	Manufacturer's Value Added	Dealer Value Added
Putt-Putt	$0.42	$0.13
Zoom	$0.30	$0.20

Dealers get less of the total value added with Putt-Putt boats, but may be perfectly happy if they are easier to sell because of Putt-Putt's greater advertising and support commitments. Dealers, as private companies, are more interested in profits measured in "dollars to the bank," not margins.

Value added can also mean reduced strategic flexibility.

Because value added is often gained by either forward or backward integration along the product/service flow chain, the potential to decrease strategic flexibility always exists. By committing more and more resources to additional parts of the same industry, the company reduces its flexibility to change its strategy. This move is usually beneficial in stable industries and can be a difficulty in highly volatile ones. (The concept of strategic flexibility is discussed in detail in Chapter 8.)

How Is the Value Added Migrating?

Value added is a key concept in industry dynamics because it is always in motion. As change occurs, value added shifts, or "migrates," in the industry. As it shifts, business definitions change.

What causes businesses to converge or diverge?

Fundamentally, this phenomenon is caused by the *migration of value* over time. No business is static. Both the business and the technological, legal, political, natural, sociological, and economic meta-processes in which the business exists are constantly changing. The only constant is change!

Value is commonly defined by the following equation:[7]

$$Value = Needs\ Met - Cost$$

To the extent customers have the information to make a choice, they tend to purchase the products and services that give them the most value.

Let's take an example that affects virtually everyone and see how the value has migrated over the last thirty years or so. Get ready for a crash course in the history of the computer sector (see Figure 7–10).

In the early 1960s, the only type of computer available was a mainframe. These devices required specialized rooms with air conditioning and false floors. They were run by wizards called electronic data pro-

Figure 7–10
Divergence of Businesses in the Computer Sector over
Three Decades

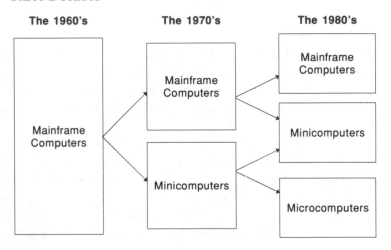

cessing (EDP) managers. Part of their mystique was the language they used. It consisted of lots of acronyms and strange words like "bits" and "bytes." These managers had power in their organizations because they managed a large part of the total information flow in the organization.

IBM "owned" the mainframe business with some 70% of market share among the Fortune 1000 during the 1960s.[8]

Unfortunately, this highly centralized approach to data processing was not loved and admired by all members of management. Some wanted more control over their computing resources. As the technology evolved, so did the products.

The next major product evolution was the minicomputer. It heralded the advent of DDP, which stood for either departmental data processing or distributed data processing, depending on which manufacturer's literature you read. Now engineering, manufacturing, finance, and each of the other departments in a typical business could have their own computing power. And when networking developed, each department could share information and computing resources with others.

Interestingly, IBM missed this divergence of the minicomputer business from the mainframe business. Other, more innovative companies like Digital Equipment, Data General, and Hewlett-Packard took the lead in the development of minicomputers.

This failure of the leading company in one business to identify the next business that diverges from it is quite common. It often happens to the best of companies. The reason it happens is that leading companies are "customer-driven," which means they pay close attention to the needs and desires of their current customers. As a result, they often miss markets that more "product-driven" companies create. A successful business with a large installed base of customers can be a major impediment to innovation. Obviously, it is important to be both customer- and product-driven.

In the late 1970s and early 1980s the value of computing power migrated again. If you want to know why the migration continued, all you had to do was ask managers how they felt about their data processing department. The typical answer I have gotten is, "They're too slow and too expensive."

The migration of value didn't happen with the advent of the microcomputer. Microcomputers were around for some time before the business truly diverged from minicomputers. It happened when the microcomputer and two software packages were combined. The specific computer was the Apple and the software packages were VisiCalc and WordStar. Suddenly, everyone had the capability to do spreadsheets and word processing on his or her desk.

With the micro- or personal computer, everyone has control over his computing power. With the evolution of technology, it is easy to put more computing power on your desk, or even in your lap, than existed in most computer rooms in the 1960s. The revolution that the microcomputer created has changed how people live their lives on a daily basis throughout the world. The divergence of businesses in the computer sector is an example of what can happen as value migrates over time.

Where Is the Profit?

There are three kinds of profit you should examine as you look across the parts of the industry. They are margins, returns, and capital appreciation (also see Chapter 3). On the margin line you will want to know what the gross margin, operating profit, pretax income, and net income are for each of the businesses. With regard to returns, you want to know the return on assets, return on invested capital, and return on equity. Finally, you will want to know whether the businesses in each part of the industry are appreciating or depreciating in value, and why.

Where Are the Economies of Scale?

In each industry the potential for economies of scale usually differs among the parts of the industry. Sometimes economies of scale are more available in component manufacturing, and sometimes they are found at the assembly stage. Occasionally, economies of scale are found even in the distribution channels. You want to know where the economies of scale are because competitors in the industry will try to gain economic power through them.

How Is the Industry Related to the Total Economy?

Economies, both world and national, go through cycles. Figure 7–11 shows the typical economic cycle of boom or bust that occurs in most economies. The dashed line shows how a discretionary product would react as the economy cycles. As the economy increases, sales of discretionary products accelerate. As soon as an economic downturn or recession is feared by the customers for the product, its sales take a dive. Typically, discretionary products recover after the economy is clearly on the way to recovery.

The dotted line shows a product that is a necessity. These products are not affected much by economic downturns or upswings. Staple foods such as bread and milk fall into the category of necessities.

Knowing what your industry's relationship to the economy is will allow you to predict cyclical changes in your business' growth rate. The only challenge is finding an economist who can predict what the economy is likely to do!

The second aspect of knowing how your business is related to the

Figure 7–11

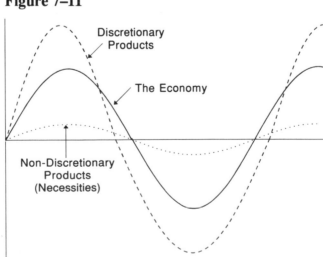

economy is to predict how each of the players will behave in each part of the cycle. Some, for example a participant with a low cost structure, may use a downturn as an opportunity to force a consolidation by lowering prices to start a price war that only he can win. Others may use an upturn in business as an opportunity to expand their share.

The more a business is affected by changes in the economy, the more changes in behavior you are likely to encounter among the players in the industry.

Trends and Discontinuities

A trend is an identifiable direction in which events are moving. Trends occur in each of the six meta-processes discussed in Chapter 3. You find trends in legal, economic, political, sociological, technological, and natural areas. The important things to determine are the trends that affect your industry and their implications.

A discontinuity is an event not on a trend line. I previously discussed the discontinuity caused by the Arab oil embargo in 1974. In more recent years, specifically in 1991, a number of discontinuities occurred. An entire war was fought in the period of a few weeks, the USSR disintegrated, and the savings and loan industry collapsed in the United States. Most discontinuities are predictable by those who are looking closely. However, for most people the above mentioned events were rather sudden and unexpected.

It is useful to ask the question, "What discontinuity might affect my business in a dramatic way?"

HOW WILL THE FUTURE UNFOLD?

To predict the future of your industry, the first step is to isolate those trends that are absolutely clear and predictable. In any industry there are usually a few trends that are sure bets. The economy is changing. New competitors are entering. Some things are highly predictable.

The second step is to ask, "Where is there instability in the industry?" Instability can be found anywhere things are out of balance. For example, anywhere that supply exceeds demand, there is a threat that that portion of the industry will undergo a shakeout or other reduction in the competition. Similarly, anytime new technology is replacing old technology, instability is present. When new strategic groups form, or old strategic groups adopt new strategies, instability is likely. Industries tend to seek stability through whatever means necessary. Given the type of instability you are facing, what changes are likely in your industry?

The third step in predicting the future is to look at the interactions *among* the major components of the industry. Figure 7–12 shows one way to structure your questions. For example, how will forces in the market cause changes in the competitors, technologies, economics, and regulatory areas of the industry?

If the market happens to be declining, competitors may fight harder to protect their revenues and maintain profits. Investment in technology will probably decline or perhaps stop. Profits will probably decline to the extent that competitors use price as a weapon to maintain share. An economic downturn will make the situation worse if the product is discretionary. The declining market might not have any effect on the legal or regulatory climate other than it might generate a source of income for bankruptcy attorneys.

By systematically looking at the interactions of the components of the industry and using some common sense, you can make fairly sophisticated and very accurate predictions of the future of your industry.

The final step in predicting the future of your industry is to ask who has the power to affect events in the industry. Typically, there are those who lead the industry in some way—whether it be in market share,

Figure 7–12

Cause Changes in the . . . .

How Will Forces in the	Markets	Competitors	Technologies	Economics	Legal/ Regulatory
Markets		?	?	?	?
Competitors			?	?	?
Technologies				?	?
Economics					?
Legal/ Regulatory					

technology, or profitability—that have the power to affect events in the industry. Whether or not they exercise that power is a matter of their choice, but players with power often use it.

WHAT ARE THE KEY SUMMARY POINTS ABOUT PREDICTING THE FUTURE?

Industries can be analyzed by examining their structures and dynamics. The first step is to draw an industry product/service flow diagram that gives you an accurate picture of the structure of the industry. By thoroughly exploring each cell in the diagram with a set of penetrating questions, you can understand the role of that cell in the industry. By looking at the economics of the industry, you can understand the relationships among the players in the industry.

So the future of an industry really is predictable. All it takes is a lot of data that you organize into information and extract value from by analyzing it to gain knowledge. The process of converting data to information to knowledge is called moving through the Knowledge Wedge (see Figure 7–13).

Knowledge is what you need to make effective decisions.

For your management team to exercise its five freedoms it is absolutely necessary that they do a complete industry analysis and make predictions of the future.

Now that you know what the past, the present, and the future look like, it is time to do what you probably wanted to do first, to evaluate how good your strategy is.

Figure 7–13
The Knowledge Wedge

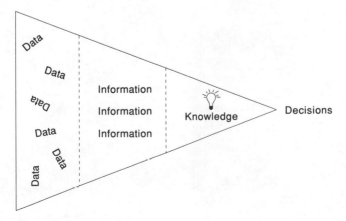

Chapter 8
How Good Is the Strategy?

"How good is your strategy?"

"Our strengths and weaknesses analysis said it was pretty good."

"You mean you haven't applied the nine tests of a business strategy?"

"Nine tests? What nine tests?"

Many managers want to start their strategy creation process by critiquing the "strengths and weaknesses" of their current strategy. For some reason, evaluation of the current strategy comes first.

By using the process discussed in this book, you have taken a different path. You have systematically built a comprehensive understanding of your business, its current strategy, and the future that your business is likely to face. The approach has been data-based and nonevaluative of your current strategy. By postponing your evaluation to this point you have substantially increased your odds of having a comprehensive understanding of the strengths and weaknesses of the strategy.

The introduction to Freedom 2, Creating the Right Strategy, explained one of the reasons why the traditional strengths and weaknesses analysis does not work very well. It tends to reveal only the typical conflicts between the functional areas of the business, such as finance and marketing's traditional conflict over pricing. Finance wants a high price; marketing prefers a low price. The other three reasons that traditional strengths and weaknesses analysis doesn't work well are that it is often (1) based too much on opinion rather than data, (2) not comprehensive, and (3) does not look at the three relevant time frames: the past, present, and future.

A better way to assess the true strengths and weaknesses of a business strategy is to employ three different families of tests: (1) performance tests, (2) consistency tests, and (3) expectancy tests. These three families of tests look at the strategy in the past, present, and future. You must use all three perspectives if you are to gain a comprehensive understanding of the real strengths and weaknesses of your strategy.

Within these three families there are a total of nine different tests that are useful in evaluating a business strategy (see Figure 8–1). Each test looks at a different facet of the strategy and yields somewhat different results than the others.

There are only two secrets to using these tests to understand the strengths and weaknesses of any strategy. You must (1) get the best possible data, and (2) apply all nine tests.

The quality of an evaluation is directly proportional to the quality of the data used to perform each test. Unfortunately, many people have

Figure 8–1

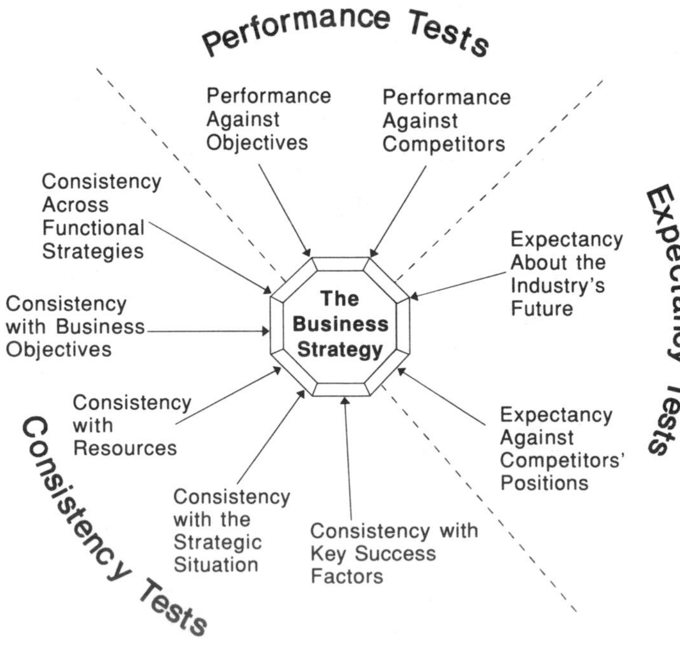

biases about data. They do not understand that they must get four types of data in order to effectively do an evaluation.

The four types of data (shown in Figure 8–2) are used in different tests. The performance tests tend to use objective data, but it can be either quantitative or qualitative. The consistency tests use both objective and subjective data. Expectancy tests use only subjective data because you are looking solely into the future with these tests. Since you cannot know the future with certainty, all of the data is subjective, but it can be either quantitative or qualitative.

A saying in the field of total quality control (TQC) is very relevant here: "Without data, all you have is another opinion." While opinions can be valuable, good data drives out opinions. When you can get objective data, you should employ as few opinions as possible.

A problem I encounter frequently is that some people are trained in certain ways of thinking. For example, scientists and engineers tend to be trained to use objective and quantitative data, so they may not be as comfortable with the other types. Other people have thinking patterns in which everything tends to be subjective and they fail to get the appropriate objective data to use in the strategy evaluation.

Figure 8–2

	Quantitative	Qualitative
Objective	Financial Statements	Fact Statements
Subjective	• Budgets • Forecasts	Opinions

Regardless of your biases about data, it is absolutely essential that you apply all nine tests when evaluating a business strategy. In many situations a strategy will successfully pass eight of the nine tests and fail just one. That failure, however, can mean that the business does not have a bright future. It may even mean that the business is no longer viable.

Let's look at the three families and the nine tests that they comprise.

HOW WELL HAS THE STRATEGY PERFORMED IN THE PAST?

Performance tests have some common characteristics. First, all performance tests are historical in nature, because there has to be some performance to examine. Second, when looking at performance tests you are looking at both the quality of the strategy *and* the quality of its implementation (i.e., the systems, organization, and people). In a business that has performed poorly it is often difficult to tell whether the poor performance was due to the quality of the strategy or how well it was implemented.

The differences in the performance tests are created by the differences in the criteria against which the business' performance is measured. The two basic types of performance tests are performance against objectives and performance against competitors.

Performance Against Objectives

Every business has objectives. Some businesses have stated objectives, and some only have unstated objectives. Most have both.

What are objectives?

Objectives are desirable ends to be achieved. They are sometimes called goals or targets. I do not try to make fine distinctions among these terms because I have never found any consistent way to do it.

Before measuring performance against objectives you need to ask another question: "Performance against *whose* objectives?"

All objectives are subjective. There is no such thing as an objective objective. Therefore, different people who have a stake in the success of the business may have different objectives for it.

There are at least two primary categories of people who set objectives for a business: management and stakeholders. Let's look at management first because the most direct way to examine performance against objectives is to let management set the objectives and then measure them on their performance.

Performance Against Management's Objectives

There are usually several levels of management objectives. The ultimate objective is, of course, to increase shareholder wealth. However, that particular objective is difficult to achieve directly because of capital market effects. One way to think about it is that management's job is either to increase shareholder wealth faster than the capital markets are growing, or to preserve shareholder wealth when the markets are declining. "Relative shareholder wealth" is the key concept for management.

Most measures of shareholder wealth, however, are a bit difficult to relate to the business strategy in a direct cause-and-effect manner over time. Therefore, most business objectives have to do with revenue and profit. Other frequently seen objectives include social responsiveness, market share, quality, and the like. However, in most cases the fundamental objectives that are measured over time are revenues and profits.[1]

At the functional level, for example marketing or production or R&D, there can also be specific, functional objectives. Marketing may have a market share objective. R&D may have a new product introduction target. Production may have a cycle time objective. Each of these is a specific objective that contributes to revenue and profits.

The application of the test of performance against objectives is usually quite straightforward. It simply requires you to identify over time the objectives for the business. The more stated and unstated objectives you can identify, the more complete the test can be. Once the objectives have been identified, simply measure performance against those objectives.

I have been surprised by how few companies measure their performance against objectives over more than a one-year time period. Many will compare the current year to the previous year, but few look at performance over a multiyear time period.

Performance always achieves, exceeds, or falls short of objectives. The operative question in each case is "Why?" The fault may lie equally in the objectives as in the strategy or its implementation.

Managers have several philosophies about objectives:

- "Objectives should always be something you strive for but never achieve."

- "Objectives should be relatively easy to achieve because you want people to be successful. Success breeds more success."
- "Objectives need to be realistic. They should stretch your capabilities a little bit without making things so difficult that you fail often. It is important to succeed most of the time."

When evaluating the strategy's performance against objectives, you need to understand that *how* the objectives were set makes a difference. Perhaps they were set too low and the performance is not as good as it looks. Perhaps they were set too high and the performance is actually better than it looks. Some understanding of the subjective element of performance against objectives enhances your ability to make assessments about the strategy and how well it is being implemented.

In a medium-sized public company that made plumbing fixtures, the family that controlled over 50% of the stock held all of the key management positions. A harder driving bunch would be tough to find. The seventy-five-year old father was the chairman and CEO. His oldest son and daughter each ran divisions of equal size. One division handled all of the business east of the Mississippi, the other all of the business to the west. While relations were friendly, the rivalry between the son and daughter was intense. Each wanted to ascend to the top job when the patriarch finally retired.

When we plotted actual results against the relevant three year plans, they looked like Figures 8–3 and 8–4. As you can see, actual

Figure 8–3

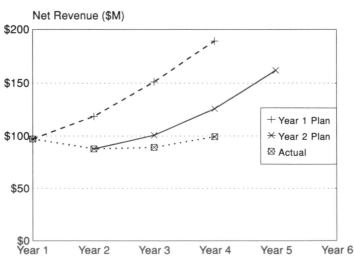

Net Revenue ($M)

Figure 8–4

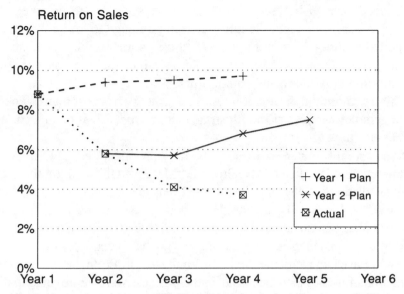

Return on Sales

performance was nowhere near the business objectives. The siblings had let their desire to outperform each other push their objectives out of the realm of reality. Since they had also tied their management team's bonuses to the achievement of the objectives, no one had earned a bonus for several years and morale was at an all-time low. What should have been perceived as good performance in a tough business was actually perceived as failure because objectives were not being met.

When the team revised its objectives, they were more realistic, but still aggressive. Performance met the objectives, bonuses were granted, and an upward spiral of both morale and performance began.

Performance Against Stakeholders' Objectives

There are actually two names for this test. The more formal name is the stakeholder test. A stakeholder is simply that—someone who has a stake in the success or failure of the business. The more descriptive name is the "minefield test."

The general manager running a business is like the captain of a ship that has to pass through waters that have been mined. The mines are actually the minimum needs that must be met for each significant stakeholder in the business. Creditors must be paid, customer requirements must be met, and shareholders must earn a return on their investment if their needs are to be met. If a stakeholder's needs are not met, the manager's ship runs into the mine, causing damage to his ship that can range from minor to fatal. Figure 8–5 shows some of the typical stakeholders in a business. Other stakeholders might include creditors, the community, regulators, and competitors.

Failure to run this evaluation test on a strategy has cost many general managers their jobs. Let me illustrate with a true, albeit disguised, example.

"Mr. Profitability" took over as the new president and CEO of AAA Amalgamated, Inc. from "Mr. Growth." Mr. Profitability did a thorough analysis of the business and determined that the strategy that was being followed had some significant flaws that needed to be remedied. He moved quickly to make those changes, including some personnel changes among key managers in the business who had been protégés of Mr. Growth. Based on a rational economic analysis, Mr. Profitability was doing all the right things. Financial results in the business were improving rapidly.

But Mr. Profitability forgot about one stakeholder.

Mr. Growth was still on the board of directors and held significant stock in the business. Unfortunately, Mr. Profitability's actions were making Mr. Growth's tenure as CEO look bad. Other directors were starting to wonder why Mr. Growth hadn't made the changes Mr. Profitability was making.

Figure 8–5

Mr. Profitability was fired.

The reasons given were the standard "disagreements between the board and management on policy matters."

Mr. Profitability was really fired because he failed to run the mine-field test before he implemented his new strategy. One key stakeholder's needs were not met and his mine blew up.

Mr. Profitability could have found ways to do virtually everything he wanted to do and still meet the needs of all of his significant stakeholders, if he had asked three fundamental questions:

1. Who are the stakeholders in the success or failure of my strategy?
2. What is each one's stake?
3. How well is my strategy performing to serve that stake?

Mr. Profitability's problem was that he did not adequately meet the needs of the former president and major shareholder. Note that those needs were not necessarily rational, economic needs, but they were still important needs that a stakeholder was willing to act upon.

Obviously, the above story, although true, had to be disguised to protect the innocent (and the guilty). More public examples are available, however.

In the spring of 1992, General Motors' board of directors "revolted" and took "strategic control from management."[2] Lloyd E. Reuss was demoted from the presidency of GM and Chairman and CEO Robert C. Stempel was removed as chairman of the executive committee of the board. In October of 1992, Stempel resigned from GM.

This drastic action was unprecedented in the history of General Motors. Why did they take this action and why at that particular time? After all, GM's financial results had been poor for years. The apparent answer is that GM's top management was not meeting the needs of key stakeholders, its outside directors, in demonstrating sufficient leadership to turn around the results at GM.

John Akers at IBM and James Robinson at American Express lost their jobs in 1993 because stakeholder requirements were not adequately met. Stakeholders in a business often provide complex challenges for general managers. Their needs often conflict, and it is difficult to meet all of them, but a significant part of the job of a general manager is to balance the performance of the strategy in such a way that the dynamically changing needs of the various stakeholders are met over time. Managers who can do this are termed "politically astute." Managers who can do this *and* deliver outstanding economic results are sought out and promoted to bigger jobs very quickly.

Performance Against Competitors

A second category of performance test is to look at the performance of the strategy against direct competitors wherever possible. By "wherever possible" I mean on any dimension for which you can get data that could have meaning. One example of how different performance can be among competitors can be seen in the luxury lodging industry. When comparing the operating profit margins of Marriott, Hilton, and The Four Seasons for the years 1989, 1990, and 1991, it becomes apparent very quickly that Hilton performed almost twice as well as the other two companies (see Figure 8–6).

By comparing the detailed strategies of these three competitors, it is possible to begin attributing results to certain strategy elements. Differences in the mix of owned versus franchised hotel revenues, pricing strategies and the financial structures of the three probably account for the differences in results.

Figure 8–6
Operating Profit Margin in Lodging Operations, 1989–1991

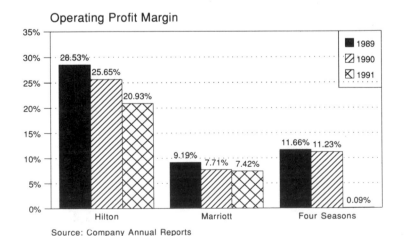

Source: Company Annual Reports

HOW CONSISTENT IS THE STRATEGY TODAY?

Consistency tests look at the strategy as it exists at a point in time—usually the point in time at which the current strategy was identified in detail, as described in Chapter 6. In many ways, consistency tests are tests of the logic of the strategy. They require the use of simple common sense to determine whether or not there is consistency between and among strategy elements.

The differences among the consistency tests are determined by the different perspectives from which you are checking for consistency. The five tests check consistency (1) across functional strategies, (2) between functional strategies and objectives, (3) between functional strategies and resources, (4) between functional strategies and characteristics of the strategic situation, and (5) with key success factors/models of success.

Consistency Across Functional Strategies

One professional service firm developed a very interesting strategy. They segmented the market in such a way that they were able to serve the high end of the market by targeting only the clients who wanted the highest-quality professional services. The company also put in place a production strategy which consistently produced the highest-quality service in the market. Unfortunately, the results weren't very good. The firm was running at breakeven.

Once they looked at consistency across the elements of their strategy it was easy to see why the results were poor. The firm's high-quality service was also a high-cost service to produce. Unfortunately, it was being priced with services that were aimed at the average quality market. The costs were driving all of the profitability out of the business.

It is not uncommon to find that some elements of a strategy are inconsistent with others. The reason this happens is that different functional strategies are often developed by different people without thorough coordination. Marketing develops its strategy, and manufacturing does its own, and R&D does its own, and so on down the line.

Usually the one strategy that is most often a check and balance for the other three is the financial strategy. The process of annual or semiannual budgeting is a useful way to control various strategies and make them consistent.

Figure 8–7 shows the way in which you can apply consistency tests across elements of the strategy. In Chapter 6 you identified a business

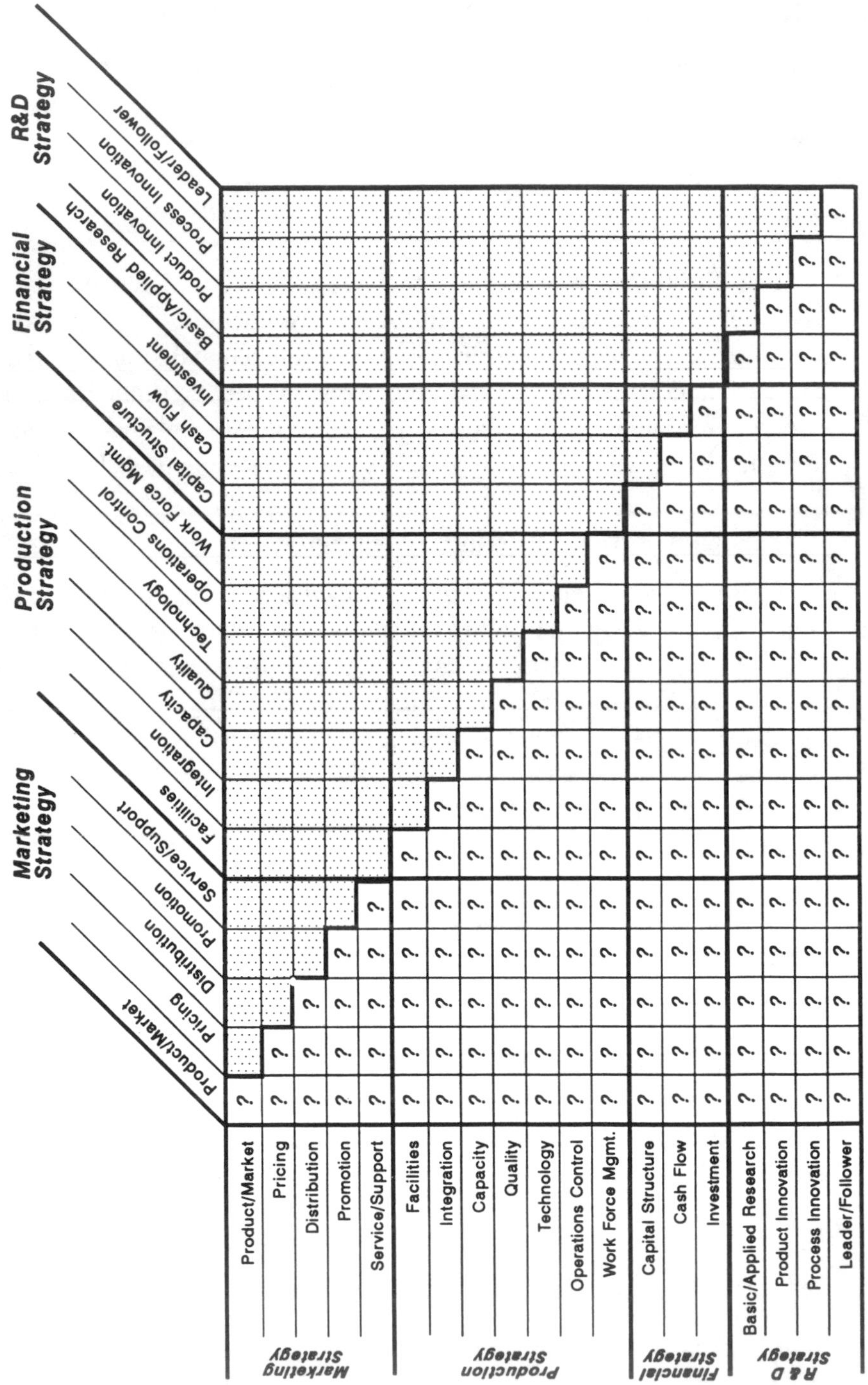
Marketing Strategy
Production Strategy
Financial Strategy
R&D Strategy
Product/Market
Pricing
Distribution
Promotion
Service/Support
Facilities
Integration
Capacity
Quality
Technology
Operations Control
Work Force Mgmt.
Capital Structure
Cash Flow
Investment
Basic/Applied Research
Product Innovation
Process Innovation
Leader/Follower

Figure 8–7

strategy. Now you take each element of the strategy, starting with the product/market strategy, and ask if it is consistent with every other element of that strategy. Since you start at the top and work down, the process works as it appears in the diagram in Figure 8–7.

Consistency Between Functional Strategies and Business Objectives

One well-known personal service organization had over four thousand individual outlets throughout the world. This particular service business had been very successful at identifying and dominating a market with over 80% of the available business. Unfortunately, the management was not happy with their results at the time I entered the scene. Although profitable, the business was not growing. In fact, it had been stagnant for three years. When they ran the tests for consistency among the functional strategies, the tests came up amazingly clean. Each element was in line with every other element.

However, when we compared each functional strategy with the objectives, we discovered the problem. One of the objectives for the business was to grow revenues and profits consistently at 20% per year. The cash flow strategy, however, was to milk every dime of cash out of the business to pay dividends to the shareholders. It's just not possible to milk all the cash out of a business and simultaneously grow it. Growth usually requires an expenditure of cash.

To perform this test, all you have to do is take each element of the strategy and ask whether it is consistent with the business objectives. Remember, it is important to test it against both the stated and unstated business objectives.

The interesting question that often comes up when you find an inconsistency is whether the objective or the strategy is incorrect. If there is an inconsistency, which direction does it flow—from the strategy to the objective, or the objective to the strategy?

In the example cited above, the objective was wrong. It was not possible to grow 20% per year given the market growth rate and the highly dominant market share position of the company. That much growth simply was not available on a yearly basis. A 5% per year growth objective was much more realistic. When the objective was lowered and the cash flow strategy was also modified slightly to supply the necessary funds for slow growth, the strategy and the objective became consistent and logical. Performance subsequently improved.

What are other typical inconsistencies? One of the most common in-consistencies is that an objective is set to grow much faster than the market, and the strategy has no demonstrated way of taking share away from the competition. A second is to have the objective of being the technology leader in the industry and a product development strategy that is funded with a below average percentage of sales. As you can see, each element of strategy can be inconsistent with one or more objec-tives.

Consistency Between Functional Strategies and Resources

A business strategy might be brilliant, but if you don't have the re-sources to implement it, it is relatively worthless. Resources include money, people, raw materials, facilities, and time. Each is important in its own way.

Money is particularly important in high-growth situations. When growth is abundant it eats cash. One formula that I have found espe-cially useful is the sustainable growth rate formula (see Figure 8–8).[3]

While the formula looks complicated, it isn't really. It's just a short-

Figure 8–8

$$SGR = \frac{b(NP/S)(1+D/E)}{(A/S) - [b(NP/S)(1+D/E)]}$$

SGR = Sustainable Growth Rate of Revenues

b= Retention Rate of Earnings = $\frac{\text{Net Income - Dividends}}{\text{Net Income}}$

NP/S = Net Profit Margin
D/E = Debt-to-Equity
A/S = Assets-to-Sales Ratio[1]
S = Most recent annual sales

Assumptions behind the Sustainable Growth Rate formula:
• The SGR is an average over time that assumes a steady state of the variables (D/E, A/S, NP/S, b)
• Assets are fully utilized (i.e. there is no slack or excess capacity that could be used to support additional growth)
• Depreciation charges are sufficient to maintain the value of operating assets
• All interest expenses are incorporated in the target net profit margin

[1]If the company is carrying excess cash on the balance sheet, it must be taken out of cash *and* shareholders' equity.

cut that holds your financial structure (see Chapter 4) constant and tells you what rate of growth your current cash flows will support. In essence, it is a simpler way of looking at your growth possibilities than creating detailed pro forma balance sheets and income statements.

The two fundamental questions about money are: (1) does the business have enough cash flow to support its operations, and (2) does the business have enough capital to make the necessary investments on an ongoing basis? Obviously, these two questions are interrelated as is shown in the sustainable growth rate formula. However, it is also necessary to look at a capital plan for the business to ensure that the company has either the capital in-house or the business strategy to support raising additional capital in the form of equity or debt. Therefore, you may want to look at similar businesses and see if the business can expand its debt or issue new equity.

It seems that all managers complain that they can never find enough of the right kind of *people* and keep them in their organization (see Chapter 14). The problem is not that there are not enough good people—the problem is that the science of sourcing and selecting appropriate people is still in the dark ages. If you study the research on interviewing, for example, you will learn that the typical interview is no better than chance as a predictor of success. If you do a typical selection interview you might as well flip a coin to predict success.

When you test functional strategies against resources, you are looking at the people in the organization to see if they have the combination of skills and motivation needed to implement the specific strategies that have been selected. The analysis starts with top management and goes through at least the functional managers and perhaps their direct reports. Two questions are fundamental:

1. Does this person have the skills necessary to implement the strategy?
2. Does this person have the appropriate type and level of motivation to do the job?

The first question can be tested fairly simply. Has the person done this task before. How well? If the person has never done it before, how is the company going to ensure he or she has the skills necessary to be effective in implementing that element of the strategy?

Motivation is discussed in more detail in Chapter 14. For this particular test, however, you need to know what motivates a person and whether or not the incentive system you have in place is consistent with that pattern of motivation.

Suffice it to say, if you do not have skilled and motivated people, you do not have the people resources necessary to implement the strategy. If so, you are lacking a critical resource for the success of the strategy.

In many businesses *raw materials* are in short supply or somehow allocated. You need to make sure that you have plentiful sources of raw materials that will enable you to move forward in implementing your strategy.

Facilities can also be a hindrance to continued success. In some businesses, facilities cannot be expanded fast enough to meet demand for products or services and business is lost to competitors. For example, in the passenger airline business, boarding gates are sometimes in short supply at busy airports. Do you have enough facilities to meet your current and projected demand?

Time is a resource, and there is rarely enough of it. In business strategy, both time and timing are important. *When* you do something is often as important as *what* you do. Is there enough time to take the actions dictated by the strategy?

Is time used effectively as a competitive weapon? The company that can get its new products to market faster has a decided advantage over a slower competitor.

The importance of both time and timing is illustrated by a story from the management book publishing business. Two rival books were being prepared on a "hot topic." The publisher of one book, scheduled for publication six months later, overheard at a cocktail party in London that his rival's book would be out in only four months. After several frantic international calls in the middle of the night, it was decided to accelerate publication of the first book. It hit the bookstores three months later and became a huge best-seller. The second book was an also-ran.

Consistency Between Functional Strategies and the Strategic Situation

Every business faces certain characteristics in its strategic situation. Recall the life cycle example in Chapter 3. One question you need to ask is, "Is the business strategy consistent with the stage in the life cycle of the business?" If you are following a strategy that is aimed toward growth, but the business is mature, the strategy must be designed to take significant share away from the competition. Otherwise the strategy and the stage in the life cycle are inconsistent.

Similarly, if you are following a strategy that would be appropriate to a declining business, such as milking cash from the business, and you are in a growth business, you are accelerating the decline of your market share and giving up the market to the competition. This may be perfectly acceptable to you, but you need to know that you are doing it.

A second aspect of your strategic situation is the level of strategic flexibility you have adopted. Strategic Flexibility is the ability to change your strategy in response to changes in the business' environment. For example, a new competitor enters the scene or a new technology becomes available. How fast can you change your strategy to respond to these events?

Figure 8–9 shows the relationship that exists between strategic flexibility and profit margins in most businesses. Typically, you trade flexibility for profitability. This happens because as you fine-tune the strategy for increased profits, you make commitments that reduce flexibility. For example, you might backward-integrate to capture more of the value added in your business by making components for your products. Similarly, you might forward-integrate into the distribution and sale of your products and services. You might build a plant that is dedicated with a single technology to making a particular product.

If you want more flexibility, you probably won't integrate forward or backward, and you won't commit to a single technology or channel of distribution. You will stay highly flexible. However, this flexibility probably means that you give up some margins. In most cases, flexibility costs money.

The strategic goal is to get to Point A on Figure 8–9. This is the point at which you are both highly flexible and highly profitable. The extreme example is a legal, unregulated monopoly in a growth business. Anytime you can find one of those, please give me a call. I'll be happy to invest.

It may not be as difficult as you think to find that Point A business. If you can find a growth business in which you can gain dominant market share through some means other than low price alone, it is likely that you will get very close to Point A.

What is the right amount of strategic flexibility? Unfortunately, this is one of those questions to which the answer is, "it depends." It de-

Figure 8–9

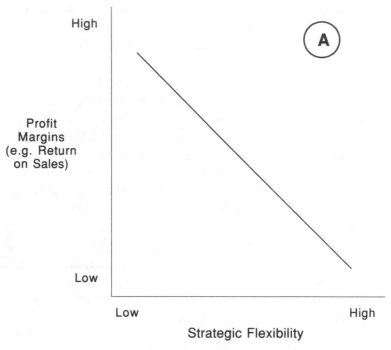

pends on how much stability you have in your business. In highly stable businesses you can make the choice to give up flexibility in order to gain margins. In highly volatile businesses it's probably better to stay flexible. Your industry structural analysis should have given you some sense of how volatile your particular business is.

In one highly volatile business in which the products were big ticket discretionary items, one manufacturer adopted a strategy of backward integration that gave his company the lowest variable cost, highest fixed cost structure in the industry. During the growth cycle of the economy, the company was much more profitable than its competitors. During recessions, the company lost more money than competitors. During one particularly long economic downturn, the lack of strategic flexibility eventually cost the company its market leadership position.

Consistency with Key Success Factors/Models of Success

I explained the key success factor test in Chapter 2 when I wrote about defining the business. With this consistency test you check to see if the strategy is consistent with the key success factors that are isolated in that test. It amazes me that whenever I run this test the management team knows what the key success factors are, but they have failed to effectively implement at least one of the action items needed to achieve all of the key success factors. Managers often know what they need to do, but don't do it.

Another twist on this test is to look for models of success in similar businesses. Find out what people have done in businesses that are like yours on most dimensions. Model their success and then test your strategy against it. This is another way to determine whether you are strategically positioning your business in the same way other successful companies have in the past.

HOW WILL THE STRATEGY PERFORM IN THE FUTURE?

There are two fundamental expectancy tests that you need to run. These tests are interrelated and often give slightly different slants on the same theme. One uses the predictions of the future developed in the industry structural analysis. The other asks you to become your competition.

Comparing the Strategy Against Predictions of the Future

The result of the industry structural analysis described in Chapter 7 was a set of specific predictions about what is likely to happen in your industry. In this test, take each of those predictions and ask whether the strategy has a way of coping with that event as it occurs. Invariably there will be some elements of the future that the current strategy has not anticipated. The more dynamic the business, the more the future is likely to contain elements that are not fully anticipated by the current business strategy.

Comparing the Strategy Against Likely Competitor Positions

This is the point in the process in which you get to become the competition. The secret to doing this is to get into the minds of the competitor's management team and think the way they think. The better you are able to do this, the more effective this test will be.

I have often told the story about a client and friend of mine named

Fred Wenninger. When I first met Fred he was the general manager of Hewlett-Packard's Fort Collins Systems Division in Fort Collins, Colorado.[4] His division was in direct competition with a division of IBM.

Fred is a particularly bright person. He had completed his Ph.D. in electrical engineering at a young age and had done a number of things in his life, including becoming a ham radio operator and a skilled pilot of both fixed-wing airplanes and helicopters. In addition to his work at HP, Fred personally farmed several thousand acres of wheat and millet in Colorado and Oklahoma each year. He was very much a down-to-earth, casual person who occasionally showed up at work in cowboy boots, jeans, and a western shirt. He sometimes flew to work in his helicopter and landed in the division's parking lot.

When Fred first heard about this test, he really took it to heart. He bought IBM's competing product and had his team tear it apart so that they could understand exactly how it worked. He read books on IBM, and learned as much as he could about the IBM managers running the competing division.

I knew that he had made the transition, and "become" the competition, when he showed up at our strategy evaluation meeting wearing a dark blue suit, white shirt, and striped tie. He even walked and talked differently. Actually, the transition was not quite complete. I knew that it was still Fred playing a role as his IBM competitor because he was wearing his cowboy boots!

Fred did a great job, and you need to do the same to effectively become the competition and develop a strategy to attack your own business. As you begin to become the competitor and develop that strategy, ask yourself the following three questions:

1. Who are we? (What are our values and beliefs?)
2. Why are we here?
3. What are our objectives?

This is one of the most useful of all the tests because it enables you to attack your own weaknesses in a nonthreatening way. It usually yields significant results that enable your team to see things in their own business that they had not seen before. Some teams have developed such powerful strategies while "playing" the competition that they have insisted all notes from the session be destroyed so that they could not inadvertently fall into the hands of the enemy.

WHAT ARE THE KEY SUMMARY POINTS ABOUT EVALUATING A BUSINESS STRATEGY?

The traditional strengths and weaknesses approach to strategy is not effective because it primarily yields the traditional conflicts between the functional areas in a business. To evaluate a business strategy thoroughly, you must apply nine tests that look at the strategy's past performance, current consistency, and expected performance. All nine tests must be applied in order to thoroughly understand the complete set of strengths and weaknesses of the current business strategy. Failure to apply any one test can cause you to miss an important perspective on your business that could illuminate a golden opportunity or a fatal flaw.

Now, on to the most challenging and creative part of the process. I'm sure you want to know what alternative strategies you might pursue.

Chapter 9
What Are
the Alternative Strategies?

"How do you know there isn't a better strategy for your business?"

"I don't."

"Well, if you explore the entire performance envelope for your strategy, you will know."

"Performance envelope? What's that?"

There is a basic formula in business: SOW = SOR. That formula stands for same old way equals same old results. If those results have not been good, the formula implies: SOW = SORry!

Even if the results have been good, there might be a better way.

Exploring alternative strategies is a requirement for anyone with Business Sense. Effective general managers always look for a better way. You know that the world is changing constantly, and alternatives will be needed at some point.

All of the work done to identify the current strategy, predict the future, and evaluate the current strategy has led to this, the most creative part of the strategy formulation process. This is where you must explore the "performance envelope" of alternative strategies that are available. Every airplane, automobile, or boat has an envelope of performance of

175

which it is capable. So does every business strategy. You want to push your thinking to the edges of the envelope so that you can thoroughly explore all of the things you could do to make the business perform in different ways. (See Figure 9–1.)

Why is this effort necessary in a successful business? Because no business stays the same for long. You must know the contingency strategies available to you long before you need them. You need to prepare yourself for making the changes that are indicated by those strategies. And you need to know what will "trigger" the use of a contingency strategy.

When businesses are in trouble it's easy to get the management team to look at alternatives. Unfortunately, by the time it is clear that a business is in trouble, the alternatives are usually fewer in number and less attractive. The time to save a business is *before* it gets into trouble, not after.

It is more difficult to get the management teams of successful businesses to be creative. Their successes have reinforced their behaviors to the point that they often do not want to look at the challenging task of developing alternatives. They think they already know all of the answers and don't have to change. This is perhaps the most common reason that businesses get into trouble in the first place. Complacency about the dynamics of change causes many management teams to wait until the danger signals are so strong that they are in a position of having to save their businesses, rather than preventing the problem.

There are many ways to encourage creativity, and many different strategies that any given business can follow. By answering the follow-

Figure 9–1
Exploring the Performance
Envelope

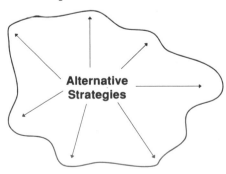

ing eight questions, you will create alternative strategies that will cover most of the "performance envelope."

1. What is the minimum fix alternative?
2. What happens when we change objectives?
3. How could we change the defining factors?
4. What are the ways to reframe the business?
5. Is there a different strategy if the business is product-driven vs. customer-driven?
6. What if we play like the competition?
7. How would the strategy be different if we became an objective observer?
8. How could we model success in another business?

Each method is described in some detail below.

WHAT IS THE MINIMUM FIX ALTERNATIVE?

The minimum fix alternative is exactly what it says. The objectives for the business are kept the same as they have been in the past. The team of managers is then directed to use the comprehensive list of strengths and weaknesses developed in the evaluation of the strategy to develop an alternative strategy. The assignment is simply to play to the strengths of the business and fix the weaknesses. This should be done with the minimum possible incremental investment of resources.

The minimum fix process was used to great advantage by a company in the business forms industry. After the evaluation of the strategy it was clear that one of the weaknesses was the pricing strategy. The company's historical pricing strategy was to be the premium price provider of the products in its business. Special deals would then be made to give discounts to each major account.

When I asked the management team how many major accounts they had, the answer was four hundred. When I asked them how many "special deals" there were, the answer was also four hundred!

Their public pricing strategy had alienated a number of customers who perceived them as selling a commodity product at a premium price. This misplaced image in the market cost the company a tremendous amount of business. The irony was that due to their "special deals" their actual prices were competitive but they had a "premium price" image.

The alternative strategy they developed was to create a new price sheet that reflected reality and did not portray an image of being the premium price provider. This decision, combined with one other strategy change—an expansion into 20% of the country where they were not yet competing—led this company to increase sales 2.7 times in a period of just two years, while maintaining profit margins.

The above example illustrates why it is always important to try the minimum fix alternative. Sometimes very small changes in strategy can make huge differences in results.

WHAT HAPPENS WHEN WE CHANGE OBJECTIVES?

Changing objectives is a method of creating alternative strategies that has two major variations. The first is to change the *value* of the objectives that you are trying to achieve. The second is to change *what* the objectives are that you are trying to achieve. Let me illustrate how each works.

Assume, for the moment, that the business has just two objectives, revenue growth and profitability, as measured by return on sales. Figure 9–2 shows four different ways to change the values of these objectives that would lead to the creation of different business strategies. Cutting both objectives in half, doubling both, or doubling one and cutting the other in half should help you to create strategies that are different from

Figure 9–2

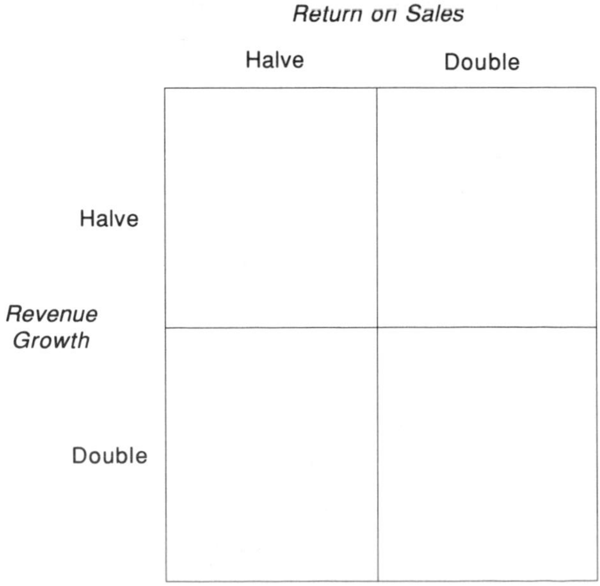

Return on Sales

	Halve	Double
Halve		
Double		

Revenue Growth

the one you are currently following. If they don't, something is wrong with the strategies you are formulating.

You learn something particularly interesting by doing this exercise. You learn to identify the specific elements of your business strategy that the management team reaches for when it wants to change either revenue growth or profit margins.

For example, one high-technology company was entering a new business using a new technology. When they were asked to double their profitability and halve their sales growth objectives it became evident that improving the performance of the product and targeting niche markets with specific value added features would be the appropriate strategy.

When they were asked to double revenue growth and halve profitability, the appropriate strategy was to push to make the product a standard in the industry by concentrating major efforts on cost reductions to drive prices down while simultaneously marketing the products to both the large original equipment manufacturers (OEMs) and to the aftermarket through computer dealers.

Obviously, Figure 9–2 is a simplified example. You can change objectives up and down by any percentage you wish. The point is to explore those areas that would change in the strategy if you change the *values* of the objectives of the business.

Another thing you might learn is something that happened to one of our clients. This company was in the bulk freight transportation and distribution business. (Before you knew how to define a business, you might even have called them a railroad or a trucking firm!) When they did this exercise they found that they could not double either their revenue growth or their profitability and still be within the envelope of feasible alternative strategies. Given the constraints of their business, including a severe geographic constraint, they were unable to create a strategy that had a likelihood of achieving either aggressive objective.

The net result? Their best strategy resulted in a $22 million loss. I guess that's better than some alternatives which would have lost $100 million and put them out of business.

The second major way to change objectives is to change the *type* of objective. One simple but powerful way to do this is to change the profit objective from a profit margin to a return on investment. Now the focus is on *both* the margin that can be attained and the amount of capital that is required to achieve that margin. In comparing two businesses with equal margins but different capital intensities, the one with the lower capital intensity is preferred if your objective is to achieve a high return on investment.

Try making this simple change from a profit margin to a return on investment objective and see what it does to your strategy. I suspect it will generate a different alternative strategy. When you focus on return on investment your strategy will probably emphasize both the ways to get margins up and the ways to reduce the needed investment.

You can also play with making changes in the time frame of your objectives. What happens if you focus on a one-year time frame versus a three- or five-year time frame for achieving your objectives?

HOW COULD WE CHANGE THE DEFINING FACTORS?

Using each of the four factors that define a business, change them one at a time and see what that change does to create new alternative strategies. Note that if you change more than one factor at a time, you are possibly headed for a new business. If you change two factors at a time you are headed for the gray area. Let's look at several examples of what happens when you change one factor at a time.

What happens if you change the needs met by the current product or service? Originally in-line skates were designed as training devices for cross-country skiing and speed skating. A good friend of mine road-skied on in-line skates with ski poles to stay in shape. I remember when he visited us in 1980 in Palo Alto. People followed him around, trying to find out what he was doing. By changing the needs met by in-line skates from a training device to a combination outdoor roller and ice skate, a whole new market emerged for them.

By changing the technology in a ballpoint pen to a porous point felt tip, a new type of pen was created. It serves many of the same needs and is produced using many of the same technologies as the ballpoint pen; however, the technology in the new product created a slightly different product that generated new revenues.

Baking soda was a useful part of many recipes. Its chemical properties, however, had other features that were useful for different purposes. Baking soda could absorb odors and an open box of it became an effective refrigerator deodorizer. By changing the emphasis on the needs met by a particular product a new, niche market was developed.

By systematically changing each of the four factors that define a business, you can create new strategies. You might even create a new business if you change more than one of the four factors.

WHAT ARE THE WAYS TO REFRAME THE BUSINESS?

"Reframing" is a concept from the field of communications. A reframe is usually some type of reversal. It was used with great effectiveness by President Reagan in his second set of debates against a younger, more energetic-appearing contender. At the end of the first set of debates Reagan appeared tired and a bit confused. In short, Reagan's age had become an issue. During the second debate, when the inevitable question came up, Reagan was ready. The reporter asked, "Mr. Reagan, do you think age should be an issue in this campaign?" Reagan, with his patented smile and a tilt of his head, replied "No, I don't think my opponent's youth and inexperience should be an issue in this campaign." Even his opponent Mondale laughed. The age issue disappeared.[1]

There are at least seven ways to reframe your business as you explore alternatives.

Turn a Weakness into a Strength

This is a wonderful trick, if you can pull it off. The classic example, of course, is the Post-it Note. Post-its were born when an adhesive was discovered that failed every test 3M put it to. Thus, the adhesive that wasn't really an adhesive became the basis for Post-it Notes.[2]

7-Up did a similar reframe. Originally positioned in the market as a lemon-lime soda, 7-Up was just another soft drink. Its light, bubbly taste did not give it a strong position to compete against the myriad of colas until it became "The Uncola."

Reframe the Type of Business

Kodak and other leading photography companies realized years ago that they are not in business to sell cameras; they are in business to sell film. This is a classic reframe from a hardware business to what is often called a "razor blade" business. (In a razor blade business you might give away the razors in order to sell the blades.)

Another classic reframe of the type of business is to change the profit model by changing your expectations from a business that you earn profits on today to a business that is a development business. This, of course, is what has happened to many sports teams over the years.

In 1992 the San Francisco Giants were estimated to be losing at least a million dollars.[3] This loss was on revenues of approximately $51 million. However, the team was purchased in 1976 for "about $9 million," and in 1992 was worth somewhere between $100 and $125 million.[4] In late 1992 owner Bob Lurie agreed to sell the team for approximately $105 million. A compound annual return on investment of over 16% made the team a reasonably good investment.

Reframe the Relative Value of Parts of the Product or Service

Is the value of Apple's Macintosh computer in the hardware or the operating software? It can be argued that the real value is in the graphical interface that makes the Macintosh so easy to use. Maybe Apple is really a software company in competition with Microsoft.[5]

What alternative would you follow in your business if the value was in the software and not the hardware? What if it's support and service, not the equipment? What if it's the stability of the relationship, not your particular equipment? What if it's your ability to give credit terms, not your products? All of these questions are important as you try to reframe the source of the value in various parts of your product or service.

Reframe the Competition

If you are in the casino business at Lake Tahoe, you could consider your competition to be the other casinos in the area, casinos in Las Vegas, or other attractions that people could chose over you. What would be different about your strategy if you reframe the competition to be Las Vegas? Napa Valley? Disneyland?

This technique is particularly useful when your product or service is somewhat different than or in between others'. However, it can be used with virtually any business.

Herb Kelleher built an airline that has been profitable since 1973 by reframing the competition from other airlines to ground transportation.[6] Operating Southwest Airlines over a number of short-haul, point-to-point routes like Dallas to Houston, Southwest offers low-cost, no-frills service that competes effectively with automobile and bus transportation alternatives.

Reframe the Value of the Product or Service

Many products are valuable for more than one use. Aspirin may be bought to relieve headaches, but used to prevent strokes. Baby-wipes can be bought to keep the baby clean but also used by Mom to remove make-up. Antacids are intended to relieve stomach distress, but can be used as a source of calcium.

Reframe Mass Market vs. Niches

If your product or service currently serves a mass market, what niches could it serve with minor changes in features? Conversely, if the product currently serves one or more niches, what would it take to make it a mass market product?

In the 1970s 35mm cameras were niche products used only by professional or serious amateur photographers. When auto-focus and auto-flash features were added in the 1980s the PHD (push here dummy) 35mm cameras opened up the mass market.

Reframe the Channels of Distribution

If your product currently goes through distribution, what strategy would be needed to sell it to OEMs? If your product currently sells in retail stores, what would it take to sell it through discount chains? There are a wide variety of possibilities when you start looking at channels.

One recent example is Packard Bell, a company which grew to some $800 million by 1991.[7] Packard Bell was essentially a computer clone manufacturer that followed a strategy quite similar to other computer clone manufacturers, except that it chose a different channel: mass merchandise retail outlets.

Dell Computer was created on a similar reframe of the channel. Originally Dell only sold its products direct to end users over the phone. Both companies developed their strategies by reframing the channels of distribution.

IS THERE A DIFFERENT STRATEGY IF THE BUSINESS IS PRODUCT-DRIVEN VS. CUSTOMER-DRIVEN?

In the early 1990s many books were written on how to be customer-driven. While being customer-driven is certainly something every company should do, most companies should also be product-driven. The dangers of being *only* "customer-driven" or *only* "product-driven" are so severe that they could be fatal.

For example, customer-driven companies often miss the next market.

IBM missed minicomputers, Hewlett-Packard missed workstations, and Ford missed minivans. One of the biggest hindrances to innovation in any company is to be market-driven and focused only on your current customers. They're the ones whose needs you have mostly met and whose future needs are likely to be incremental. They won't tell you what the next big market is because it's not them!

Many people don't know that they want a new product until they have an opportunity to experience it. Where was the hue and cry for Post-It Notes or instant cameras? How many of us knew we needed PCs before they came along? Those were not products that were developed by customer-driven strategies.

On the other hand, being product-driven can lead you to develop products for which there are no customers. Hewlett-Packard's entry into the personal computer business is a good example. A strong value within the HP culture has always been to "make a contribution," usually meaning a technical contribution. When HP entered personal computers, its contribution was a "touch screen." Unfortunately, few people wanted a touch screen and the product failed.

One way to develop alternative strategies is simply to ask three questions:

1. What would my strategy look like if it were heavily customer-driven?
2. What would my strategy look like if it were heavily product-driven?
3. What would my strategy look like if it were both customer- and product-driven?

By using each of these three perspectives you should create three different strategies.

Each is important, and depending on the likely evolutionary path of your business, you may choose to be more product- or customer-driven. The process of being customer- and product-driven is illustrated in Figure 9–3.

The market is defined as everyone who buys the products and services supplied by your business. You don't want a market, however, you want customers. When you are product-driven *and* customer-driven you combine the forces of product positioning and market segmentation to get people in the market to have positive feelings about your offerings and practice buying behaviors that are in your favor.

Figure 9–3
Customer- and Product-Driven
Strategies

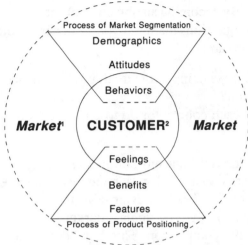

Process of Market Segmentation
Demographics
Attitudes
Behaviors

*Market*¹ CUSTOMER² *Market*

Feelings
Benefits
Features
Process of Product Positioning

¹Everybody who buys substitutable products/services.
²Only those who buy your product/service.

WHAT IF WE PLAY LIKE THE COMPETITION?

Put the competition's management team, with all of their biases, values, and beliefs, in charge of your business. This is called a "management transplant"! While this isn't possible in a literal sense, it is possible to do it by studying the values, beliefs, and backgrounds of the competitor's management team. Since you have been competing with them, you can probably predict the types of moves they would make if they were to take over your business. Give them your business by becoming them, and do what you think they would likely do given the strengths and weaknesses of your current strategy. This test is usually not only valuable, but a lot of fun. Can you imagine what would happen if Ben & Jerry were put in charge of Häagen-Dazs? What if Lee Iacocca ran GM? How about John Sculley at IBM?

HOW WOULD THE STRATEGY BE DIFFERENT IF WE BECAME AN OBJECTIVE OBSERVER?

To use this method effectively you need to step outside the competitive battle in your business. The point is to become as objective an observer of your own business as you are of other businesses. By doing so you can watch the battle unfold over time, through history and into the future. It is important to look *both* at the past and at what is likely to happen in the future. By becoming an objective observer you are able to ask two fundamental questions that help you to generate alternative strategies. The questions are:

1. What can these competitors do that will enhance their collective position?
2. What can each competitor do to enhance its individual position?

The first question is the one most often overlooked. Sometimes cooperation (to the extent that it is legal) is the best policy. Often more can be gained by not going head-on against your competition and instead staking out very strongly a particular market niche and leaving other niches open for the competition. This has been done effectively in a number of different industries.

The same process can be used for observing your company and your customers. If you objectively observe the communication between the company and the customers, you can get a different perspective than when you are responding to the customers directly. Sometimes it's easier to see things when you are an objective observer.

HOW COULD WE MODEL SUCCESS IN ANOTHER BUSINESS?

Another way to generate creative alternatives is to look for success in a business that has similar characteristics but is not a direct competitor. This is the way a number of companies get started. For example, I suspect that Office Club got some of its ideas for its successful strategy by modeling Price Club. Price Club was started in 1976 by the father and son team of Sol and Robert Price. They created the membership warehouse club and originally sold memberships only to businesses. As time progressed, they expanded membership to many other groups. The stores contained business and personal merchandise in large quantities and at very low prices. The markup on most items was less than 10%.[8]

Office Club opened its first membership warehouse in January, 1987.[9] The concept for Office Club was essentially the same as for Price Club, except that the goods being sold were office products.

Sometimes the same people can take what they learn in one business and use it as a model to become successful in another. The founders of Fry's Discount Foods started Fry's Electronics. Both were large discount outlets using similar principles for success, even though the first business was a supermarket and the second an electronics superstore.

WHAT ARE THE KEY SUMMARY POINTS ABOUT DEVELOPING ALTERNATIVE BUSINESS STRATEGIES?

An exploration of the performance envelope of alternative strategies is important if you want to understand the possibilities for your business. By exploring a complete set of alternatives, you will be better prepared for the changes that are likely to occur in your business over time. When changes do occur, you will be prepared with appropriate contingency strategies.

The primary ways of generating alternative strategies for your business include:

1. Make the minimum changes that would fix the weaknesses and play to the strengths of the current strategy
2. Change the value and type of objectives
3. Change the defining factors of the business
4. Reframe the business
5. Switch to or from a customer-driven or product-driven approach
6. Play like the competition
7. Become an objective observer
8. Use a model of success from another, similar type of business

The exploration of alternative strategies is a fascinating process. It is only limited by the creativity of those involved, and the time available. At some point, however, it is time to decide what strategy to follow.

Chapter 10
What Strategy Should We Follow?

"What is the ultimate objective of every business?"

"I don't have any idea. Could there be just one?"

"Sure there is. It's to increase shareholder wealth."

"Then why do businesses behave so differently?"

"Because the shareholders get to define 'wealth.'"

The alternative strategy you choose to implement depends on the objectives you are trying to achieve. Since all objectives are subjectively set, you have a problem. How do you know what objectives to attempt to achieve?

There are answers if you know where to look.

Until now we have talked about the specific objectives for the business. Because it could have been confusing, I have not mentioned the primary constraint that exists on every business' objectives. Those are the constraints imposed by the business' owners.

The shareholders always set explicit and/or implicit *boundary objectives* for the company they own. Boundary objectives are the shareholders' definition of wealth; they set the limits within which

189

management must work. Within the constraints of the boundary objectives, and considering the realities of the business, management must set the *specific objectives* for the business.

WHAT ARE BOUNDARY OBJECTIVES?

Boundary objectives can be anything the controlling shareholders want them to be.

If the controlling shareholders want to keep a certain number of family members employed or somehow supported, that becomes a boundary objective. Management must choose strategies that fulfill that objective.

A classic case is provided by the controlling shareholders of Joseph Schlitz Brewing Co. in the middle 1970s. At that time the company was in a serious competitive battle with Miller Brewing Company and Anheuser Busch Inc. In 1976 Schlitz paid out 39.6% of its net income to shareholders as dividends. In 1977, when earnings dropped to $19.77 million, the dividend per share did not change, and the company paid out 99.99% of its net income as dividends!

A former president of the company was asked why he left.

> . . . Satchell said he left because he concluded he would never be free to run the company as he felt it should be run. "There were not many family members in management," he said, "but the family did influence the company behind the scenes."[1]
>
> Some 500 family members owned 75% percent of Schlitz's stock; even at the recent depressed price of about $12 a share, those holdings were worth roughly $270 million. At 68 cents per share, the family collected $15 million annually in dividends. Uihleins and their in-laws held eleven of the sixteen board seats. Three of the family-connected directors ran small privately-held businesses; the others included a retired Schlitz executive, a retired neurosurgeon, an IBM program manager, and two men who devoted their time to managing their own investments.[2]

Performance of the company continued to deteriorate. Dividends were cut to $.54 per share in 1978 and $.20 per share in the first half of 1979 and then were stopped.[3] Schlitz was sold to Stroh Brewery Company of Detroit, Michigan, in 1982.

In a private company, a wide range of boundary objectives can be observed. I once visited an oil exploration company whose primary stockholder was an avid collector of western art. The hallways of corpo-

rate headquarters were filled with expensive pieces of art, all owned by
the corporation. Woe to the general management team that followed
any strategy in the exploration efforts that would put the company's art
collection in jeopardy!

Although it is a large, multibusiness company, Hewlett-Packard provides an excellent example of how boundary objectives work. As corporate cultures go, HP's is revered as one of the finest in the world.
Many management books use HP as the example of a highly people-
driven company. The "HP Way" with its strong values-driven approach
to management is held up as a model for other corporations. Profit shar-
ing, management by walking around (MBWA), the "next-bench syndrome," free coffee, and an implicit "no-layoffs policy" (until the acquisition of Apollo Computer, anyway) have become legend.[4]

But the data shows a different picture of HP's performance (see Figure 10–1).

Stockholders have this nasty habit of measuring their wealth from the
stock's peak value. While they are somewhat forgiving when that

Figure 10–1
Hewlett-Packard Quarterly Financial History
First Quarter 1986–Fourth Quarter 1990

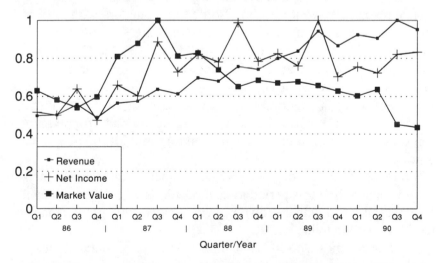

Note: Market value calculated using the ending weekly stock price per quarter. HP's year-end
is Jan. 31. Thus, HP's Q1 (end 4/30) is matched with calendar Q1 (end 3/31).
Source: HP Annual Reports and MicroQuote II, a CompuServe Service.

wealth declines due to general stock market declines, even then they expect management to outperform the market and certainly the competition. Any decline in wealth due to poor revenue and/or earnings performance is much less likely to be viewed with benevolence.

From the third quarter of 1987 until the fourth quarter of 1990, HP's ending quarterly stock price dropped from $61.125 per share to $31.875 per share. The company's total market value dropped from $18.1 billion to $7.9 billion.[5] HP shareholders literally lost 56% of their wealth by holding onto the stock throughout this period. Many "voted with their feet" and sold the stock. During this same period, the Dow Jones average decreased from 2565 to 2528 (1.4%) and the S&P 500 Index decreased from 318 to 316[6] (0.6%). Obviously, HP's stock was not outperforming the market.

What happened at HP?

Unfortunately, the second quarter of 1988 saw a decline in both revenue and earnings. This downturn heralded a period in which HP's revenues grew rather steadily from quarter to quarter, but earnings became highly erratic.

At many companies, the above sequence of events would have been cause first for alarm and then for significant change. A different board of directors might have blamed top management and made a change. Some might have brought in a "turnaround specialist."

(Have you ever wondered how some top managers with definitive styles would fit in companies other than the ones they run? Wouldn't it be interesting to know what Jack Welch, the CEO at General Electric, would have done at HP? Welch was known as "neutron Jack" during his early years at GE when he was cutting out unprofitable businesses and staff operations. After his examination of some businesses, it was said that it was just as if someone had dropped a neutron bomb. The buildings were still standing, but all the people were gone!)

But HP's board did not go outside. A number of top level HP managers did leave during this period to take positions with other companies. Whether this attrition in the top ranks was significantly greater than normal is difficult to tell.

Other companies who suffered similar declines in market value during the same time period became targets of takeover specialists. After all, the 1980s were what *Fortune* called "The Deal Decade."[7] During that decade, "counting friendly and hostile deals, more than a third of the companies in the Fortune 500 industrials were swallowed up by other concerns or went private."[8]

But not HP.

Why not? Because it would have violated the boundary objectives of the controlling stockholders. Through outright ownership and the power of personal influence, David Packard and Bill Hewlett "controlled" the Hewlett-Packard corporation. As a practical matter, no significant changes in strategy could be made without their agreement.

They created the HP Way, and it has served their customers, employees, and shareholders extremely well since the company's founding just prior to World War II. It would take more than a 56% drop in the company's value to cause them to change something that had worked so well since 1939.

For Bill Hewlett and David Packard, maybe other things, like making a contribution, always were more important than money.

What happened at HP, instead of a top management overhaul or the sale of the company, was classic HP.

> With the company he founded 51 years ago beset by financial and strategic crises, 78-year-old David Packard has emerged from retirement and taken back the helm of Hewlett-Packard Co. by reasserting the management style that helped make the firm Silicon Valley's most famous pioneer.[9]

When asked in an October 29, 1990, interview about problems at the company, Packard responded,

> These problems were, in part, a reflection of the economy in the last decade. There's been a lot of concern about hostile takeovers, about financial wheeling and dealing, instead of about basic management. And there's been attention to a structure called "matrix management," in which responsibility is so diffused that nobody knows who the hell is responsible for what.[10]

As Packard discussed the situation, his concern for employees and shareholders became evident:

> We have 90,000 people in the organization. Bill and I feel a very solemn responsibility to those people. They joined the company, many of them, because of the HP Way. We have a tremendous number of shareholders who became shareholders because they had confidence in our policies. We have a responsibility to make sure those things on which their faith was exhibited are satisfied with the continuation of those policies.[11]

Packard's continued faith in his company's strengths, and especially its values, was reinforced by repeated emphasis:

> Bill and I, and I'm sure John Young, still believe that HP is one of the world's best companies. We have all the fundamentals in place: outstanding people, good technology and good management practices. We've worked through some tough times before. I think if you look at the thing objectively, our company has a better capability than almost any of our competitors. We know that these corporate values are right and that our business direction is sound. All in all, we are very optimistic about HP's prospects in the years ahead.[12]

Finally, Packard gave his view of the workings of the stock market:

> I want to add one other thing. There's been too damn much concern in this whole industry about quarter-by-quarter profits. We're going to concentrate on those things which strengthen our company for the long run and not pay as much attention to quarter-by-quarter profits as in the past. What this will do to the short-term price of our stock, I don't know. But in the long run, it's going to get the stock price up where it should be.[13]

Clear enough? Any questions about what the chairman of the board and largest single stockholder wants? Or what some of his boundary objectives are?

Management must effect a turnaround within the tenets of the HP Way.

The results of David Packard's and others' efforts were exactly what has come to be expected of HP (see Figure 10–2). Although not at its peak value by the third quarter of 1992, HP's stock had regained more than half of the value it had lost.

In widely held public companies with no identifiable controlling group of stockholders, the boundary objectives tend to be much more limited to financial measures. For example, an investment in the company needs to return what other equally or less risky alternative investments would return.

Even when the stock is widely held, some investors or investor groups may attempt to impose other types of boundary objectives on companies. Some investor groups will not invest in companies that do business in South Africa because of that country's apartheid policies. Others will not invest in companies that they believe are harming animals in research or in some way damaging the environment.

Figure 10–2
Hewlett-Packard Quarterly Financial History
First Quarter 1986–Third Quarter 1992

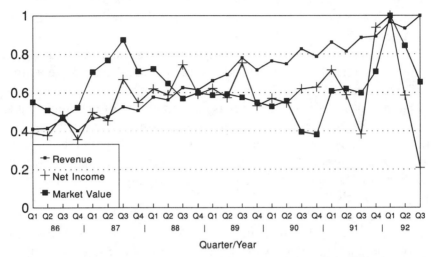

Note: Market value calculated using the ending weekly stock price per quarter. HP's year-end is Jan. 31. Thus, HP's Q1 (end 4/30) is matched wtih calendar Q1 (end 3/31).
Source: HP Annual Reports and MicroQuote II, a CompuServe Service.

An entire approach to investing, labeled "ethical investing" by its proponents, has been created.

Mutual funds are probably the easiest way to get into ethical investing. And although their holdings often overlap, each of the dozen or so funds defines "socially responsible" in a different way. For instance, the New Alternatives Fund specializes in non-nuclear energy companies such as Burlington Resources, recyclers such as Wellman and waste-to-energy converters such as Wheelabrator Group. Working Assets, a money-market fund, invests in commercial paper issued by companies with progressive labor practices (female and minority advancement, day care, or generous profit-sharing plans), such as Quaker Oats and Pitney Bowes, and in community development banks, such as the New York Job Authority.[14]

Whatever the boundary objectives, management must either find a way to meet the minimum requirements or convince the shareholders that they must change their boundary objectives. The former is usually a lot easier than the latter.

WHAT ARE SPECIFIC OBJECTIVES?

Many managers think they can set any objectives they want, once they understand the boundary conditions set by the stockholders. After all, the stockholders are the only ones who can directly hire and fire top management.

In practice, management *can* set any objectives it wants. But it would be a serious mistake not to consider some practical requirements that need to be met.

One requirement is to have a reasonable number of accomplishable objectives. A business can have an infinite number of objectives. Not only can there be overall business objectives, but every functional strategy and each element of each functional strategy can have an objective attached to it. In fact, every person in the company can have one, few, or many objectives.

The discovery of the "network of objectives" gave rise to a management practice called management by objectives (MBO). Where the classic approach to MBO is used it usually turns out to be something between a partial success and a partial disaster.

What happened at one large life insurance company describes the typical scenario. In this company the entire management team was trained in the MBO approach. Then everyone set their objectives and checked them against those of their superiors. When the gun sounded to start the fiscal year, what ensued was an incredible battle over resources. Infighting among various functions, groups, and individuals began immediately. The MBO program created so much distrust that it was eventually dropped.

MBO should have been MBOS: management by objectives and strategies. Without allocation of resources among the various strategies that are being employed throughout the organization, MBO doesn't work.

The boundaries surrounding your specific objectives for any business can be discovered by asking two questions:

1. What are the stakeholder (other than stockholder) requirements for the business?
2. How do the characteristics of the strategic situation limit the objectives?

What Are the Stakeholder Requirements?

Remember the minefield test from Chapter 8? This is where you get to employ it in reverse. Any strategy that is to be effective must meet the needs of the various stakeholders at some minimum level. Apart from the stockholders, these stakeholders might include the company's board of directors, its employees, its creditors, outside regulators, and, of course, management.

We have already dealt with the needs of stockholders by determining the boundary objectives. While some would make stockholders equal to other stakeholders, they deserve a special place because they are the only stakeholders who can directly hire and fire top management. Business Sense requires that managers in a business pay careful attention to the people who have the power to hire and fire them.

A lot has been written about the role of the board of directors in a corporation. Fundamentally, the board represents the stockholders. As we move further into the 1990s, boards of directors will likely become even more active in their role in managing top management.

Every stakeholder is "the most important stakeholder" in one situation or other. However, customers and employees are always near the top of the list. Your strategy must meet the minimum requirements set by customers for your products and services. Your strategy must provide value to the customer.

Without employees, you do not have a company. Therefore you cannot employ just any business strategy. The employees' needs must be met.

Your creditors must be paid. Therefore any strategy that does not generate enough cash flow to pay the creditors could lead to loss of the business.

Your community has needs. How closely you relate to the community probably varies by business. For example, if you are in the daily newspaper business you play a major role in the community and are expected to abide by certain ethical and professional standards.

Regulators also play an important role in one way or another. If you are producing semiconductors you need some way to meet the regulatory requirements for disposal of hazardous chemicals. It is a fact of life that every business must meet the minimum needs of some regulators.

Finally, management has a certain level of needs as well. The needs for challenging work and advancement are important and must be recognized.

How Do the Characteristics of the Strategic Situation Limit Objectives?

Three characteristics of the strategic situation must be taken into account when setting objectives. The first characteristic is the *stage in the business life cycle* (see Figure 10–3).

When the business is in the *introduction* phase, the objectives have more to do with successful product launching and gaining market acceptance than with financial goals.

During the *growth* phase of the business, adequate margins to sustain growth become particularly important. Demonstrating profitability in the form of return on investment (ROI) is a key to attracting future investors. There is some debate about the importance of market share during the growth phase.

Is market share an important objective in your business?

Market share is not important in every business. It is only important when it allows one competitor to build barriers to entry or success—for example, by using large economies of scale—against others. As one competitor builds market share, economies of scale can allow it to produce products at significantly lower cost and use that lower-cost position strategically against competition. There are very few "always" in business, but it is *always* best to be the low-cost producer of total value added.

Similarly, market share is important when it allows one competitor to

Figure 10–3

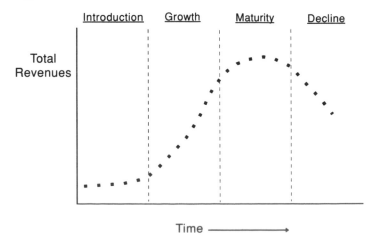

build a brand identification or reputation that would keep others out of distribution channels.

Finally, market share is important when a battle is raging over standards. The classic battle between VHS and Beta formats in the VCR business illustrates the point. Incompatible products will find the battle for market share important when the follow-on sales of related products (for example, razors and blades) is an issue.

Apple Computer recognized the importance of market share in 1991 when it slashed prices dramatically on its Macintosh computer line. Apple has always been incompatible with IBM's operating system, forcing customers to make a choice about the computing platform for their applications. Once Apple saw its market share slide to very low levels, it implemented a price-slashing strategy to regain share so that a critical mass of its Macintosh operating systems would get into the marketplace. Without this critical mass, software developers and makers of peripherals would focus more on IBM and ignore Apple.

When a business begins to *mature*, the growth objective for the business becomes critical. When market growth is no longer sufficient to sustain the desired growth of the company, the alternative is to take share from the competition. If an objective is set to take share, clearly the strategy selected must be able to meet that objective.

In a *declining* phase of the business, a decision must be made about the appropriate objectives. Should they be to decline with the market, or fight for share? The answer probably revolves around the economics of fighting for market share. It doesn't make a lot of sense to fight the competition for market share if the result is that you accelerate the decline of your shareholders' wealth.

The second characteristic of the strategic situation that is a constraint on the objectives which can be set is the *level of strategic flexibility* of the business (see Figure 10–4).

If a business is not very flexible and the chosen strategy calls for a great deal of change, failure is likely. The strategy must be consistent with the business' level of strategic flexibility. The strategy can also be designed to change the level of flexibility. However, this process usually takes some time, especially if you want to move from a low- to a high-flexibility position.

The final characteristic that must be considered is the business' position in The Chess Game (see Figure 10–5).

If a business is in the lower left-hand corner of The Chess Game,

Figure 10–4

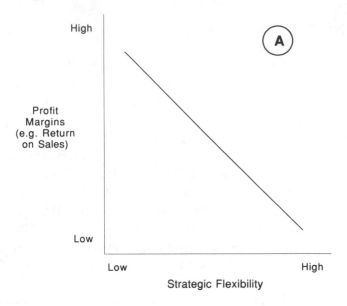

Profit Margins (e.g. Return on Sales)

High

Low

Low   High

Strategic Flexibility

Figure 10–5
The Chess Game

FEATURES

		Fewer	Same	More
	Lower	80/20 features that meet "must" requirements. Price battle, must be LCP.*	Price battle, must be LCP*	Differentiated Big Winner
PRICE	Same	Loser	Execution is Key	Differentiated Winner
	Higher	Big Loser	Loser	Must have the features people will pay for.

*LCP = Low cost producer.

200

significant changes need to be made in order to move to a more desirable position. If, on the other hand, the business is in the upper right-hand corner of the board, it is in an advantageous position and the advantages should be exploited.

WHAT DOES IT TAKE TO BALANCE THE OBJECTIVES?

Once all of the boundary objectives and constraints on specific objectives have been examined, the remaining area of freedom is determined. More often than not you will find that the limitations have placed too many constraints on your objectives. Some balancing is required. It is a rare case when management can freely set objectives without constraints.

Within the area of freedom, the question is "Now how do you set the final objectives?" The answer is: You use judgment.

It is not enough simply to set the objectives as high as possible. Companies can be, and often are, too profitable in the short run. They fail to make needed investments in technology, people, or facilities, and find themselves in trouble somewhere down the road. Judgment is needed to balance objectives in a way that enables the business to be successful for as long as possible.

The best approach I have seen to setting practical objectives comes from research done on entrepreneurs by David C. McClelland at Harvard.[15] McClelland replicated this research around the world in many different cultures. Fundamentally, what he did was give people a ring toss game and let them set up the rules for success. Some people would set the post (that they were going to toss the ring onto) so close that it was a sure thing that they would be successful every time. Others would place it so far away that it was virtually impossible to be successful more than one try in ten.

The people who were most likely to be successful entrepreneurs were the ones who set the post far enough away that tossing the ring onto the peg was a challenge, but an achievable one. In my experience, too, setting challenging but achievable objectives is the best way to set objectives for the performance of a business.

WHAT IS THE APPROPRIATE TIME FRAME FOR BUSINESS OBJECTIVES?

Have you noticed that everyone thinks they need a five-year plan? It always amazes me that venture capitalists require a five-year plan for a startup business. Even though the product hasn't been developed yet, they want a five-year plan for the business. Five-year plans for startups are usually obsolete within the first six months.

Why is it that everyone thinks that the appropriate time for setting a strategy and objective is five years? The answer is that in 1917 the Soviets started doing five-year economic plans. From then on, five years was adopted as the appropriate time frame for every business, even though the Soviets never achieved any of their five-year plans.

If you think about this for half a minute you'll realize that it's ridiculous. Let's look at a couple of examples. The time frames for the strategies for a compact disc (CD) manufacturer and a public utility are significantly different. In the CD business in 1992, I would have defied anyone to make predictions for more than eighteen to twenty-four months into the future. There were huge uncertainties about digital audio tape (DAT) and how it would impact CD sales. The last three years of a five-year plan in that business would be meaningless.

In the utility business, at least in North America, it takes twelve to fifteen years to build a new fossil fuel plant. (The time frame on nuclear power in the United States is infinity. Don't bother even trying to plan one of those.) If you are only planning for five years you could be out of capacity for many years and not know it because you didn't plan far enough in advance.

There are two rules of thumb you can use to set an appropriate time frame for your strategy. The first rule is that the strategy should be set for that time period for which you can make reasonably good predictions. Whether it's only six months or it's twenty years, that's the time frame for which you should have a strategy.

The second rule of thumb is that your strategy should encompass your longest lead-time decision. Therefore, if it takes ten years to build a new plant to produce your products, you'd best have a strategy and set of objectives for at least ten years into the future.

The challenge arises when your longest lead-time decision is much farther out than your ability to predict the future. For example, let's say your longest lead-time decision is ten years, but your ability to predict the future is five. In this case what you have to do is make a strategic bet. You simply must make your best decisions given the information you have under these high levels of uncertainty, and hope they work out. The only alternative is to fail to make a key decision and doom your business to poor performance or possibly failure.

HOW DO WE FINALLY SELECT THE STRATEGY?

Once you have narrowed down the objectives you can cycle back to the alternatives developed previously. In reality this is an iterative process.

In my experience the world breaks down into two kinds of people. There are those who think that they must set their objectives first and then choose the strategy to meet the objectives. And then there are those who want to develop the strategies to see what's possible, and then set the objectives. I've found that people are pretty much divided fifty–fifty between the two camps. This conflicting set of thinking styles is one of the major reasons that management teams have difficulty getting closure on the selection of a strategy and a specific set of objectives.

It doesn't matter which you do first, as long as you do both iteratively. Come up with a set of objectives that are circumscribed by the boundary objectives of the shareholders, the limiting factors of the stakeholders, the characteristics of the strategic situation, and what can be done. Select a time frame for the strategy and objectives that fit within your longest lead-time decision and your ability to predict the future. If you do these things it is usually fairly easy to choose a specific strategy that you and your management team can agree upon.

WHAT ARE THE KEY SUMMARY POINTS ABOUT CHOOSING A BUSINESS STRATEGY?

Two kinds of objectives are important when you choose a strategy from among the many alternatives available to you.

The first are boundary objectives and they are set by the owners of the business. Boundary objectives are the shareholders' definition of wealth. They set the limits within which management must work. Boundary objectives can be anything the controlling shareholders want them to be.

Within the limits imposed by the boundary objectives, management can set the specific objectives for the business. The most appropriate specific objectives (1) meet the minimum needs of all the stakeholders in the business, (2) fit with the characteristics of the strategic situation, and (3) can be accomplished with reasonable certainty. To meet all these requirements, some balancing is usually required among the naturally conflicting objectives for a business.

Although many people think that everyone should have a five-year plan, that time frame may not be appropriate for your business. The appropriate time frame for which to set objectives is bounded by how far into the future you can make predictions with reasonable certainty, and what your longest lead time decision is. In some businesses the appropriate time frame for objectives is less than a year. In others it may be twenty years.

Now that you have your new strategy, let's take on the challenge of creating a mission and a vision for your business.

Chapter 11
What About Missions and Visions and Such?

"What's the mission of your business?"

"Our mission is to be the biggest and best at what we do."

"And what is that?"

"Well, it's a little hard to explain."

You may think the above conversation is a little facetious. It's not.

Let me share with you the mission statements of three well-known companies without their names attached. See if you can identify the companies.

Mission A

_____ is committed to providing our customers with the world's highest level of satisfaction with our products and service.

To accomplish this, we will emphasize the importance of our most valuable resources, our people and our partners, through participative and respectful working relations.

This commitment to the customer, our people and our partners is essential to our prosperity and our ability to provide a reasonable return to our stockholders.

Mission B

- Provide differentiated products and services of recognized superior value to discriminating customers worldwide.
- Pursue businesses in which we can be a leader based on one or more of our strengths.
- Build and maintain a productive work environment in which high levels of personal satisfaction can be achieved while conforming to our Code of Worldwide Business Conduct and Operating Principles.
- Achieve growth and above-average returns for stockholders, resulting from both management of ongoing businesses and studied awareness and development of new opportunities.

Mission C

Our primary enterprise objective is to increase the value of shareowners' investment by managing our resources and serving our customers better than and more efficiently than our competitors.

We will grow in markets where we can create enough advantage to earn a good return for our shareowners. We will redeploy resources from markets where we cannot.

By achieving our objectives, we expect to reward our shareowners, whose continuing investment in the Company is vital, and to reward our employees, whose creativity and commitment to winning through teamwork is the key to our competitiveness.

Can you identify the companies to which these mission statements belong?

It's difficult isn't it?

Let me make it easier. I'll tell you the names of the three companies and you match the company with its mission. Sound fair? The three companies are Chrysler, Navistar (formerly International Harvester), and Caterpillar. Can you match them with their respective missions?[1]

If you can't, does it mean that these companies' missions are interchangeable? Now there's a thought to ponder for a minute.

WHY DO MOST COMPANIES WANT A MISSION AND/OR VISION STATEMENT?

Mission and vision statements have been a management rage in the late 1980s and early 1990s. It seems that every company has to have them, even if they don't know what they are or what purpose they serve. While writing this book, one of my associates called fifty different companies to ask for their mission and/or vision statements. Of the fifty, thirty-nine said they had them and would fax them to us. I was absolutely amazed that 78% of the companies actually had developed mission and/or vision statements.

When I read them, I was also surprised at how worthless most of the statements were. Most sounded alike and would not inspire anyone to take any action.

There are a number of reasons that companies would like to have mission and/or vision statements.

Effective mission and vision statements are inspiring. They touch deep human needs for great challenges. Whenever an individual, a group, or company has a crystal clear purpose, the level of commitment and motivation is visible.

Proponents of mission and vision statements seem to use the same three examples, none of which come from the world of business. Key excerpts from each of the three are reproduced below.

Winston Churchill gave some of the most descriptive, stirring speeches of all time. One of his most famous was his assertion that:

> We shall not flag or fail. We shall go on to the end. We shall fight in France, we shall fight on the seas and oceans, we shall fight with growing confidence and growing strength in the air, we shall defend our island, whatever the cost may be, we shall fight on the beaches, we shall fight on the landing grounds, we shall fight in the fields and in the streets, we shall fight in the hills; we shall never surrender.[2]

John F. Kennedy created a mission statement that challenged a nation in his speech to Congress on May 25, 1961.

> First I believe that this nation should commit itself to achieving the goal, before this decade is out, of landing a man on the moon and returning him safely to earth. No single space project in this period will be more exciting or more impressive to mankind, or more important for the long-range exploration of space; and none will be so difficult or expensive to accomplish.[3]

And who could fail to be inspired by Martin Luther King's speech at the Civil Rights March in Washington, D.C. on August 28, 1963?

> I have a dream that one day on the red hills of Georgia the sons of former slaves and the sons of former slaveowners will be able to sit down together at the table of brotherhood.[4]

When the challenge is great and the speaker has some ability to communicate a deep human purpose, the mission and/or vision statement can be a powerful, inspirational tool.

Not many businesses are as exciting or challenging as fighting the dreaded Nazis, putting a man on the moon, or striving for racial equality and brotherhood.

Apple Computer certainly attempted to create a stirring, powerful message with its mission statement.

> It is Apple's mission to help people transform the way they work, learn and communicate by providing exceptional personal computing products and innovative customer services.
>
> We will pioneer new directions and approaches, finding innovative ways to use computing technology to extend the bounds of human potential.
>
> Apple will make a difference: our products, services and insights will help people around the world shape the ways business and education will be done in the 21st century.

Apple's statement certainly contains some major challenges. Although the challenges are somewhat more vague than Churchill's or Kennedy's political statements cited above, there is a strong sense of purpose embodied in this mission statement.

One reason managers are seeking to develop mission and/or vision statements is that people like simple answers. Wouldn't it be great if you could have an effective, one-sentence explanation of what your company is about? Think about what a powerful motivating force that would be.

A second reason that people want simple, powerful statements has to do with the limitations of our minds. In a classic 1956 article in *The Psychological Review,* George Miller explains that we can consciously deal with only seven (plus or minus two) significant bits of information at one time.[5]

One implication of Miller's experimental finding is that no one can deal with the totality of a business strategy at one time. There is simply too much information. People will be overwhelmed. If you can encompass your strategy in a powerful, motivational communication device like a mission statement, then you can use that statement to drive the strategy's implementation.

But what are your mission and vision in practical, Business Sense terms?

WHAT ARE THE LIMITS TO MISSION AND VISION STATEMENTS?

Missions and visions are not your business strategy, although they should be consistent with it.

Nor are they the foundation on which you build your strategy. Mission and vision statements are derived from the strategy, not the other way around. Trying to develop a mission or vision before choosing a strategy forces managers to try to create an approach to the business out of thin air. It rarely, if ever, works.

In an excellent article in the *Harvard Business Review*, Gerard Langeler, one of the founders of Mentor Graphics, explained how Mentor fell into what he calls "The Vision Trap." Langeler described the series of visions that the company adopted at its founding. The failure of one vision, dubbed "Six Boxes"[6] for the six businesses in which Mentor aspired to leadership, illustrated one of the dangers of vision statements. Langeler described what happened after the failure of Six Boxes:

> Middle management was most affected by the failure of Six Boxes, and it was middle managers who came to me and asked for a new direction, a new sense of purpose—a new vision. By now, vision at Mentor Graphics had most definitely become a thing apart. There was no suggestion that the new vision should rise organically from the company's particular competencies, opportunities, or strategies. The process was to be external. I was expected to order a *vision du jour* from some talismanic menu. If correctly chosen and properly cared for, it would somehow cure the ills afflicting the company.
>
> . . . I now sought a vision based not on the current business environment but on broader, more abstract issues. By ratcheting up the vision one conceptual level, I could save it from the volatile dictates of the marketplace. This seemed an excellent idea. It was not. In fact, it was completely the wrong approach. As I was to learn, *the more abstract the vision, the less effective it is and the greater its potential for mischief* [italics added]. But I didn't know that in 1987.[7]

Mission and vision statements are *not* definitive guidelines for making major decisions. Anybody who makes major decisions based on a one- or two-sentence understanding of his or her business is crazy, incompetent, or both. This kind of misguided thinking is what gets management teams into very deep trouble.

Mission and vision statements are not the generic statements that apply to every business. The mission statements that opened this chapter became generic because they were done at the corporate level. Each of the three companies illustrated in Missions A, B, and C is in multiple businesses and the resultant mission statements had to apply to all businesses. This approach simply does not work. Mission and vision statements are usually not effective at the corporate level unless the corporation is in one business, or just a few, closely related businesses.

Mission and vision statements are not able to communicate everything to everyone. The term "vision statement" is an oxymoron. A vision is a picture of the future. If one picture conveys a thousand words, how many words does it take in a statement to create a picture of the future? If you need to communicate everything to everyone, give them a written statement of your business strategy.

Mission and vision statements are not a solution. They will not cure what ails your business. If the results aren't there, creating a mission or vision statement will not create what's necessary to get results. For that, you need to complete all of the previous steps illustrated in this book and then develop the mission or vision statement.

Finally, mission and vision statements are not the same thing. Although the terms are often used interchangeably, they are fundamentally different concepts.

WHAT ARE PRACTICAL MISSIONS AND VISIONS, AND HOW ARE THEY DIFFERENT?

Your mission is what you *do* as a business. You don't just have a mission, you go on a mission. You can tell whether you're on course or not because a mission has certain explicitly or implicitly measurable results attached to it. You either accomplish a mission or you don't, and everyone can tell one way or the other.

Let's take a look at a couple of reasonably effective mission statements. Canadian National Railroad's mission statement is clear, concise, and everyone can tell whether they are achieving it or not:

> To meet customers' transportation and distribution needs by being the best at moving their goods on time, safely and damage free.

Likewise, the Saturn division of General Motors has a reasonably clear (although grammatically muddled) mission statement:

[To] Market vehicles developed and manufactured in the United States that are world leaders in quality, cost and customer satisfaction through the integration of people, technology and business systems and to transfer knowledge, technology and experience throughout General Motors.

Likewise, it is fairly clear at any point in time whether or not Saturn is achieving its mission for General Motors.

Your vision is a word picture of what you will become as you successfully accomplish your mission. CN Rail also has a viable vision statement:

As we accomplish our mission, CN Rail will be a long term business success by being:

- Close to our customers
- First in service
- First in quality
- First in safety
- Environmentally responsible
- Cost competitive and financially sound
- A challenging place to work

Can you envision the challenge that it will be to fulfill CN's vision?

The real role of mission and vision statements is to be communication devices. They're the simplest, most concise communication links possible between your business strategy and its implementation. They're useful, succinct reminders of what you do and what you are becoming. They position the business in the minds of the people in the company, the customers, the suppliers, the investors, and the competitors.

If the business is to be positioned effectively, the mission and vision must be *unique*. If they're to serve as motivators, they must be *inspiring*. Herein lies the challenge. Is your business unique and inspiring? Can you make it so?

HOW DO YOU DEVELOP EFFECTIVE MISSION AND VISION STATEMENTS?

Having answered questions 1 through 5 of the strategy creation process (see Chapters 6 through 10), you have all of the tools you need to create effective mission and vision statements.

Starting with the business strategy, you need to create a statement of *what you do*. The statement needs to emphasize the unique aspects of your approach to this business. No one else is accomplishing Saturn's mission. It is unique in all the world, and therefore very powerful.

As you develop your mission statement, you need to recognize that missions can have a limited life. The more specific the mission's outcomes are, the more you will need to develop a new mission once you achieve those outcomes. Once the United States landed a man on the moon and returned him, NASA needed a new mission. Sometimes the second mission is the more difficult one to develop.

Vision statements are often more lasting and less specific. They're a *statement of what you will become as a company if you repeatedly and successfully accomplish your mission.* At this point in the process I've found it most useful to ask "What will it do for us if we accomplish our mission?. . . What will it do for others?" These questions usually help to paint the word picture of what you will become.

It can be particularly useful to develop several alternative mission and vision statements. Because these are typically succinct statements consisting of one or a very few sentences, they may mean different things to different people. You need to test the mission and vision statements on various stakeholders inside and outside the company. When you get the right statements, a consensus usually evolves around it.

WHAT ARE THE KEY SUMMARY POINTS ABOUT MISSIONS AND VISIONS?

Mission and vision statements are the management rage of the 1990s. Many companies have developed and disseminated such statements.

Effective mission and vision statements are inspiring. They provide succinct, powerful answers to complex questions such as "What does your company do?"

But these statements are neither your business strategy nor the foundation upon which you build your strategy. They do not provide you with definitive guidelines for making major decisions, and they cannot communicate everything to everyone about your business strategy.

Your mission is what you do. You go on a mission and you can tell whether you are on course or not because there are certain implicit or explicit results attached to it. To develop a mission statement you should start with your business strategy and create a statement of what you do. Better mission statements emphasize the unique aspects of the value your business creates.

Your vision is a statement of what you will become if you repeatedly and successfully accomplish your mission. It is a word picture of your future.

Now that you have completed the strategy development process and met the mission and vision challenge, it is time to begin developing the right systems with which to implement your strategy.

FREEDOM #3:
Developing the Right Systems

"What is the one constant in business?"

"The only constant is change!"

"Right, and what is it you need to keep up with change?"

"I need the right information in the right form at the right time."

"Is that what you get in your company?"

"Not very often."

If a business strategy is a set of decisions that are made to position the business in its constantly changing, complex environment, then it follows that a key part of the general management team's job is to make those decisions. The quality of your team's decision making is directly proportional to (a) the quality of your decision-making process, and (b) the quality of the information that you feed into the process.

Historically, the problem has been that the quality of the decision-making processes has been far superior to the quality and quantity of information available to run through them. Thus, general managers have had to rely on their "judgment" in making strategic decisions. There is an old saying about judgment. "Good judgment comes from experience. Experience often comes from bad judgment." Clearly, learning to make good decisions by first making bad decisions and suffering the conse-

215

quences is a less than desirable way to become successful at general management.

Judgment is required when making decisions under conditions of uncertainty. The higher the uncertainty, the more judgment and less decision-making skill is required. The way businesses (and many other organizations) have historically dealt with the problem of decision making under uncertainty is to focus on the organization structure. Decisions that can be systematized are made routine, and delegated to the lower levels of the organization. Those decisions for which the decision-making process is unclear, or the information is unavailable, rise to the top of the organization. The most difficult decisions, those called dilemmas, rise all the way to the top of the organization. There the general manager's role, as designated by the organization structure, is to make the toughest choices.

In his 1962 classic, *Strategy and Structure*, Alfred Chandler explored the relationship between the evolution of an enterprise's strategy and its organization structure. Part of his thesis was that structure should follow strategy.[1] Sometimes it does, and sometimes structure is changed in an attempt to revitalize a losing strategy.

The world of management has been revolutionized since 1962. Specifically, general management changed dramatically with the advent of the mainframe, and mini- and microcomputers. The power of these machines has been compounded exponentially by the advances in data and voice communications.

General managers now have technology that can allow them to look at their business from multiple perspectives. Given the right systems, a manager can delve into any internal operation in his business to learn its current status. Many managers get daily reports that contain, in one or a few pages, more information on the status of their business than their fathers could get on a quarterly basis. Some managers even have on-line reports that give them the latest information on changes in their customer base and new strategies being employed by their competitors.

Decisions don't need to be made under nearly as much uncertainty as they did in 1970, 1980, or even 1990. More and better information is available now than in any time in the past. The quality and quantity of information available to make difficult decisions continues to grow. There will always be dilemmas to challenge the wisest general manager and his team. The trick is not to artificially make something a dilemma when it isn't.

The primary relationship is no longer between strategy and structure. Almost every organization structure is obsolete when it is installed. Structures are the rigid components in a fluid world. Although necessary, they often get in the way.

The new relationship is between strategy, systems, and structure. The quality of the information about the business is what makes the difference in the decisions that are made and how well they are implemented. As information has increased in both availability and importance, systems have come to play an increasingly important role in business success. Information systems have become the nervous system of the business, gathering and processing information so that the brain, the general management team, can guide the enterprise on its course and transform its structure whenever necessary.

"Get the data!" is the cry of the modern general management team. Companies with better information can make better decisions. They have a better chance to serve their customers and beat the competition.

Placing a higher priority on developing the necessary systems than creating or changing the organization structure is a radical notion. But it is the way things work best in rapidly changing, information-intense businesses. General managers who exercise their third freedom by developing the right systems will create more effective strategies and implement them better.

Now that you are aware of the full importance of systems, let's explore the systems you will need.

Chapter 12
What Systems Do We Need?

"Do you have a management information system in your business?"

"Of course. We've spent a lot of time and money developing a state-of-the-art system."

"Great! Let's go look at the latest information on your customers and competitors."

"Um . . . well . . . that's not part of the system."

The term management information system (MIS) simultaneously means everything and nothing. What's in an MIS, anyway? What are the necessary components? How is it linked to the business strategy and the organization structure?

In most businesses, the MIS is an historical accident that occurred when accountants and computers collided.

Whenever I am introduced to a new company, I am very interested in learning what their MIS contains and how it enhances managers' ability to manage. Invariably, I find a system that is very good at reviewing the status of last month's business and providing an audit trail for the accountants. What I *don't* very often find is good information on customers and competitors.

Think about that for a few seconds and you'll realize how ridiculous it is. If two of the keys to success in any business are to serve your

219

Figure 12–1

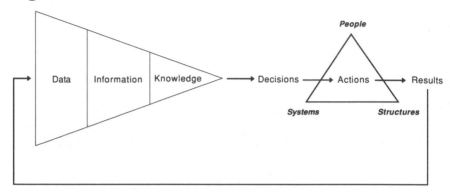

customers and beat the competition, where's the information—in the so-called management information system—that will help you to do so?

Managers exercise their third freedom when they implement the right systems.

The right systems for the business are those that get the right information to the right people at the right time so they can make the best possible decisions and create better results. The common element of all systems and processes is that they are information-based. In concept, a business should have appropriate systems for managing all of the activities shown in Figure 12–1.

WHAT'S THE DIFFERENCE BETWEEN A PROCESS AND A SYSTEM?

A system is a "routinized," sometimes automated or computerized, process. Please note that all systems are processes, but not all processes are systems.

All management is some form of process. Whether you are managing one person or 10,000 you are engaging in behaviors that can be broken into steps. Those steps are related to each other in some sequence. Managers with Business Sense actively manage their management processes. They identify their current processes, improve them, and know when to convert processes to systems. They also know when to apply the appropriate process or system.

There are literally hundreds of specific management processes, far too many to discuss here. There are, however, three generic management processes that are used to create most specific processes.

The single most pervasive, generic management process is the traditional *problem solving process*. It has six steps:

1. Define the problem.
2. Gather data about the problem.
3. Develop alternative solutions to the problem.
4. Define the criteria for selecting a solution.
5. Select a solution from the alternatives.
6. Implement the solution.

The quality of the results you get from using the problem-solving process is directly proportional to your ability to define the problem accurately. The process tends to work very well on small, incremental problems. It does not work well on large, complex management challenges like creating the right strategy for the business. For that level of issue, you need a holistic process that can solve many smaller problems simultaneously. The creative management process described in "Freedom #2: Creating the Right Strategy" is such a process.

In other situations, you may want to use the *scientific process* in which you create and test hypotheses. This process is particularly good for tasks like the test marketing of different versions of a product in representative markets before actually launching one particular version into the total market.

All management processes can be characterized as primarily (1) *information* gathering, processing, and/or distribution, (2) *incentive* creation or distribution, or (3) *decision-making* processes. Some management processes are more effective and efficient if they are turned into systems.

The most common systems are information systems where large amounts of data need to be consistently gathered, organized, and disseminated on a routine basis.

When a manager of a retail store wanders around the store talking to employees to learn what merchandise is selling, he's using an information gathering process. When he looks at the sales report generated by recording the product numbers off the bar codes on the products as they pass through the checkout stand, he's getting information from a system.

Incentive processes exist in every business. There must be some incentive for the people who work there. The incentives can be quite straightforward. When I asked the division manager of a well-known electronics company what the incentive was for him and his management team to be successful in their new business, his reply was, "Incentive? Our incentive is that we get to keep our jobs!"

When the general manager of a business decides at the end of the year the amount of each person's bonus for that year, she is employing an incentive process. If the incentives in the business are spelled out clearly at the beginning of the year and are based on a formula, for example a percentage of profits allocated proportionally based on salaries, the business has an incentive system.

The advantage of an incentive system is in its apparent fairness. No personal bias is applied at the last minute. Any bias built into the system is usually known to all who participate in the incentives. The disadvantage is that no single system, no matter how complex, can reward all positive behaviors or match everyone's motivation patterns. For example, the issue of whether salespeople should be on commission or salary depends on what provides motivation to the specific people in the sales organization.

When office supplies are reordered based on the office manager's judgment about current inventories getting low, the business has an inventory decision-making process. If automatic reorder points are created, the business has an inventory decision-making system.

Processes, especially decision-making processes, may or may not produce the same results when they are applied at different times. In a management process, judgment is used by the people gathering the information, and the person making the decision. Human judgment, which may be defined as "the capacity to make reasonable decisions, especially in regard to the practical affairs of life,"[1] can vary over time.

Systems produce replicable results. If you put the same data into a system a number of times, it will give you identical output each time. In a system, any judgment that is required is built into the system as "rules." Judgment is applied automatically through the rules.

The quality of any management process or system is directly proportional to (a) the quality of the data fed into it and (b) the quality of the method used to turn the data into information and knowledge.

All systems are GIGO (garbage in, garbage out) processes. The quality of data is measured by its accuracy, timeliness, and completeness. Unfortunately, there is usually a cost to acquiring data which must be balanced against its quality. In general, the more important the decision, the more complex the information that needs to feed into the decision-making process. It is rare indeed to be able to make significant decisions with perfect information. Some of the data used to create the information is either wrong, old, or incomplete. In most cases, however,

80% of the valuable information comes from 20% of the data. The trick is to spend your resources on acquiring the right 20%!

The quality of the method used to organize the data into information, and analyze the information to extract value (i.e., knowledge) from it is directly proportional to that method's ability to deliver answers to management's questions. If management wants to know why customers buy a competitor's product and the method of analysis is only to analyze opinions from salespeople and not customers, the quality of the method may be in question.

HOW DO YOU TAKE A PROCESS/SYSTEM INVENTORY?

You've probably heard the manager's lament. "Human beings can make mistakes, but if you really want to mess things up, use a computer!"

The "information age" has created "information overload." Many managers complain that their company's systems generate entirely too much information that is in the wrong form and too old to be useful.

Processes and Systems for Strategy Creation

Whether your business is in this predicament or is humming along like a well-oiled machine, the first step in aligning the systems with the business strategy is to complete a process/systems inventory. The first step in this inventory is to take each element of the business strategy (see Figure 12–2) and ask what processes and/or systems are being used to make each decision represented in the strategy. Each process and system should be categorized into one of the six boxes shown in Figure 12–3.

Let's look at an example. If you are in the highly competitive business of making and selling three-and-a-half-inch form factor, Winchester technology, hard disk drives to original equipment manufacturers (OEMs) for IBM compatible computers, you might have a pricing strategy something like the following:

We will use a cost-based strategy to price our disk drives to yield a 20% gross margin. We will drive costs down at a rate commensurate with increases in volume. In doing so, we will endeavor to be the price leader in the business with our prices equal to or lower than the competition's directly competing products. If necessary we will give up margins in the

Figure 12–2
Examples of Key Elements of a Product Business Strategy

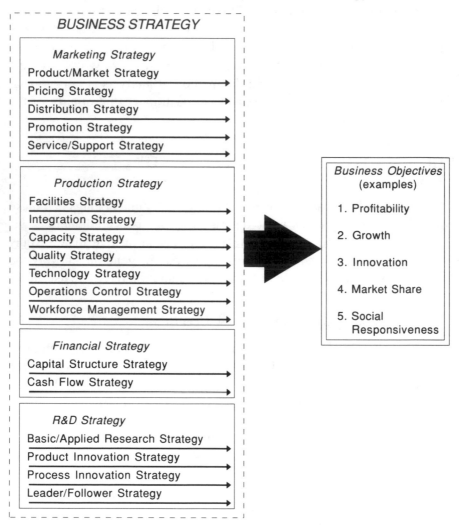

short term in order to beat our competitors in high volume deals and maintain a position as the volume leader.

Obviously, your pricing strategy is a primary competitive weapon that you plan to use with great force in your business.

It's possible that you can create such a strategy based only on the opinions of your experienced general management team. If so, you have an opinion-based decision-making process.

Figure 12–3

	Process	System
Information		
Incentive		
Decision Making		

It's more likely, however, that you want to have some significant information before choosing such a pricing strategy. Without good information on certain factors, the stated pricing strategy could be a formula for losing money. For example, at a minimum you want to know:

1. *What are our costs?* If your costs are higher than the prices in the marketplace today, you could have a serious problem.
2. *What are our competitors' prices?* It is difficult to price your products competitively if you don't know your competitors' prices.
3. *How much do our costs decline with increases in volume?* If increased volumes do not yield lower costs, should you be chasing volume?
4. *What are our competitors' costs?* If the competition has a lower cost structure than you do, using price as a competitive weapon could be a self-defeating strategy.
5. *How is our volume likely to increase with price reductions?* If price reductions do not increase total volume enough, you are intentionally lowering your total revenue and unless your costs have gone down more than you have cut prices, your total profit will also decline.

The information to answer the above five questions can be obtained by asking your finance and accounting departments to source the necessary data and do the analysis. By doing so, you would create an information gathering process.

If you have a cost accounting system, a competitor intelligence system, and a market research system, you may already have the information you need. In this case your decision-making *process* would be supported by several information **systems.**

In either case, the process/system inventory, when completed for all elements of the business strategy, tells you exactly what processes and systems you have in place that can assist you in developing your business strategy. Unless you consciously change the processes and/or systems you use, you are likely to get the same quality of strategy the next time you make these decisions. Improving the quality of your processes and/or systems is likely to improve the quality of your strategy.

Processes and Systems for Implementation

There is also some combination of systems and/or processes used by the people in the organization structure to **implement** each strategy decision. These processes and systems need to be identified and categorized. For example, the next time you introduce a new product, you will need to set a price for that product. What processes and/or systems will you use to do it?

If you are the product manager responsible for setting the exact price, you might have to source all of the relevant information from various parts of the organization and the marketplace. If the customer, competitor, market research, and cost accounting systems are in place and computerized, you might be able to access all of the information on-line. Some companies even have pricing models (i.e., systems) that combine all of the relevant information, apply certain pricing rules, and set the prices for their products.

The simple process of "flowcharting," that is, drawing a picture of the steps in each strategy development and implementation process and system, is a very powerful tool for starting the improvement of both processes and systems.

Figure 12–4 shows a flowchart of the pricing system in a company

Figure 12–4
The Old Pricing System

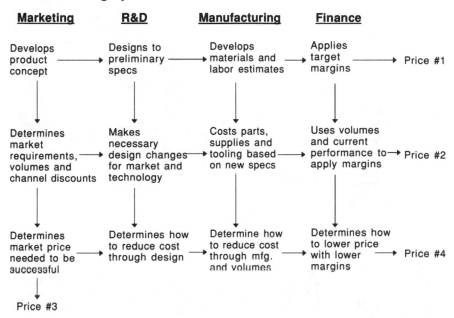

Marketing	R&D	Manufacturing	Finance	
Develops product concept	Designs to preliminary specs	Develops materials and labor estimates	Applies target margins	Price #1
Determines market requirements, volumes and channel discounts	Makes necessary design changes for market and technology	Costs parts, supplies and tooling based on new specs	Uses volumes and current performance to apply margins	Price #2
Determines market price needed to be successful	Determines how to reduce cost through design	Determine how to reduce cost through mfg. and volumes	Determines how to lower price with lower margins	Price #4
Price #3				

that introduced a new line of products every nine to fifteen months. At first blush it appears to be fairly orderly and logical.

In reality, the pricing process was creating a lot of frustration. At the point in time when the product manager went to set a price for the latest product to be launched, he learned that no two departments had the same price in mind. Four prices had been discussed by various groups at various times and none had been finalized. Repeated meetings had been held with various sets of people participating. New information was injected into the process randomly with its importance being only partially understood.

After the management team flowcharted their process for implementing the pricing strategy, it was easy to see why there was so much frustration. The decision-making process was full of "open loops" instead of feedback loops.

The process was redesigned to function as shown in Figure 12–5. The process was vastly simplified, and the appropriate people with adequate information were involved at the right points in the process. Most of the frustration with the pricing process disappeared overnight.

Figure 12–5
The New Pricing System

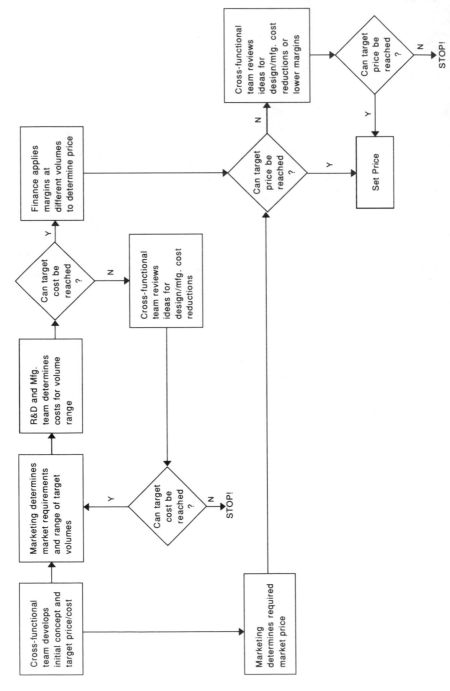

WHEN SHOULD WE CREATE A SYSTEM?

There is only one system that every business is required to have. Every business must have an accounting system. This system may be slips of paper kept in a shoe box and reconciled once a year at tax time, but some form of accounting system is necessary to know whether or not the business is making money.

All other potential systems for a business are optional. Decisions can be made, and results can be obtained by using processes, systems, or in most cases a combination of the two. Your process/system inventory identifies what processes and systems you are currently using in the business, but which ones should be used?

The first step is the easy one. Eliminate each process and system that does not contribute directly to creating or implementing the business strategy.

Information Systems

Since all incentive and decision-making systems are extensions built on information systems, the second step is to determine what information systems are needed in the business. An information system, as opposed to an information process, is needed any time the information required to create or implement the business strategy is extensive, dynamic, important, and accessible. After all, a system is relatively useless if the needed information is limited, static, unimportant, or inaccessible.

How do you tell if an information system is necessary?

Since information is the lifeblood of any business, you need to map the business' circulatory system. This is done by identifying the information *needed* to create and implement each element of the business strategy. What information do you need about your current activities, results, customers, and competitors? What historical information and what projections into the future do you need?

Figure 12–6 shows the basic format that can be used to map a business' information circulatory system needs. When the suggested analysis is completed, what typically happens is that certain categories of information are extremely valuable in a number of places for decision making and implementation. These categories of critical information should be prioritized and become the basis of the desired information systems for the business.

Although each business is somewhat different, most have needs for

Figure 12–6

Information Needed to Create and Implement Business Strategy

Business Strategy Elements	Internal Operating Information	Competitor Information	Customer Information
Marketing Strategy			
Product/Market			
Pricing			
Distribution			
Promotion			
Service/Support			
Production Strategy			
Facilities			
Integration			
Capacity			
Quality			
Technology			
Operations Control			
Workforce Management			
Financial Strategy			
Capital Structure			
Cash Flow			
Investment			
R&D Strategy			
Basic/Applied Research			
Product Innovation			
Process Innovation			
Leader/Follower			

information systems to deal with current performance, costs, customers, and competition. Current performance and costs are the information categories most often tracked by accounting and control systems. Current performance information tends to be accessible and controllable. Most companies do a good job of having adequate systems for this internal information.

Some companies do an excellent job of tracking their costs, but many do not have effective cost accounting systems. Cost accounting can be as much art as science. Traditional standard cost systems provide one method of estimating costs. The relatively recent development of activity accounting is another method that may allow businesses to track costs more accurately. Fundamentally, activity accounting measures those activities that truly drive costs.[2] It provides more accurate cost information for management decisions.

Most companies do not do a good job of tracking information systematically on customers and competitors. All too often, customer information consists of what management learned on its last customer visit. Competitor information is what was read in last month's trade journal. While information on customers and competitors is accessible, it is external to the day-to-day operations of the company and is often erroneously perceived to be difficult to get.

To illustrate to top management how much they can learn about their competitors with just a little effort, I like to give each member of the team a copy of their competitor's annual report, 10-K, and any recent feature articles from major business publications. I then give them two assignments: (1) "Identify your competitor's business strategy" (using the method described in Chapter 6) and (2) "Become the competitor and develop a strategy to beat _____" (their current employer).

I have done this exercise with senior managers of multibillion dollar companies and of small companies. In every case they were surprised at how much they could learn.

Two companies, Cypress Semiconductor and Frito-Lay, illustrate how differently information systems can be employed in different businesses.

Founded in December of 1982, Cypress Semiconductor Corporation compiled an outstanding record in a highly cyclical and competitive business. In a 1990 article entitled "No Excuses Management," T. J. Rodgers, founder, president, and CEO of Cypress, described the extensive use of information systems in his company:

> If everyone in our company made ordinary business decisions in a commonsense way, we would be unstoppable. It turns out that very few people, at our company or anywhere else, make ordinary business decisions in a commonsense way. Most companies don't fail for lack of talent or strategic vision. They fail for lack of execution—the mundane blocking and tackling that the great companies consistently do well and strive to do better.
>
> At Cypress, our management systems track corporate, departmental, and individual performance so regularly and in such detail that no manager, including me, can plausibly claim to be in the dark about critical problems. Our systems give managers the capacity to monitor what's happening at all levels of the organization, to anticipate problems or conflicts, to intervene when appropriate, and to identify best practices—without creating layers of bureaucracy that bog down decisions and sap morale. . . .
>
> How do we measure success at Cypress? By doing what we say we are going to do. We meet sales projections within a percentage point or two every quarter. We don't go over budget—ever! . . .

Technological change drives the semiconductor industry, and several of our management systems help us make decisions about technology assessment and product development that are quite specific to our business. *But most of our management systems (and certainly the most important ones) address the universal challenges of business—motivating people to perform effectively and allocating resources productively* [italics added]. To succeed over the long term, we have to do at least four things better than our competitors:

1. Hire outstanding people and hold on to them.
2. Encourage everyone in the organization to set challenging goals and meet them.
3. Allocate key resources (people, capital, operating expenses) so as to maximize productivity.
4. Reward people in ways that encourage superior performance rather than de-motivate superior performers.[3]

Within two years of the publication of Rodgers' article, Cypress lost business at a key account to a major competitor. The company's earnings declined and it announced the first layoff in company history:

... For a number of years the idea that Cypress and its outspoken president T. J. Rodgers would lay off workers was unthinkable, in part because Rodgers had created what many felt was a model semiconductor manufacturing company: lean, aggressive, well managed and profitable. But in recent months the $300 million company's earnings have deteriorated dramatically as prices fell on its primary products—a type of memory chip known as static random-access memories or SRAMs—and shipments of its microprocessor line slowed.[4]

Part of Cypress' problem may have been due to aggressive competition from Texas Instruments:

The hard times at Cypress have also been exacerbated by concerns that Texas Instruments Inc.'s new SuperSPARC microprocessor—introduced last week—will grab a lion's share of the Sun Microsystems Inc. workstation market away from Cypress. Only about 15 percent of Cypress' total sales are in microprocessors for Sun workstations, but they are a highly profitable segment, analysts said, and vital to the company's profit future.[5]

Whether Cypress would regain its lead role with Sun remained to be seen:

Analysts said TI has the edge with Sun now, because Sun engineers worked closely with TI designers to create the chip. But if the TI chip does not perform as expected, Cypress could have an opportunity to sell the HyperSPARC chip to Sun, which can switch processors in a computer in less than a week, said Michael Slater, editor of the Microprocessor Report in Sebastopol.[6]

Cypress' market value dropped from $687 to $425 million in a period of twelve months from the third quarter of 1991 to the third quarter of 1992.[7] Is it possible that Cypress' extensive, *internally focused* systems caused it to miss key developments in its customers and competitors?

What's wrong with the San Jose-based company? That depends on who you want to believe. The most optimistic view comes from Rodgers and Half Moon Bay analyst Mike Murphy, who say Cypress is suffering mostly from last year's purchase of the Minnesota chip-production facilities of Control Data. The extra overhead is eating into the bottom line, they say. But over time, they add, who can argue with buying a $100 million plant for only $14 million.

"That was one of the great buys of all time," Murphy said.

Unfortunately, the semiconductor plant isn't Cypress' only problem. Profits on the company's single biggest product line—static random access memory (SRAM) chips—have shriveled up in a sea of competition. Business with one of the company's biggest customers, Sun Microsystems, has fallen. Cypress was the leading purveyor of microprocessors for Sun's top-end but aging line of servers and work stations. Now Texas Instruments has the commanding edge as the chip of choice for Sun's pending new family of products.

Some Cypress critics add that Rodgers' micro-management style is the biggest problem of all. Rodgers is too domineering to build a sufficiently strong core of second-tier executives, they say.[8]

Frito-Lay is also in a highly competitive "chip" business. Since 1987, Frito-Lay has built increasingly sophisticated information systems to use in managing its business.

... The Plano, TX-based snack foods maker distributed hand-held computers to some 10,000 truck route sales representatives who deliver Frito-Lay products to 400,000 locations varying in size from the huge metropolitan grocery store chains to rural general stores. The reps use the computers, manufactured by Fujitsu Ltd., to track 100 branded products in about 250 sizes, so that the first place supermarket personnel touch Frito-Lay products is at the checkout counter. . . .

"We have made significant, concrete savings," says Charles S. Feld, vice president of management services, who along with sales operations vice president Ronald A. Rittenmeyer, won the award [from the Society for Information Management] for Frito-Lay. "The ramifications have been in sales and stales."

Stales are products that pass their freshness date; Frito-Lay must pull stales off store shelves to maintain high product quality. . . .

Because the hand-held computers reduce the amount of paperwork that needs to be done, sales reps can spend an average of three to five hours more a week to call on customers with new promotions or merchandising proposals. In addition to boosting productivity, the system has boosted morale. It has helped free route salespeople from the rigors of the 10- to 12-hour workdays that were once the norm on Mondays (restocking shelves after heavy weekend shopping) and on Fridays (stocking up for the coming weekend).

Managers have also benefitted, as the up-to-date reports of activities on each route makes them better equipped to monitor individual workloads, trade off stops between sales reps, or consolidate routes.

Among the other strategic advantages gained from installing the system:

• Better control of marketing programs. The effect of a new promotional campaign on sales can now be gauged in two days. Before, Frito-Lay had to wait until a campaign had run its course to determine its success.
• Closer links between raw materials purchasing and manufacturing, distribution, and inventory systems. Such links are critical with a business in perishable products.
• More chances at future business opportunities, including links from the hand-held computers into a supermarket's computer system, an experiment that is currently underway in California.[9]

Once the company had the basic system in place, it began the development of a sophisticated decision support system.

. . . There was one overwhelming reason for undertaking the project, says [Steven] Gleave [director of systems development]. "Now that we have all this data coming in, we had to ask ourselves, 'What do we do with it?'"

He explains that the system will be divided into two separate parts for two different groups of users, both of whom will distribute the valuable information from the handheld computer network. An executive information system (EIS) will contain a broader, more general set of information for top-level executives in the company's corporate headquarters in Plano, Texas, and a business operations system will provide more detailed information to managers of individual divisions.[10]

Even the president of the company uses the system.

Employees as high up as President and Chief Executive Officer Robert Beeby use the system. One day, Beeby spotted red numbers on the screen, meaning sales were down in the central region. "I punched up another screen display and located the problem: Texas," he wrote in Comshare's annual report. "I tracked the red numbers to a specific sales division and finally, the chain of stores."

Beeby discovered that a local company had successfully introduced a new white corn chip. Frito-Lay immediately put a white-corn version of Tostitos into production and had it on shelves in a few months.[11]

Obviously, Frito-Lay's information systems are both internally and externally oriented. They are used in operations as well as in developing business strategies. Information systems can be used to create a competitive advantage.

Incentive Systems

Incentive systems create a known relationship between results and rewards, activities and rewards, or both. Although almost every combination of result, activity, and reward has been put together somewhere, managers with Business Sense know that there is no such thing as the perfect incentive system. The best incentive systems support an incentive process by using the four types of data discussed in Chapter 7 to create a relationship among rewards, activities, and results.

The foundation of any incentive system is to create a relationship between results and rewards. For example, an incentive compensation system that rewards the top management team with a bonus for achieving certain levels of revenues and profits is a results-oriented incentive system.

Every person in the organization is there to achieve some results. What are the desired results? How can incentives be tied to those results?

Perhaps the most frightening thing about results-oriented incentive systems is how powerful they are in providing motivators to people. More than one company has been known to ship defective products, or "stuff" their distribution channels with products that haven't been ordered, so that management could make their year-end numbers and get their bonus.

In one case, the activities of management were almost bizarre. In December of 1987 top managers at Miniscribe, a disk drive manufacturer, actually shipped disk drive boxes filled with bricks instead of their product. The false shipments were supposed to be valued at $4.37 million. They were shipped in order for management to achieve their year-end objectives and receive a bonus.[12]

The SEC later demanded the return of some bonuses and profits earned on insider trading of stock.[13]

What kind of incentive would it take to get you to ship bricks instead of your real products?

Getting the incentive system tuned just right is rarely a simple task.

A system that rewards salespeople for the number of sales calls made, rather than the actual sales made, is an activities-based incentive system. In general, the only time you should use an activities-based incentive system is when it is nearly impossible to measure results. When this occurs managers with Business Sense ask why the activity is being undertaken. If there is no measurable result, how will the activity benefit the business?

Some parts of some jobs are very important to the long-term health of the business, but the results are difficult to measure. Part of every manager's job is to develop his replacement. This is an important task in any company but it is particularly important in a high growth business, exactly where managers have the least time to engage in development. Unless these development activities are an explicit part of the incentive system it is unlikely that many managers will spend time on them.

To be effective, incentive systems have to offer a means to achieve rewards that (a) provide incentives that are motivating to individuals and groups, and (b) match the business strategy. Chapter 14 covers motivation in some detail. For now, just note that incentive systems are not effective motivation tools unless they are perceived as fair and competitive.

Incentive systems can easily be in conflict with the business strategy, especially when multiple, potentially conflicting incentive systems are at work. In one company, the sales force earned commissions based on total dollar volume of product sold. Top management's bonus was based on achieving specified levels of revenues *and* profits.

As often seems to be the case, the easiest products to sell in the product line were the ones with the lowest margins. They were the most price competitive with the market leader.

Guess where the sales force spent its time?

Clearly if this behavior continued, top management was not going to hit its targets and get a bonus.

The obvious answer to this problem is to put the sales force on an incentive system that rewards them for both revenues and profits, right? Not necessarily. That solution might make the situation worse. Instead of missing just the profit target, management might now miss both the revenue and profit targets!

There are at least three other solutions that need to be explored before changing the incentive system for the sales force. First, is there some way to cut the costs of the products that are easy to sell and thereby increase the profit margins? Second, is there a way to make the products that aren't selling more competitive so they are easier to sell? Third, if the structure of the business has changed to such a degree that both the strategy and the objectives need to change, can the incentive system be modified to reflect new targets?

Clearly the third alternative is the most dangerous. If management realizes that they can't clear the bar at its current height, they may simply lower the bar. Managers with Business Sense resist this activity, even if it is personally painful in the short term.

The more complex the job, the more necessary it is to have an incentive process supported by one or more incentive systems. Incentives need to be available to managers and employees based on doing the right things for the short- and long-term health of the business.

Decision-Making Systems

There is a clear difference between a decision-making system and decision support systems. The latter are really information systems that support the making of decisions by people. The former actually make specific decisions, depending on the information fed into them. A decision-making system must be able to come up with more than one answer or decision. The simplest systems may have only two answers, "yes" and "no."

In the inventory reorder system mentioned earlier, the system periodically checks the level of supplies in inventory by subtracting the materials checked out of inventory from the starting supply levels. The level of remaining supplies is then compared to a predetermined "rule." For example, if the level of supplies in inventory is above X, do not reorder. If it is below X reorder amount Y. With a technology known as electronic data interchange (EDI), the order can be placed electronically with the vendor and delivered on a prearranged schedule. The vendor may have a decision making system that checks your credit record for past payments to determine whether or not to extend credit for this order. Assuming your credit passes muster, the vendor's electronic order entry system can ship your supplies on schedule. When the supplies arrive at your loading dock robots can pick them up and place them in inventory, with no human interaction having taken place. The process is seamless and requires no human decision making.

In general, decision-making systems make sense when the decisions are repetitive, routine, and the rules for making them can be specified. The way to decide if a system should be developed and installed is to determine if the savings in management time and the combined improvements in speed, accuracy, and reliability of decision making justify the cost.

Even complex decisions can be done by decision-making systems if you are willing to make the investment. These "expert systems" are often useful when there aren't enough people with high enough levels of skill to go around. Using the science of artificial intelligence, experts have developed systems that will do speech recognition, advise doctors in diagnoses, and detect flaws in products as they come down the production line.

The biggest potential problem with any decision-making system is that it is static once it is created until the rules in it are changed or a feedback loop is created in the system's own data base. Decision-making systems do not have a mechanism for learning, but they can update the results of their decisions in such a way that the data base provides more complete information in the future.

WHAT ARE THE KEY SUMMARY POINTS
ABOUT SYSTEMS?

Most companies have management information systems that provide good information on internal operations. Unfortunately, most are sadly lacking in information on customers and competitors.

Processes and systems are used for both strategy formulation and implementation. A system is a "routinized," sometimes automated or computerized, process. Businesses often have systems for (1) information gathering and distribution, (2) incentive creation and distribution, and (3) decision making.

To determine what processes and systems you need, you have to take a process/system inventory. By looking at the information you need to formulate and implement your business strategy, you can create appropriate systems that will support your general management efforts.

So far you've learned how to choose the right business, create the right strategy, and design the right systems. Exercising these three freedoms, once you know how, is challenging. Once you've exercised them, however, you are in a position to effectively design the right organization structure.

FREEDOM #4:
Designing the Right Organization Structure

"What's the best way to organize any business?"

"I don't know. Can there be just one?"

"Sure there is. It's the structure that most effectively gets the right information to the right people at the right time."

"That would be great!"

The purpose of any management team running a business is to make and ensure the implementation of decisions that result in an increase in shareholder wealth. The purpose of the organization structure is to provide a framework in which the flow of information necessary to accomplish management's job can occur.

Many people are unhappy with the structure of their organization. Complaints are frequent and reorganizations are common (see Chapter 13 for the reasons why managers reorganize so often).

Some management experts believe that structure is *the* leading cause of business problems. Noted author, speaker, and consultant Tom Peters has written:

> During a recent seminar, an executive asked what share of business problems "come from (organization) structure, from human-resource prac-

241

tices and from top-management decision making"? My answer startled him: structure, 50 percent; systems (my addition), 35 percent; people (that face I see in the shaving-mirror each morning is a "person," not a "human resource"), 15 percent; top-management decision making, zero.

Our chiefs are hardly flawless decision makers. And the notion that "people are everything" is incontestable. I nonetheless contend that top managers make lousy decisions and people fail to shine largely because burdensome structures and misaligned systems get in the way.[1]

Some structures are obsolete by the time they are installed. Customers and competitors are changing so rapidly in some fast-paced businesses that the information flows needed to make and implement appropriate decisions change more quickly than the structures, especially the more rigid ones, can adjust.

And yet, an organization structure is a necessity if the business is to function. Without some structure, the information would not have appropriate pathways to follow, and responsibility for decisions would not be taken. The trick is to match the organization's structure to the information flows that are required to make and implement the best possible decisions.

When the organization structure fits the business, its strategy, and the information requirements, the result is a thing of beauty. The business hums along like a well oiled machine—or a super-conducting computer chip, if you prefer. Goods and services are delivered on-time, on-quality. Each element of the business operates at the lowest possible cost. Decisions are made carefully and correctly. Participants in the business can do their jobs and enjoy their work. In short, business is a pleasure.

So let's proceed with answering the fundamental question, How should we organize ourselves?

Chapter 13
How Should
We Be Organized?

"What is the number one tool used by managers to create change in companies?"

"Oh that's easy, it's reorganization. Our company does it all the time."

"Does it work?"

"No, not usually."

Why do companies reorganize so often?

It's because redesigning the organization is the easiest management freedom to exercise. It may be difficult to change the business, the systems, or the people in the short run, but the organization's structure is easy to change. Management has total control.

The business strategy is often as easy to change as the organization structure, but some managers don't know how to define a business accurately, much less what a business strategy is. Everyone knows what an organization structure is because organization charts are such powerful visual images. "Now if we just move these boxes around like this . . ."

Managers reorganize for several reasons.

When the results aren't good enough, management has to show it's doing something, so it reorganizes the business. Sometimes even large companies reorganize quite frequently:

> Digital Equipment Corp. sidelined three senior executives in the besieged computer maker's second sweeping reorganization in as many months. The surprise move underscored an air of crisis at the nation's second largest computer maker, based in Maynard, Mass., and set the stage for a new round of layoffs as it scrambles to stanch further losses . . . .
>
> A spokesman portrayed the reorganization as an effort to bring product engineering closer to customers. But to some, it suggested disarray. "It's incredible," said Ray P. Stevens, an analyst with Dean Witter Reynolds Inc. "They had just created this organization in February" and given Mr. Strecker significant new responsibility.
>
> But Digital was stunned by an unexpectedly deep third-quarter loss of $294.1 million, as revenue fell 7.6% to $3.25 billion for the period ended March 28. When the loss was disclosed April 9, executives hinted at sweeping new measures to restore profitability.[1]

Sometimes companies reorganize because outside experts tell them they should. One senior executive told me about his experience with an internationally known consulting firm.

> We hired this firm to come in and tell us how we should be organized. They brought in a team of people and interviewed all of the top executives. They recommended that we divisionalize and decentralize our operations, which we did.
>
> Three years later, our performance hadn't improved. In fact, it had gotten a little worse, so we hired the same firm to figure out what was wrong. They interviewed all of the executives and told us to go back to our old centralized, functional organization structure!
>
> I think they make a living by switching companies around depending on the latest fad. I figure they'll be back in another few years to tell us to change again.[2]

Some companies are so lacking in data, information, and knowledge about their business that they become opinion-driven, political organizations. In these companies, reorganizations herald the winners and losers in the never-ending political battles. Although there may be some politics in any reorganization, particularly in larger companies, any business that reorganizes on a solely political basis is well on its way to failure.

Reorganizations often occur when a new president takes over the business because it is one method that the new leader can use to put his or her "stamp" on the organization. It's such a common event that it is usually expected when a new person moves into the top job.

Some managers try to structure the organization around the people they have rather than around the business strategy. The implicit argument is that you should force the structure to fit the talents of the people rather than the requirements of the business. Although it can be a temporary fix, this approach doesn't work very well for very long. What you are really trying to do with this effort is to fit the *strategy* to the talents of the people you have. The strategy is the set of decisions you must make in order to position the business in its complex environment. Unfortunately, the success of the business is driven by your ability to implement the strategy and if the people you have do not have the skills and motivation necessary to implement the strategy, you will fail.

It's true that everyone has strengths and weaknesses, but if you cannot find people with the skills you need, or you can't afford them, then you must question the viability of your business. Some businesses are lousy businesses because they require superstar people who simply are not available in large numbers or at economic costs. One class of these businesses is known as "hit" businesses (e.g., "hit" records, "hit" movies, or bestselling books), and the superstars quickly evolve into independent contractors whose fortunes wax and wane with their ability to create another hit.

Some reorganizations occur because the company is in a lousy business or has a bad strategy and is getting poor results. No reorganization is going to solve those problems.

Can reorganization cause changes in strategy?

Absolutely! But the most difficult way to create a change in strategy is to reorganize and hope the reorganization will cause an appropriate change in strategy. Why not change the strategy directly? After all, the strategy is only a set of decisions. Make different, and better, decisions.

The time to reorganize your business is when the organization is, for whatever reason, not enabling the systems to deliver the right information to the right people at the right time so they can develop and implement the right strategy.

WHAT ARE THE WAYS TO ORGANIZE A BUSINESS?

When I ask executives how many ways there are to organize a business, the typical response I get is "Hundreds!"

That answer is technically correct if you count all of the minor variations that are available. But there are only four basic organizational forms that work for a business.[3] They are shown in Figure 13–1. Each is appropriate for some strategies and not others. Note that I am discussing only the ways to organize a single business, not the multiple business corporation. The processes for doing the latter are beyond the scope of this book.

The most basic form of organization is the *entrepreneurial* form, or the basic work group. It consists of a manager and a group of workers. Everyone does and is responsible for everything in this form of organization.

Although the entrepreneurial form of organization has been around since the beginning of recorded history, it is being rediscovered in the early 1990s. Described as the lean, flat organization where employees are empowered, it is being heralded as the wave of the future. It's really just the old highly focused, customer- and product-driven, understaffed, undercapitalized entrepreneurial organization. It works because entrepreneurial organizations have to be highly focused on the process of creating, selling, producing, delivering, and supporting something of value. If they're not, they die.

The second basic organizational form is the *functional* form. In this

Figure 13–1
The Four Ways to Organize a Business

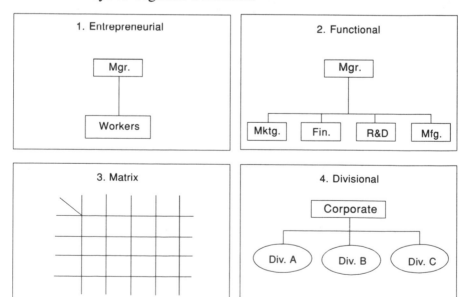

form of organization the tasks that make up the processes of the business are broken out and managed separately. The typical functional organization has separate functions for marketing, finance, production, research and development, and administration. These functions can easily serve as checks and balances on each other.

For example, would you like to go to a hospital, a place you go when you are very sick or seriously hurt, that is run with an entrepreneurial form of organization? The staff is very lean and decision making is pushed to the lowest possible level. Employees are encouraged to innovate and mistakes are widely tolerated.

No thanks! I'll take a good old-fashioned functional organization for my medical care.

The third form of organization is the *matrix*. This is the organizational form of last resort. It requires so many interactions among people without clear authority to get something done that it should never be used unless nothing else will work. In many businesses, especially those doing project work that requires flexible teams, nothing else *will* work. Consulting and construction businesses often must be organized as matrices.

The fourth form of organization is the *divisional* structure, most often found in firms that are in multiple businesses. Single business firms may also use it when it is necessary to separate organizational units, for example, to create geographical divisions. It may be the same business in Asia, Europe, and the United States, but to run it effectively you may need three divisions.

HOW DO YOU LINK BUSINESS STRATEGY, SYSTEMS, AND ORGANIZATION STRUCTURE?

Two fundamental forces determine the appropriate structure for any business. These are the forces of *accountability* and *diversity*.

Accountability

Accountability occurs when a position in the organization's structure is vested with the authority to implement some element or elements of the business strategy and is then held responsible for success. An accountable organization is an effective and efficient organization.

Whenever possible, accountability should be single-point: Ultimately, there should be one person who clearly has primary responsibility for the implementation of each of the elements of the strategy. That person should have the authority to take actions commensurate with his or her responsibility. Anything less will cause conflict and confusion.

Where accountability does not exist, elements of the strategy do not get implemented properly and sometimes don't get implemented at all. It's all well and good to say that in a modern, free-form organization in which all participants are empowered, "everyone is responsible for everything." Managers with Business Sense know that when everyone is responsible for everything, no one is ultimately responsible for anything. There is a significant difference between an organization in which each person takes responsibility for getting results and one where everyone is collectively held accountable for results. In the latter, what do you do when results are not achieved? Without single-point accountability it is very difficult to focus an organization on results.

The basic test, a *task test* of accountability, is to go down your list of strategy elements (see Figure 13–2) and ask what position in the organization is responsible for implementing that element of the strategy. When the structure of the organization has been matched properly to the business strategy, you will get clear-cut answers. When it has not been effectively matched you find either that no position is accountable for that strategy element, or that the position being held accountable is overloaded and is not able to implement everything. The latter is becoming more prevalent as companies downsize by slashing management's ranks without reducing the work.

A second basic test is the *process test* of accountability. In this test you need to look at the interlinked processes that create the value in your business. Many times these processes will cut across functional boundaries. For example, who is accountable for getting information from the customers to the people who create, sell, produce, deliver, and support the products and services of your business? Who supplies the information on competitors?

If it's not happening, it's because no one is clearly accountable.

Diversity

The process of matching an organization structure to a strategy requires an understanding of the concept of *diversity*. Diversity is the opposite of homogeneity and it is what drives the choice to move to increasingly complex forms of organization. Diversity can exist among

Figure 13–2
Examples of Key Elements of a Product Business Strategy

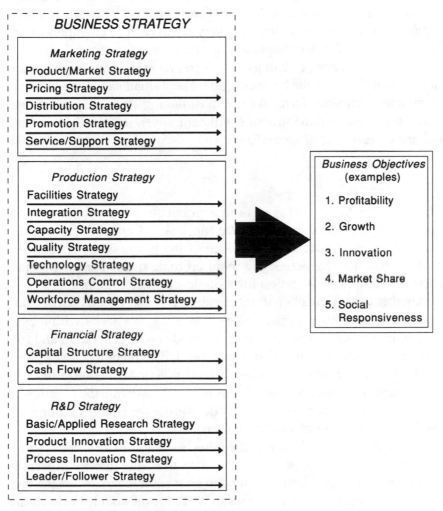

and within the products and services, the technologies, and the markets that define the business.

The Entrepreneurial Form

The simplest form of organization consists of a manager and a group of essentially interchangeable workers. This form is appropriate when there is so little diversity among the products/services, markets, and technologies of the business that specialization is not needed. With a little management, everyone can create, produce, and sell the products and services of the business. A small farm, a convenience store, a boutique, or an early stage startup company could each be examples of appropriate places for an entrepreneurial structure.

Even large companies can use the entrepreneurial form of organization if the unit size of the business can be kept small enough to function in an entrepreneurial form. As the minimum practical organizational unit grows, however, the structure will naturally, if informally, gravitate toward some degree of specialization.

The Functional Form

The first form that most organizations gravitate to is the functional organization, organized by task. Here the tasks of creating, producing, and selling the products and services of the business are specialized enough that different people are required to do them. This is the most common form of organization for a single-business company.

Another form of functional organization is the so-called "horizontal" organization which is organized by processes, not tasks within processes. Examples of processes might include order generation and fulfillment, integrated logistics, and commercialization of technology.[4]

The difference between the horizontal functional organization and the vertical functional organization is in how you define the function of the work group. Is it responsible for delivering the results of a process (horizontal) or the results of a task (vertical)?

Each approach's weakness is the other's strength. The vertical structure requires coordination among the tasks to ensure that the processes are completed properly. Results tend to be measured by how well a task is done, not necessarily what the result is. The results of the business are only measured at the general management level because that is the only place all of the tasks come together. Because the tasks are somewhat naturally in conflict, checks and balances can occur early in the process, and remedial action can be taken. In the horizontal form of organization, results—as they relate to the overall success of the business— are more easily measured at the individual process level. It's easier to hold the order generation *and* fulfillment process team responsible for revenues. Unfortunately, there are fewer checks and balances early in the process. A misguided process team can do a lot of damage before anyone blows the whistle because it's only when results are known that corrective action can be taken. The horizontal form thus requires short cycle times in its processes so that corrective actions can be taken quickly.

The type, amount, and timeliness of information to run the horizontal organization is different. More information on customers and competitors is required more often to enable the horizontal organization to function.

The Matrix Form

When diversity grows within any one of the four elements that define the business (i.e., customer needs met, product/service features, technologies used to make the product/service, and the technology in the product/service) a matrix form of organization may become appropriate. For example, assume that your business is to make air-to-air missiles and sell them to the U. S. Air Force. Air-to-air missiles are the kind used to shoot down one aircraft from another aircraft.

Your organization is structured in the classic task-based functional form. After a review of your strategy, you decide to go after two other markets, the Navy and the Army. Your market studies tell you that selling to them will be quite different. Although you can sell them virtually identical missiles, perhaps with different numbers on them and with different color paint on the outside, the buying process each uses is different. Each branch of the military perceives its missile requirements as unique. The Air Force requires a comparative "fly-off" among competing missiles. The Navy wants special testing to ensure that the missiles will work effectively under carrier aviation conditions, and the Army wants to test fire the missiles from helicopters.

When the diversity in markets is great enough that the job requires more than one person or small team to do it, you have two choices for your organization structure. You can stay with your functional organization and designate market managers within the marketing function (see Figure 13–3), or you can create a matrix organization. A matrix organization would look like Figure 13–4: Across the top you have market managers for each of the three markets, Air Force, Navy, and Army. Down the left side you have the classic functions of a business, including production, finance, research and development, and marketing.

Figure 13–3

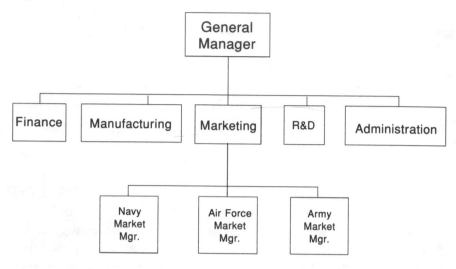

When you design a matrix organization, one dimension contains the elements of the business that are the most diverse and therefore require the most specialization. The other dimension of the matrix contains the elements of the business that are the most homogeneous and therefore can be managed as units.

So, how do you choose between the functional organization with market specialists in the marketing organization (i.e., Figure 13–3) and a matrix organization with market managers for each target market (i.e., Figure 13–4)?

You use your predictions of the future. If you think the future will allow you to continue to sell virtually the same missiles to all three branches of the military, then only the marketing approach will be different among the three markets and you can keep the functional form. If, however, you believe that the requirements of the three markets may lead you to increasingly customized products for each market, you probably need to change to a matrix form so that the market manager can be given more direct contact and influence with the R&D and production functions.

The great advantage of the matrix structure is that it allows a focus on similarity and diversity simultaneously. In the above example, you can focus on the economies of scale that are available in developing and producing similar products, while simultaneously focusing on the perceived unique needs of three different market segments.

Matrix organizations are inherently the most difficult form of organi-

Figure 13–4

Market / Function	Air Force	Navy	Army	
Production				
R & D				
Finance				
Admin.				

zation to manage because they are designed to violate the single-point accountability rule. Responsibilities and authorities are automatically muddled in a matrix organization, making the form inherently unstable. Matrix organizations work much like helicopters fly: with lots of thrashing about and a sheer force of will.

A matrix organization should never be used unless nothing else will work to implement the chosen strategy. When one dimension of your business has a lot of diversity, and the other three are homogeneous, no other form will work as well as a matrix.

Some businesses are predisposed to the use of matrix organizations. For example, any business that does project work such as construction, consulting, or government contracts is predisposed to a matrix form. Projects are another way to specialize the organization by customer.

Matrix organizations can be created to deal with diversity in the geographic location of customers or any other segmentation variable.

Matrix organizations work well in dealing with the diversity in product lines. Procter & Gamble, General Foods, and R. J. Reynolds are each examples of companies who have product managers for specific brands of products within one business, whether it is laundry detergent, coffee, or cigarettes.

The Divisional Form

The only function in a business that does not lend itself to being "matrixed" is finance. Finance deals with money and money has no diversity. It is purely homogeneous!

The rarest form of organization for a single business company is the divisional organization. But it does occur and is appropriate in some situations. Continuing with the air-to-air missile example used above, assume that you want to expand your sales to the military services in Europe. This brings a geographic diversity to your strategy that was not present before. The geographic diversity could be handled by either the functional or matrix organization discussed above. The choice between the two would once again depend on your expectations about the future direction of the business.

As you attempt to sell your missiles in Europe, you learn that the military services in Europe are willing to use the same technologies as the American military, but they want moderately different features in their missiles. The dimensions, explosive power, and weight need to be different to fit their aircraft and mission profiles.

Now you have diversity along a second dimension of the business. When the diversity becomes sufficiently large that you see the beginning of a potential divergence of the European business from the U. S. business, you divisionalize. The divisional organization works best in a single business when you have diversity on two of the dimensions that define the business. It is most appropriate when a single business is in the process of becoming two businesses.

WHAT ARE THE KEY SUMMARY POINTS ABOUT ORGANIZATION STRUCTURES?

Reorganization is one of the most often used and least effective tools for creating change. General managers sometimes reorganize (1) in an attempt to improve results, (2) because the "experts" tell them they will be more efficient, (3) in order to meet some political need in the organization, or (4) to try to use the skills of the people they have.

The time to reorganize your business is when the organization is, for whatever reason, not enabling the systems to deliver the right information to the right people at the right time so that they can develop and implement the right strategy. The forces of accountability and diversity are the primary determinants of the appropriate choice of organization structure for a business.

The four choices of organization structure for a business are the entrepreneurial, functional, matrix, and divisional forms. Each can be appropriate, depending on the type of accountability required and the amount of diversity that exists in the business.

A business strategy is a set of decisions. An organization structure is a diagram of accountabilities. To create a living, breathing, successful business, you will need to get the right people.

FREEDOM #5:
Getting the Right People

"Is your number one problem getting and keeping enough good people?"

"Sure, isn't that every manager's biggest problem?"

"It wouldn't be a problem if you were in a great business and had a winning strategy."

"I never thought of it that way."

In the early 1990s Microsoft was in a great business with a powerful strategy and excellent results. DEC's core business, minicomputers, was an average business with a questionable strategy and results that were so poor that in 1992 the company had its first layoff in the company's thirty-five-year history.

Guess which company was able to hire great people and get them to take a pay cut to come on board?

> . . . In the 17 years since he launched Microsoft, he [Bill Gates] has followed a simple rule: "I hire smart people that are pretty high bandwidth, and I challenge them to think. I ask them to be pretty committed and to work pretty hard."
>
> New recruits usually accept a salary cut and 60- to 80-hour workweeks. And there's minimal training.[1]

Management's ability to get and keep the right people is directly proportional to the quality with which the first four freedoms have been exercised.

Great businesses attract great people. Opportunity draws talent. Conversely, the best people are often the first to leave a business when its fortunes decline. The best people are the ones who have options to work elsewhere.

Brilliant strategies, even in average businesses, convince people that they have a chance to be winners. Inadequate strategies breed a lack of confidence in good people.

Appropriate systems give people the tools they need to do their jobs. Without the right information, even the best people can accomplish little or nothing.

Effective organization structures make sense for the business and enable people to do their jobs. Structures that are not aligned with the required information flows automatically cause conflict.

The fifth management freedom is getting the right people. The right people are the ones who have the skills and motivation that will allow them to use the systems in the organization to effectively and efficiently implement the business strategy.

If you're going to turn a business enterprise from an abstract concept into a living enterprise, you must get the right people.

Chapter 14
What About People?

"What do the right people and the wrong people for your organization have in common?"

"Well, for one, they all want jobs."

"Right. What else?"

"Well, it's often difficult to tell which ones are the right ones and which ones are the wrong ones."

The difference between having the right people—the ones with the necessary skills and motivation—and the wrong people is enormous. It can be the difference between success and failure. Think about it for a minute. If you have the wrong people, it means that they do not have the necessary skills and motivation to do the job. How can you possibly be successful in that case?

Why do most CEOs say their biggest problem is getting and keeping good people? Because it is. Unfortunately, management is sometimes the cause of the problem. Many managers don't know what they want, or how to find, select, reward, and retain the right people.

Assuming that you have done the best job you can in exercising your first four management freedoms, your exercise of the fifth freedom should be driven by three key questions:

1. What people do you need?
2. How do you find more great people?

259

3. How do you keep great people?

Each of these questions is addressed in this chapter.

WHAT PEOPLE DO YOU NEED?

What makes a great person for your job?

Have you ever seen an average performer change jobs and become an outstanding performer? It happens a lot, especially with young, talented people who finally find their niche. When the person's skills and motivation match the job and the opportunity, a great person emerges. Everyone has the potential for great performance. It's the combination of the person and the situation that creates the possibility for greatness. Put any person in exactly the right situation to bring out her abilities and a great performance will emerge.

Do you build an organization around the people you have, or do you find new people to fit the organization?

To answer this question, you first have to specify all of the jobs that you need done, and the motivation needed to do each one. Then you can inventory the skills and motivation of the people you have. Maybe you will be lucky and have just the right people. Maybe the boundaries of the jobs can be redefined in such a way that your current people can do them. If not, you will need some new players.

Specifying the Job

Note that I didn't say describe the job, I said specify it.

What does the person have to *do,* specifically, to be effective in this job? If the job is a high-level management position the person may need to be able to exercise the five freedoms I've discussed in this book. If he is a first-line supervisor, he may need to be able to schedule production and have basic people-management skills.

When job specifications are too general, too many people can fill them. For example, if you are looking for someone who is intelligent and has the knowledge earned from a general business degree, there are thousands of people who fit that bill. Most of them won't be able to do the job you are trying to fill, however, because they don't have the specific skills that are required.

Be careful that you do not simply identify *traits* and think they are *skills*. Things like intelligence and sense of humor might be useful to have, but they are traits, not skills. You also may want to identify the traits you would like in the person you hire, but these are typically less important, in most cases, than being able to identify the application of a specific skill in previous experience.

If the job can't be *specified*, it can't be done. If you are having difficulty specifying the job, more work needs to be done on the organization structure and the systems before you are ready to specify and fill the job.

Once the skill specifications have been completed, you need to check them for reality. The first reality check is to see if there is someone, somewhere, who has the necessary skills. If you are looking for a twenty-four-year-old Ph.D. in biophysics who has ten years of management experience in biomedical companies, you are on a fruitless search. The only person who qualifies has already started his own company! If you have specified an unrealistic job, the only real answers are to (1) change the job or (2) change the business strategy and the organization and then the job.

The second reality check is to compare the economics of your business against the job you've specified. Can you get what you want for what you can pay? Some businesses are not viable because the people with the needed skills can and do make more money in other businesses. Some market research firms have experienced this as people who become experts in a particular industry are hired away by Wall Street firms that need research analysts with knowledge of that industry. Wall Street firms typically can pay significantly higher salaries than a market research firm because of their higher-margin financial structures.

Specifying the Motivation

In addition to skills, the other major category that needs to be specified is the ways in which the candidate self-motivates. Let me make it clear that no one can motivate anyone else. All you can do for another is provide a context in which the person motivates himself. In order to do that you must understand what will motivate him. Please note that I am using the term "motivation" in its broadest sense.

Beginning with the work of Carl Jung on psychological types,[1] and extending through the work of Isabel Briggs-Myers, who created the Myers-Briggs Type Indicator, a new method of understanding behavior has developed. A powerful set of tools for understanding and predicting behavior was developed by Richard Bandler, a co-founder of neuro-linguistic programming (NLP). Bandler developed the concept of meta-programs. Meta-programs are like operating systems for the brain. They are the filters that people use to take in their experiences and pattern their behavior. Although there are at least twenty-five meta-programs in total, some are more important than others when specifying the motivational patterns needed in a particular job.

It is not my intent to teach you how to elicit meta-programs. For that skill you should read Tad James and Wyatt Woodsmall's book *Time Line Therapy and the Basis of Personality*.[2] It shows you how to use the technology of meta-programs in both specifying the job and screening candidates. The intent here is simply to illustrate the usefulness of the concept.

Figure 14–1 shows six of the meta-programs that are particularly powerful in discerning motivational patterns. These six are shown as continua because most people fall somewhere on each continuum, not at one end or the other. Take each of the six and see what you can learn about someone.

If you ask someone what he wants in a job, does he tell you the things he wants that are positive in his ideal next job, or does he tell you the list of things he wants to get away from in his last job?

> . . . Some people tend to be energetic risk takers. They may feel most comfortable moving toward something that excites them. Others tend to be cautious, wary, and protective; they see the world as a more perilous place. They tend to take actions away from harmful or threatening things rather than toward exciting ones.[3]

There is nothing wrong with being toward one end of the Direction Filter spectrum. Each can be appropriate in the right job. In general, I think the head of company security, the corporate counsel, and the head of accounting should be people who "move away" rather than "energetic risk takers" who move toward! The head of marketing and sales probably needs to be a little more in the other direction.

The Reason Filter tells you whether someone does what he does out of necessity or because of the wonderful possibilities for the future. I once knew a manager who worked out of necessity and moved away from things. The only way for this individual to motivate himself was to think his job was in jeopardy and he might not be able to pay his mortgage or feed his family if he didn't get busy. Since his boss was at the

Figure 14–1
Meta-Programs

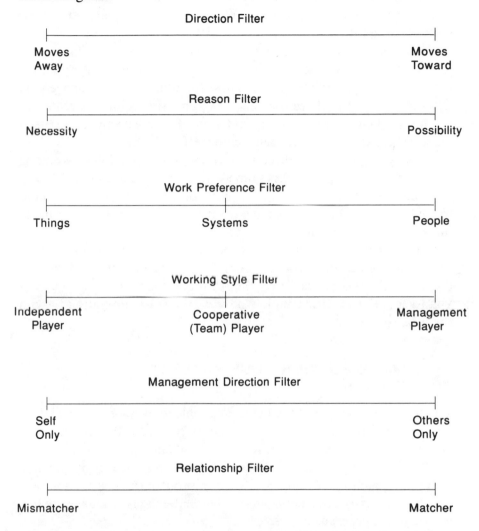

opposite end of these two meta-program continua, the relationship was doomed.

The Work Preference Filter tells you if someone prefers to work with people, systems, or things. If you have a job, for example sales management, that requires someone to work with people, a person who prefers to work with things is not likely to succeed.

The Working Style Filter tells you if someone prefers to be an *independent player*, a *team player*, or a team player who likes to run the show, also known as a *management player*. The classic mistake that seems to be repeated forever occurs when a successful salesperson who is terrific as an independent operator is made the sales manager. Unless he becomes a management player, he will fail.

Some people can and will manage themselves only. Some know how to manage others, but don't really want the responsibility. They are the office's Monday morning quarterbacks. According to the Management Direction Filter, people whose meta-programs are at either extreme will not be good managers. In order to be an effective manager a person must be able to and want to manage himself *and* others.

The Relationship Filter discerns how people see relationships among things or people. Mismatchers immediately see the differences, the exceptions or the mistakes. They make great proofreaders and quality control managers. Matchers see the patterns and relationships among things. Good consultants are often matchers.

Each job in the organization structure has certain characteristics that fit along the dimensions of the meta-programs. Knowing what those dimensions are before trying to match people to jobs enables you to spot the specific people whose methods of motivation fit with the job.

HOW DO YOU MATCH YOUR PEOPLE TO YOUR JOBS?

When you begin to match your current people to the jobs you need done in order to implement your business strategy, you will encounter four combinations of results. Those four are shown in Figure 14–2.

The obvious categories are when both skills and motivation either do or do not match. When both skills and motivation match the job, you have a potentially great performer. Your challenge is to make sure that person has appropriate challenges.

When neither the skills nor the motivation match the jobs available, you have a person on your team whom you don't need. He may be the person you like the most, or even a relative, but keeping him on the team creates a cost you probably don't want to bear. Every time I have seen an organization carry someone who had neither the skills nor the motivation to do a job, it has turned out to be bad for both the organization and the employee in the long term.

What do you do when you have people who have either skills or mo-

Figure 14–2

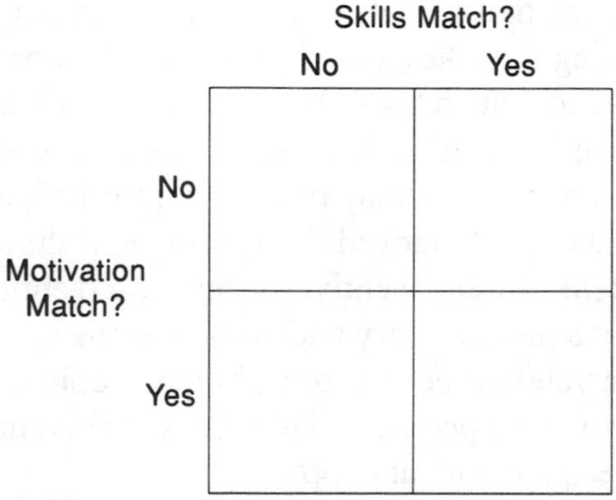

Skills Match?

	No	Yes

Motivation
Match?

No

Yes

tivation, but not both? Each is a potentially positive situation, but you have to handle each differently.

When people have the motivation that fits the job, but not the skills, you can train them, assuming they have the intelligence and raw talent required to learn the skills. Some companies actually prefer highly motivated people, and care less about their skill level. Herb Kelleher, chairman, president, and CEO of Southwest Airlines, a company noted for its employee relations, stated:

> If we can get employees with the proper attitude, we can teach them the job. But, we can't teach attitude; and if they don't have the right attitude, all the experience and intelligence they might have will do no good.[4]

Obviously, the difference between the level of skill the person has and what's needed will play an important part in determining whether you will make the investment to develop skills in a highly motivated person.

The opposite situation—high skill level but motivation that does not fit—is potentially complex.

Each person is motivated somehow, or he would never do anything. So each person has some pattern of things that lead him to take action. If a job requires one set of motivating factors and the person has metaprograms that are opposite of those requirements, the probability of success is low.

Let's say your chief financial officer moves toward possibilities, prefers to work with people rather than systems or things, is an independent player who manages himself only, and is a matcher. The first thing I would do if I were you is have an independent audit of my books! I would be concerned that his job had not been done correctly. I would look for accounting mistakes, and I would want to be assured that he had not perceived too much "possibility" in my cash balances.

If, however, the mismatches between the person's motivational patterns and the job are minor, it may be possible to change the job context in such a way that a fit is achieved. For example, if the sales manager is somewhat frightened by an incentive system based entirely on commissions, what about a mix of salary and commissions?

In some cases you will be able to train the people or change the job context in order to fit the people you have. Invariably, however, at some point you will need more great people.

HOW DO YOU FIND MORE GREAT PEOPLE?

No one has ever built a successful company quickly without an extraordinary emphasis on finding the right people. Microsoft has not been an exception.

> Finding and hiring the best is top priority in Redmond, Wash. It drives the No. 1 maker of personal computer software to visit 137 campuses, some of them four times each year. It prompted the review of more than 120,000 resumes last year and face-to-face interviews with 7,400 candidates—to hire 2,000 people. It makes Microsoft pull out the stops for folks like the Linns, two Ph.D.s who were working at a military think tank outside Washington, D.C. Explains Jeff Raikes, a senior vice-president: "You can't hire bad programmers and get great software."[5]

Almost every member of the Microsoft team gets involved in recruiting top people:

> Even Chairman William H. Gates III gets in on the act. Ask him what the most important thing he did last year was and he answers: "I hired a lot of smart people." Then he actually names them. Near the top of his list is James Allchin, the former chief technical officer at Banyan Systems Inc. His knowledge of networking software is critical in his new post as vice-president for advanced systems. "It took a year to recruit him," says Gates with the pride of the happy hunter.[6]

Although some recruits are reluctant, Gates' persistence often pays off:

> Allchin, 40, knew he was Gates' quarry. He kept deflecting Microsoft's

offer, but Gates kept coming back— visiting, calling, flying him in for dinner. Gates finally won him—at a 35% pay cut. "He convinced me of one thing," Allchin says. "If you want to change the world—and being the silly kind of guy I am, I do—I would have a bigger impact at Microsoft."[7]

When Ross Perot was building Electronic Data Systems (EDS), one of his most important efforts was recruiting people. Perot nicknamed his original team of thirty recruiters the "Wild Bunch."

> The recruiting effort was very aggressive. *Back in 1968 when EDS consisted of 300 employees, 1 of every 10 was a recruiter* [italics added]. The recruiting department had a clerk who did nothing but book airline seats and hotel rooms and a secretary who sat all day compiling and typing recruiters' reports. The recruiters had their hands on the throttle at EDS. Perot never asked them for budgets, or issued orders except to bring in as many good people as they could find. . . .
>
> The recruiters spread the mythology about Perot and EDS. They were the apostles of the horseback newsboy. The service officers who packed hotel ballrooms outside Camp LeJeune came half expecting Perot to walk on water. Of course, Perot was the master of symbols. Perot also gave the Wild Bunch its slogan: Eagles don't flock. You have to find them one at a time.[8]

You can find great people for any business. The process may be difficult and costly, but even lousy businesses can recruit outstanding people if it's done properly.

Searching for the Prospects

Ross Perot was right: "Eagles don't flock. You have to find them one at a time."

Whether they do the searching or hire an outside search firm, managers with Business Sense realize that the probability of finding a successful prospect declines as they go down the following list of priorities for places to search:

1. People in the same business performing the same function
2. People in related businesses performing the same function
3. People performing the same function in unrelated business
4. People in different functions in unrelated businesses

The last category is known as "raw talent."

The above formula indicates the order of priority of where to look to get the best people.

Screening the Pool

If you want to hire great people, you need a very intense screening process for two reasons.

First, the cost of a hiring mistake is much higher than most managers realize. Not only is there the cost of actually hiring the individual, including recruiting fees, travel, and moving expenses, but there is the cost of having him on board until you recognize your mistake. This may take six months to a year, during which time your business strategy is not being effectively implemented in the job in question. Then there's the cost of the termination and the search for a replacement. Some specialists in the field have suggested that the cost of a hiring mistake is two to three times the "mistake's" salary.

The second reason is that people want to feel special. What's special about getting a job that is easy to get? On the other hand, how would you like to be part of an elite group whose manager calls them "The Incredibles"? That is exactly what Mal Stamper, Vice President of the Everett Division of Boeing where the 747 was built, called his people when they started to produce that massive jet. It is not too surprising that they would voluntarily come in nights and weekends to build the world's largest commercial jetliner. "I remember escorting workers to their cars, telling them to go home, they'd put in enough hours," he [Stamper] said. "But they'd be back in the plant before I was."[9]

A lot of people want to be part of a special team, and they expect the screening to be tough. The face-to-face screening starts with the interview.

The research on interviewing indicates that the typical job interview is no better than chance at predicting whether or not the candidate will be successful in the job. Instead of your typical interview, you could just toss a coin and be as effective.[10]

One way to improve your odds for success is to ask the candidate to explain exactly how he did something, and that something should be on your list of skills. If he can explain exactly how he did it, he can probably do it again. If he cannot articulate it, he probably can't do it again.

Unfortunately, the typical candidate wants to explain what he was responsible for, rather than what he did. He wants to talk about his unit or team, not his specific skills. Don't accept these responses. Ask again. Have the candidate do the best job he can in telling you exactly what he did.

Task Testing

In interviewing you need to be on the lookout for the Articulate Incompetent. He is the one who can talk a good game but can't play it. Unfortunately, there are more of these people around than most of us would like to admit. They have good communication skills and little else. If you are going to hire someone to do a job, the best way to find out if she can actually do it is to test the applicant. I don't mean just a paper and pencil test (unless that's what you really want her to do) but specific tests of the kinds of work that will be part of the job. Ask a candidate for a sales job to make a sales presentation. If the search is for a technical writer, ask the candidate to write a technical document.

While samples of past work are useful, they do not necessarily tell you that this person has all of the skills needed to do the work.

AT&T and others have used Assessment Centers to both screen and promote executives.[11] In an Assessment Center experience, candidates, including current employees, are given a set of tests and exercises that simulate real job skills. Teams of executives might compete in a sophisticated business simulation. Individuals are given simulations like the "in-basket" to test their ability to handle routine executive tasks like time management and prioritization.

Reference checks are also an important part of any screening process. Although some people will tell you that reference checks are useless because "everybody has three friends," I have found that effective reference checking can be a lifesaver.

A high-technology company, of which I was a co-founder and director, was funded with venture money and the product was in the testing phase. We were ready to hire a vice president of sales and marketing. With the help of some executive recruiters we were able to find three candidates who looked good on paper. Everyone on the board of directors interviewed the three, and we unanimously agreed on our first, second, and third choices. Then we did the reference checks.

We learned some interesting things. Our number one candidate had lied on his resume. He claimed to have been the regional sales manager of a large electronics company, but he had actually been a salesman with no management responsibilities or experience. The number two candidate had conveniently omitted from his resume two companies at which he had worked. He had been terminated from both, allegedly for incompetence.

Fortunately, candidate number three checked out, and he became a very successful vice president of marketing. The only reason he had been our third choice in the beginning was that the other two candidates appeared to have stronger track records. If their resumes had been true, they would have been stronger candidates. In reality, they weren't.

Some companies have been burned so many times by "resume fraud" that they now employ private detectives to do thorough background checks on any potential hire above a certain level. One company CEO who used this technique told me that it had saved him from making a serious hiring mistake when he learned that a finalist for a senior job had been involved in misappropriation of funds at his previous employer.

Whether you need to go to these lengths to check someone out probably depends on the sensitivity and importance of the job, and the amount of information available about the candidate. As one executive recruiter advised me, however, don't be afraid to change your mind about the "perfect candidate" if some critically negative information shows up at the eleventh hour.

Hiring

The best way to hire someone is not just to sell him the job, but to sell him the business, your strategy, and his job's role in making that strategy a reality. In his book *Odyssey*, John Scully relates how Steve Jobs sold him the job at Apple Computer:

> We were on the balcony's west side, facing the Hudson River, when he finally asked me directly: "Are you going to come to Apple?"
>
> "Steve," I said, "I really love what you're doing. I'm excited by it, how could anyone not be captivated? But it just doesn't make sense."
>
> I explained that even if I wanted to join him at Apple, the financial package wasn't right. I told him I needed $1 million in salary, $1 million for a sign-up bonus, and $1 million in severance pay if it didn't work out.
>
> "How did you reach those numbers?" he asked.
>
> "They're nice big round numbers," I replied, "and they make it a lot easier for me to talk to Kendall."
>
> "Even if I have to pay for it out of my own pocket," Steve said, "I want

you to come to Apple. We'll have to solve those problems because you're the best person I've ever met. I know you're perfect for Apple, and Apple deserves the best."

"Steve," I said, "I'd love to be an adviser to you, to help you in any way. Any time you're in New York, I'd love to spend time with you. But I don't think I can come to Apple."

Steve's head dropped as he stared at the pavement. After a weighty, uncomfortable pause, he issued a challenge that would haunt me for days: *"Do you want to spend the rest of your life selling sugared water or do you want a chance to change the world?"* [Italics added.]

It was as if someone reached up and delivered a stiff blow to my stomach. I had been worried about giving up my future at Pepsi, losing pensions and deferred compensation, violating the code of loyalty to Kendall, my ability to adjust in California—the pragmatic stuff that preoccupies the middle-aged. I was overly concerned with what would happen next week and the week after next. Steve was telling me my entire life was at a critical crossroads. The question was a monstrous one; one for which I had no answer. It simply knocked the wind out of me.[12]

If you do not have a good business or a first-rate strategy, you will have a much more difficult time hiring your top candidates. Great people can recognize a company that doesn't have its act together.

Obviously, the offer and the manner in which it is made must be competitive with the other roles that great people can play. If you're not prepared to really compete, don't bother to make the offer.

HOW DO YOU KEEP GREAT PEOPLE?

Why do people leave a business?

Some are forced to leave for one reason or another. There is one tough-minded manager in a highly competitive business who insists on getting rid of his worst performers. His argument is that good people will leave to seek opportunity, which allows the less-qualified people to keep rising to the top, until you have a company of incompetents. His approach is to make a list of his people each year in each category, and get rid of the bottom 10%. By doing so he sends a clear signal that the incompetents will not be supported by the good people.

Some people leave for personal reasons. Divorces happen, spouses die, or children have illnesses, causing people to move or stop working. Sometimes people simply need change. They want to live in a different part of the country or get involved in a new industry.

Two other reasons that people make changes are dissatisfaction with the current situation and the perception of a greater opportunity elsewhere. As mentioned in the discussion of meta-programs, some people move "away" from things, and others move "toward." There may not be a lot you can do about someone having a better opportunity elsewhere, but management certainly can make a difference with regard to an employee's dissatisfaction with the current situation. Usually the dissatisfaction is real. People can't get what they want because the strategy, systems, or structure are getting in the way. These kinds of problems can be solved with better management.

Rewarding Great People

To provide an appropriate context for someone to be motivated, each person should ideally have a custom-tailored reward system. But tailored reward systems are perceived as biased, and their perceived unfairness causes dysfunctional behavior in the organization. Therefore, groups of people in similar jobs must have the same reward system.

It is possible to have different groups with different reward systems. For example, few others in the organization complain when salespeople are given an opportunity to earn more money if they sell more. Obviously, selling more of the company's products or services is in everyone's best interest. Besides, sales is the only job in the company in which people are paid to be rejected more often than accepted.

How companies reward their people also differs relative to the market for those people. Apple Computer and Microsoft illustrate the differences.

Historically, Apple paid salaries that were in the top 10% of those in their industry. When the company changed its strategy to lower prices and go after market share, it also lowered its target positioning of salaries to be somewhat more competitive with other companies.[13] Paying premium salaries while competing on price no longer made sense.

As previously noted, Microsoft has had a strategy of paying discounted salaries. Employees were often expected to take a pay cut when joining the company. Why would good people take a pay cut to go with Microsoft? There are probably several intangible and tangible reasons. On the intangible list is the value of working for a winner and leader in the industry. There is a likelihood of working with great people at the company. On the tangible list, the stock options have done well.

. . . Thomas Dimitri, a novice programmer who turned down a higher-paying job to join Microsoft last year, has already made a paper profit of $150,000 on options he can exercise in 1995. He is also eligible for a performance bonus of up to 15% of his salary every six months.[14]

Inevitably, the company's growth will slow and the mix of compensation will have to change if the company is to keep great people. Some analysts already point to the difficulty of continuing Microsoft's historical growth rates of almost 50% when its annual revenues exceed $3 billion and it is facing increased competition from Apple and IBM.[15]

There is a reward system to fit every person's motivation pattern. Lincoln Electric has a waiting list of applicants to work in its piecework pay- and profit-based bonus system that provides significant potential for those willing to work hard. The company has no paid holidays and paid vacation is less than average, but the company hasn't had a layoff in over forty years. In 1990, Lincoln Electric employees earned an average of $9–16 per hour versus an average of $11.35 per hour for comparable workers in the Cleveland, Ohio, area where Lincoln is located. This no frills approach meets the needs of many who are willing to make the inherent tradeoffs.[16]

Whatever the reward system you choose, it must fit the economics of your business. The motivational patterns of the people you have in your organization must fit the reward systems you choose.

Challenging Great People

You already know how to challenge great people, because you are a great person. Remember a time when you were challenged, and you were able to do your best and got outstanding results? I'll bet it was when . . .

You were in a situation with boundless opportunity. The possibility to grow and profit from the opportunity was clear.

You knew what direction to go. The path to success was on the map you had drawn.

You had the information to enable you to not only move forward effectively, but to correct any missteps along the way and get quickly back on track.

You organized in a way that would allow you to follow the map exactly.

You had the team to back you up. Each person was skilled in his
job and motivated to do it.

WHAT ARE THE KEY SUMMARY POINTS ABOUT GETTING THE RIGHT PEOPLE?

The right people can make all the difference between success and failure in your business. If you don't have the right people, it means that
you don't have the people with the combination of skills and motivation
necessary to turn the right strategy into good results.

Getting the right people is always a challenge because there is so
much variability among individuals. The job is easier, however, if you
have chosen a great business, created a brilliant strategy, developed effective systems, and designed an efficient organization structure. You
may even find that great people seek your business as a place where
they'd like to work.

Matching the right people to your business requires an assessment of
their skills and motivation. There are several good ways to assess skills,
and the methods for doing so are fairly well known. Motivation can be
assessed by using the relatively new concept of meta-programs.

Finding, hiring, and keeping great people will require continuous use
of your Five Freedoms as your business moves forward in its dynamic
environment.

Now that you know about all Five Freedoms, what do you do next?

Conclusion

"Now that you know, in detail, what your Five Freedoms are, what should you do with them?"

"Exercise them!"

"That's right. You've broken the code."

The Five Freedoms are your key to managing the one constant in business—change.

There is nothing magic about the Five Freedoms that create your Business Sense. They are simple, although not always easy, to implement. To exercise them effectively you must maintain constant vigilance. Both the world around you and your business are changing. Therefore, you must constantly exercise your freedoms if you want to create and sustain success.

The amount of growth, profit, and diversification potential in your business does make a difference. If you are looking for a business, choose a great one, not a lousy one. If you are already in a business, figure out how good it is and take appropriate action. If you are in a truly lousy business, don't be afraid to get out of it and find a better one.

Once you are in a business that you want to—or have to—stay in, create a brilliant strategy. If you are in a great business, a brilliant strategy will rapidly enhance your shareholders' wealth. The ultimate strategy may be a legal, unregulated monopoly in a great business, but you can create incredible results with lesser, but still sterling strategies. Even in lousy businesses somebody, somewhere usually makes some money by creating a brilliant strategy and implementing it well. Try to be that somebody.

Develop the right systems that will enable you to get the right information to feed your decision-making processes, make the best possible decisions, and create the right incentives for your people.

Figure out what information you need to stay on top of your constantly changing business and create the systems that are necessary to get that information and turn it into knowledge. While information on the current operations of your business is essential, information on customers and competitors can often be used to create knowledge that can give you a competitive advantage. Use that knowledge to make strategic decisions and implement them effectively.

Organize to optimize the flow of information necessary to run your business in its dynamic environment and keep it on track to your targeted results. Use the fundamental concepts of single-point accountability and diversity to fit one of the four fundamental types of organization structure to your business. If the organization and the information systems are synchronized with your business strategy, the business can run smoothly and efficiently.

Finally, get the right people. If they are part of the general management team, they can participate in exercising the **Five Freedoms**. If they work for your general management team and have the right skills and motivation, they will be instrumental in continuing to make the business successful.

That's it. The difference between what successful and unsuccessful general managers do isn't very complicated, is it?

It's just Business Sense.

Notes

Chapter 1. What Is Business Sense?

1. James J. Mitchell, "Sears Is Looking Stupid as Well as Guilty," *San Jose Mercury News,* June 16, 1992, p. 1F.
2. "Sears' Scandal: Classic Bungling of a Crisis," *San Jose Mercury News,* June 29, 1992, p. 6D.
3. John R. Wilke, "Digital Disbands Group, Sidelines Three Officials: Move Suggests Air of Crisis as Concern Reorganizes Second Time This Year," *Wall Street Journal,* April 20, 1992, p. B8.

Freedom #1. Choosing the Right Business

1. Kathy Rebello and Evan I. Schwartz, "MICROSOFT," *Business Week,* February 24, 1992, p. 62; and company annual reports.
2. "Value of Microsoft's Stock Tops IBM's," *Peninsula Times Tribune,* January 22, 1993, p. 1B.

Chapter 2. What Is a Business?

1. See Peter F. Drucker, *The Practice of Management,* New York: Harper & Row, 1954, Chapter 6, pp. 49–62.
2. Ibid., p. 49.
3. Theodore Levitt, "Marketing Myopia" (September-October, 1975). According to the *Harvard Business Review* Levitt's article was seventh on its all-time best-seller list as of April 8, 1992.
4. Ibid., p. 45.
5. Ibid., p. 45.

6. See "Winnebago Industries Inc. and the Recreational Vehicle Industry," HBS Case Services, Harvard Business School, Boston, MA 02163, Case #9–375–092, 1974.

7. Information from Sheila Davis, Public Relations Department, Winnebago Industries, April 2, 1992.

8. I am sure that my thinking on this topic has been influenced by discussions with Dick Remelt and by his excellent book *Strategy, Structure and Economic Performance,* Division of Research, Graduate School of Business Administration, Harvard University, Boston, MA, 1974. Another ground-breaking work in this area is Derek F. Abell's *Defining the Business: The Starting Point of Strategic Planning,* Englewood Cliffs, NJ: Prentice-Hall, 1980. The approach taken here is different, but clearly builds on the thinking of these two scholars.

9. Debbie Fields, *One Smart Cookie,* New York: Simon & Schuster, 1987, p. 76.

10. Kevin McManus, "The Cookie Wars," *Forbes,* November 7, 1983, pp. 150–152.

11. Charles C. Kenney, "Fall of the House of Wang," *Computerworld,* January 17, 1992, pp. 67–69.

12. Joseph Nocera, "What Went Wrong at Wang?" *Wall Street Journal,* February 26, 1992, p. A8.

13. In a classic article in the March 1956 *Psychological Review* (Vol. 63, No. 2), pp. 87–97, George A. Miller of Harvard wrote about "The Magical Number Seven, Plus or Minus Two: Some Limits on our Capacity for Processing Information." Miller suggests that most people's limits of conscious processing of pieces of information are "seven plus or minus two."

Chapter 3.   How Much Growth Potential Is There?

1. Initial public offering price from Value Line. Price at the time company was taken private provided by Ruth Theis, Director of Internal Audit, Harte-Hanks Communications, by phone on March 31, 1992.

2. Conner Peripherals eclipsed Compaq's record in 1987 with $113 million in revenues.

3. Conner also eclipsed this record by reaching $1 billion in revenues in just its fourth year of operation.

4. Michael Allen, "Compaq's Profit Dropped by 60% in First Quarter," *Wall Street Journal,* April 28, 1992, pp. A3 and A6.

5. MicroQuote II, a CompuServe service.

6. Genentech numbers are from Genentech's annual reports 1980–1989 and from Diane Hobbes of Genentech Investor Relations. Amgen's numbers are from Standard & Poor's 1990 and from Sarah Crampton of Amgen Investor Relations.

7. "Genentech Reports Fourth Quarter and Year End Results," *Business Wire,* January 16, 1992.

8. Amgen 1991 annual report.

9. HP Corporate Archives.

10. Peter M. Senge, *The Fifth Discipline: The Art and Practice of the Learning Organization,* New York: Doubleday Currency, 1990, p. 62.

11. "The Best Small Companies," *Business Week,* May 27, 1991, pp. 85–90.

12. The composite score is "the sum of 0.5 times its rank on return on total capital, plus 0.25 times each of its growth ranks." Ibid., p. 85.

13. Bruce Hager and Richard Brandt, "Where Did They Go Wrong?" *Business Week,* May 27, 1991, p. 84.

14. Alan Deutschman, "America's Fastest-Growing Companies," *Fortune,* October 5, 1992, pp. 59–82.

15. F. Peter Model, "Will There Even Be Another Airline?" *Frequent Flyer,* June 1992, pp. 27–40.

16. Janice Castro, "This Industry Is Always in the Grip of Its Dumbest Competitors" (interview with Robert Crandall), *Time,* May 4, 1992, pp. 52–53.

17. "Foes in HDTV Race to Split Victor's Pot," *San Jose Mercury News,* May 8, 1992, p. 3G.

18. "Interactive TV Evangelism: TV Answer Is Overselling Its Prospects to Investors, Some Say," *San Jose Mercury News,* May 16, 1992, pp. 12F and 19F.

19. Model, "Will There Even Be Another Airline?" p. 28.

20. Mary Vogel, Corporate Communications, H&R Block, by telephone on November 4, 1991.

21. Micheline Maynard, "'91 Auto Sales Worst In A Decade," *USA Today,* October 4–6, 1991, p. B1.

22. Compiled by the Motor Vehicle Manufacturers Associations from R. L. Polk & Co. data.

23. Howard G. Chua-Eoan, "How Do You Double the Value of a Trabant? Fill'er Up!" *Time,* January 1, 1990, p. 39.

24. Jacques Ellul, *The Technological Society,* New York: Knopf, 1964.

Chapter 4.   What Is the Profit Potential?

1. The exact form of ownership varies widely. Some are "professional corporations," others are Subchapter S companies. The point is that the owners find some way to take the earnings from operations out of the business without suffering the double taxation that owners of a typical corporation are hit with on dividends paid on their stock.
2. Catellus Development Corporation 1991 annual report.
3. Portland General Electric 1979 annual report and Art Greisser, Operations Accounting, Portland General Electric, May 29, 1992.
4. The average bond yield of all corporate bonds issued by Fortune 500 companies in 1986 (214 issues) was 8.81%. The variance of the yield was 2.69 while the standard deviation was 1.64. The average bond yield for all corporate bonds issued by Fortune 500 companies in 1991 (182 issues) was 8.73%. The variance of the yield was 1.26 while the standard deviation was 1.12.

   Using a corporate tax rate of 34%, we calculated the average cost of capital by using the equation *Cost of Capital = Average Yield × (1–t)* where *t* equals the corporate tax rate. The resulting costs of capital for Fortune 500 companies in 1986 and 1991 were 5.81% and 5.76% respectively.

   The same analysis was completed for the 1993 Fortune 500. The results were as follows:

		Earnings Exceeded Cost of Capital in 1986?	
		Yes	*No*
Earnings Exceeded Cost	*Yes*	84	14
of Capital in 1992	*No*	65	96

   These data were not used in the text because of the complexity of explaining the impact of FASB 106 on several companies' earnings. For example, the Fortune 500 listing noted that 143 companies' earnings were impacted negatively by 10% or more in 1992.
5. This analysis does not take into account the actual cash return on invested capital. Due to non-cash expenses, such as depreciation

and amortization of goodwill, ROA may not reflect the cash returns the company actually realizes.

6. The best estimates we could get came from Mr. Bill Schultz, vice president of engineering and operations, General Aviation Manufacturers Association, May 28, 1992, by phone. Mr. Schultz noted that the certification costs, excluding development costs for a four-passenger, fixed-landing-gear plane that is *not* certified for instrument operations in weather are between $750,000 and $3,750,000. He also noted that certification costs are typically only 10–35% of development costs.

7. "Kodak Exits Instant-Photo Field Today," *San Jose Mercury News,* January 9, 1986, p. 3F.

8. Martha T. Moore, "Rivals Gain Ground with Lower Prices," *USA Today,* March 3, 1992, pp. 1B, 2B. Data taken from accompanying chart titled "Mercedes Loses Edge on Luxury."

Chapter 5. Where Is the Diversification Potential?

1. Several sources provide insights into the challenges of diversification. Six of the better ones include:

E. Ralph Biggadike, *Corporate Diversification: Entry Strategy and Performance,* Boston, Harvard University Press, 1976

Michael E. Porter, "From Competitive Advantage to Corporate Strategy," *Harvard Business Review,* May–June 1987, pp. 43–59

Malcolm S. Salter and Wolf A. Weinhold, *Diversification Through Acquisition: Strategies for Creating Economic Value,* New York: The Free Press, 1979

Malcolm S. Salter and Wolf A. Weinhold, "Diversification Via Acquisition: Creating Value," *Harvard Business Review,* July–August 1978, pp. 166–176

Malcolm S. Salter and Wolf A. Weinhold, "Choosing Compatible Acquisitions," *Harvard Business Review,* January–February 1981, pp. 117–127

George S. Yip, *Barriers to Entry: A Corporate Strategy Perspective,* Lexington, MA: D. C. Heath, 1982.

Freedom #2. Creating the Right Strategy

1. James Ott, "Airline Fiscal Morass Erases Profits and Crimps Fleet Plans," *Aviation Week & Space Technology,* April 6, 1992, pp. 36–38.

2. Information regarding Southwest Airlines was taken from the following articles:

> David A. Brown, "Southwest Airlines Gains Major Carrier Status by Using Go-It-Alone Strategy," *Aviation Week & Space Technology,* March 5, 1990, pp. 82–84
>
> David A. Brown, "Southwest's Success, Growth Tied to Maintaining Original Concept," *Aviation Week & Space Technology,* May 27, 1991, pp. 75–77
>
> Subrata N. Chakravarty, "Hit 'em Hardest with the Mostest," *Forbes,* September 16, 1991, pp. 48–51
>
> Del Jones, "Southwest Flies High with Cut-Rate Niche," *USA Today,* May 7, 1992, pp. 1B & 2B
>
> Edward O. Welles, "Captain Marvel," *Inc.,* January 1992, pp. 44–47

Chapter 6.   What Is a Business Strategy?

1. I have since lost the specific reference—perhaps the rest of the text was no more practical than this definition and I threw it away!
2. I was first introduced to this analysis as a Features (Logic), Benefits, Value (Emotion) analysis by William R. Delaney of the Delaney Group, an advertising agency in Alameda, California. His process is not copyrighted and is mentioned here with his approval.
3. According to Kathleen Parker of the Public Affairs Office of L.L. Bean on April 20, 1992, L.L. Bean has one retail outlet and three factory outlets in Maine and New Hampshire.
4. "Why Tennessee?" discussion in Saturn Student Kit supplied by Saturn Division of GM.
5. Matthew Cain, "AT&T Agrees to Buy 20% of Sun over Three Years," *Electronic News,* January 11, 1988, pp. 1 & 14.
6. "AT&T Divesting Stake in Sun Microsystems," *Electronic News,* June 10, 1991, pp. 9 & 12.
7. See Peter C. Reid, *Well Made in America,* New York: McGraw-Hill, 1990 and "Employees Take the Wheel: A Study of Ownership at Avis Inc.," *New York State Industrial Cooperation Council Action Research Report Number Five,* New York: Canterbury Press, 1989.
8. Brian Dumaine, "Earning More by Moving Faster," *Fortune,* October 7, 1991, p. 89.

Chapter 7.   What Is the Future of the Industry?

1. Clearly the leading scholar in the field of industry analysis is Michael Porter of the Harvard Business School. Mike's books,

Competitive Strategy: Techniques for Analyzing Industries and Competitiors, New York: The Free Press, 1980, *Competitive Advantage: Creating and Sustaining Superior Performance,* New York: The Free Press, 1985, and *The Competitive Advantage of Nations,* New York: The Free Press, 1990, are landmarks in the development of structural analysis of industries. I had the privilege of teaching with Mike in the mid-1970s, and though I'm sure some of his early thinking rubbed off on me, the approach outlined here was developed independently during client work and executive seminars. Early versions were used at General Electric's Executive Education School at Croton-on-Hudson, NY between 1974 and 1978. The framework that is developed in this chapter has been taken from my practical experience in dealing with a large number of different businesses. It draws on the fields of industrial economics, political science, and the functional areas of business (e.g., marketing, finance, production, and R&D). Some of the concepts, particularly those related to competitive dynamics, are drawn from the study of military history and strategy.

2. Mike Langberg, "Does Nintendo Play Fair? Questions Abound About Japanese Firm's Way of Doing Business," *San Jose Mercury News,* March 3, 1992, pp. 1D–5D. (Note: on May 1, 1992 the U.S. District Court cleared Nintendo of antitrust charges brought by Atari Corp.)

3. *FCC Reports,* 2nd Series, Volumes 79, 84, 88, 90.

4. "FCC to Let Regulated BOC's Offer Enhanced Services," *Network World,* November 25, 1991, p. 6.

5. Note that this definition differs significantly from that used by industrial economists. For more information on their approach, please see:

Howard H. Newman, "Strategic Groups and the Structure-Performance Relationship," *Review of Economics and Statistics,* August 1978, pp. 417–427.

Michael E. Porter, "The Structure Within Industries and Companies' Performance," *Review of Economics and Statistics,* May 1979, pp. 214–227.

Michael E. Porter, *Competitive Strategy: Techniques for Analyzing Industries and Competitors,* New York: The Free Press, 1980.

6. Pascal Zachary and Lourence Hooper, "IBM and Apple Open New Front in PC Wars with Strategic Alliance," *Wall Street Journal,* July 5, 1991, pp. A1 & A8.

7. See Cathy Anterasian and Lynn W. Phillips, "Discontinuities, Value Delivery, and the Share-Returns Association: A Re-examination of the 'Share-Causes-Profits' Controversy," working paper from Marketing Science Institute, Cambridge, MA, p. 6. Their equation is *Value = Benefit − Price*. They take theirs from George C. Homans, *Social Behavior,* New York: Harcourt Brace Jovanovich, 1974, p. 25. Note that "Needs Met" here includes both benefits and feelings as used in the features/benefits/feelings analysis cited earlier.
8. Christine Blouke, "Competitive Dynamics in the Microcomputer Industry: Apple vs. IBM," Palo Alto, CA: FOCUS, The Management Process Company, 1990.

Chapter 8.   How Good Is the Strategy?

1. An excellent article on objectives is Charles H. Granger's "The Hierarchy of Objectives," *Harvard Business Review,* May-June 1964, pp. 63–74.
2. James B. Teece, "The Board Revolt: Business as Usual Won't Cut It Anymore at a Humbled GM," *Business Week,* April 20, 1992, pp. 30–36.
3. James C. Van Horne, *Financial Management and Policy,* 8th ed. Englewood Cliffs, NJ: Prentice-Hall, 1989, pp. 807–815.
4. Since this story took place, Fred has been the president of Bendix/King Avionics, and as I write this in late 1992 he is the president and CEO of IOMEGA Corp., makers of a variety of removable mass storage products in Roy, Utah.

Chapter 9.   What Are the Alternative Strategies?

1. Anthony Robbins, *Unlimited Power,* New York: Fawcett Columbine, 1986, p. 300.
2. Michael Gershman, *Getting It Right the Second Time,* Reading, MA: Addison Wesley, 1990, pp. 193–197. This book is full of reframes people have done with strategies.
3. Kim Boatman, "A Pitch for Financial Rebirth," *San Jose Mercury News,* April 12, 1992, p. 1E.
4. Kim Boatman, "Team Is Investment, Not Indulgence," *San Jose Mercury News,* April 12, 1992, p. 10E.
5. The argument was first suggested to me in 1987 by Steve Edelman, one of the founders of SuperMac Technologies. It has since been

put forth by Andrew S. Rappaport and Shmuel Halvei in "The Computerless Computer Company," *Harvard Business Review,* July-August 1991, pp. 69–80.

6. Subrata N. Chakravarty, "Hit 'em Hardest with the Mostest," *Forbes,* September 16, 1991, pp. 48–51.
7. Source: Packard Bell S-1 registration statement.
8. "The Price Club Story" (company literature, no printing or copyright date).
9. "Office Depot Corporate History," no printing or copyright date (Office Depot now owns Office Club).

Chapter 10.   What Strategy Should We Follow?

1. Dr. Kenneth J. Hatten, "Ferment in the Beer Industry: Schlitz-Miller," Graduate School of Business, Stanford University Case #S-BP-199, p. 11.
2. Ibid.
3. Joseph Schlitz Brewing Company 1978 annual report, and Stanley Ginsberg, "Is the Gusto Forever Gone?" *Forbes,* December 8, 1980, pp. 34–35.
4. "Hewlett-Packard Rethinks Itself," *Business Week,* April 1, 1991, pp. 76–79.
5. Hewlett-Packard annual reports and MicroQuote II, a CompuServe service. Hewlett-Packard's market value was calculated by multiplying the common shares outstanding and the ending stock price per quarter.
6. MicroQuote II, a CompuServe service.
7. Edmund Faltermayer, "The Deal Decade: Verdict on the 80s," *Fortune,* August 26, 1991, pp. 58–70.
8. Ibid., p. 58.
9. "Can David Packard Save HP?" *San Jose Mercury News,* October 29, 1990, p. 1A.
10. "Packard's Challenge for HP," *San Jose Mercury News,* October 29, 1990, pp. 1D and 7D.
11. Ibid.
12. Ibid.
13. Ibid.
14. Joan Warner, "Putting Your Cash Where Your Conscience Is," *Business Week,* December 24, 1990, p. 74.
15. David C. McClelland, "Business Drive and National Achieve-

ment," *Harvard Business Review,* July-August 1962, pp. 99–112. See also "As I See It," *Forbes,* June 1, 1969, pp. 53–57 and David C. McClelland, "Want To Be a Success: Here's What It Takes," *Science Digest,* April 1967, pp. 69–74.

Chapter 11.   What About Missions and Visions and Such?

1. The correct answers are A = Chrysler, B = Caterpillar, C = Navistar.
2. John Bartlett, *Bartlett's Familiar Quotations,* New York: Little, Brown, 1980, p. 744.
3. *Scientific Quotations: The Harvest of a Quiet Eye,* ed. Maurice Ebison, New York: Crane, Russak, 1977, p. 86.
4. *Bartlett's Familiar Quotations,* 1980, p. 909.
5. George A. Miller, "The Magical Number Seven, Plus or Minus Two: Some Limits On Our Capacity For Processing Information," *The Psychological Review,* Vol. 63, No. 2, March 1956, pp. 81–97.
6. The six businesses included computer aided engineering (CAE), computer aided design (CAD), computer aided software engineering (CASE), computer aided publishing (CAP), computer aided electronic packaging (CAEP), and computer aided circuit testing (CAT).
7. Gerard H. Langeler, "The Vision Trap," *Harvard Business Review,* March–April 1992, pp. 52 and 53.

Freedom #3.   Developing the Right Systems

1. Alfred Chandler, *Strategy and Structure,* Cambridge, MA: M.I.T. Press, 1962.

Chapter 12.   What Systems Do We Need?

1. *The American Heritage Dictionary of the English Language,* Boston: Houghton Mifflin Company, p. 709. An alternative definition is "The mental ability to perceive and distinguish relationships or alternatives; the critical faculty; discernment."
2. Debbie Berlant, Reese Browning, and George Foster, "How Hewlett-Packard Gets Numbers It Can Trust," *Harvard Business Review,* January-February 1990, pp. 178–183.
3. T. J. Rodgers, "No Excuses Management," *Harvard Business Review,* July–August 1990, pp. 84–98.
4. Valerie Rice, "Cypress Faces First Layoffs," *San Jose Mercury News,* May 13, 1992, pp. 1F & 2F.

5. Ibid.

6. Ibid.

7. MicroQuote II, a CompuServe service.

8. Steve Kaufman, "Cypress: If You've Got It, Hold On to It; If Not, Steer Clear," *San Jose Mercury News,* April 27, 1992, p. 1D.

9. Connie Winkler, "More Sales, Fewer Stales," *Computer-DECISIONS,* November 1988, p. 26.

10. Bob Francis, "Frito Lays a New IS Bet," *Datamation Magazine,* February 15, 1989, p. 75.

11. *American Demographics* March 1991.

12. Stuart Zipper, "SEC to ExMiniscribers: Pay $10M," *Electronic News,* August 19, 1991, pp. 1 and 30.

13. Ibid.

Freedom #4.   Designing the Right Organization Structure

1. Tom Peters, "50% of Business Problems Come from Structure," *Peninsula Times Tribune,* October 28, 1990, p. C1.

Chapter 13.   How Should We Be Organized?

1. John R. Wilkes, "Digital Disbands Group, Sidelines Three Officials: Move Suggests Air of Crisis as Concern Reorganzies Second Time This Year," *Wall Street Journal,* April 20, 1992, p. B8.

2. This quote is from a conversation with a participant in one of my executive seminars at the Stanford Business School. For obvious reasons, the source will remain anonymous.

3. I believe these four basic forms were first isolated by Bruce R. Scott in "Stages of Corporate Development," #9-371-294, BP 998, Intercollegiate Case Clearinghouse, Harvard Business School, 1971. (This reference is taken from the bibliography in Jay R. Galbraith and Daniel A. Nathanson's *Strategy Implementation: The Role of Structure and Process,* St. Paul: West Publishing, 1978, p. 148. It is out of print.)

4. Thomas A. Steward, "The Search for the Organization of Tomorrow," *Fortune,* May 18, 1992, pp. 92–98.

Freedom #5.   Getting the Right People

1. Kathy Rebello and Evan I. Schwartz, "MICROSOFT," *Business Week,* February 24, 1992, p. 62.

Chapter 14.   What About People?

1. C. G. Jung, *Psychological Types,* Princeton, NJ: Princeton University Press, 1971.
2. The most comprehensive and useful discussion of meta-programs can be found in Tad James and Wyatt Woodsmall's *Time Line Therapy and the Basis of Personality* (Cupertino, CA: Meta-Publications, 1988, pp. 91–146). A brief but also useful discussion can be found in Anthony Robbins' *Unlimited Power* (New York: Fawcett Columbine, 1986, pp. 253–274). This discussion draws on both of these sources and my own experience using meta-programs when interviewing people for my own and client firms.
3. Robbins, *Unlimited Power,* p. 255.
4. David A. Brown, "Southwest Airlines Gains Major Carrier Status by Using Go-It-Alone Strategy," *Aviation Week & Space Technology,* March 5, 1990, p. 84.
5. Kathy Rebello and Evan I. Schwartz, "How Microsoft Makes Offers People Can't Refuse," *Business Week,* February 24, 1992, p. 65.
6. Ibid.
7. Ibid.
8. Todd Mason, *Perot: An Unauthorized Biography,* Homewood, IL: Richard D. Irwin, 1990, pp. 82–83 and p. 87.
9. Dean Tougas, "'Incredibles' Surmounted Woods, Weather Building Big Jets," *Boeing News,* September 30, 1988, p. 1.
10. Wendell L. French, *The Personnel Management Process,* 6th ed., Boston: Houghton Mifflin, 1987, pp. 257–259.
11. Ibid., pp. 282–285.
12. John Scully, *Odyssey: Pepsi to Apple . . . A Journey of Adventure, Ideas, and the Future,* New York: Harper & Row, 1987, p. 90.
13. Rory J. O'Connor, Mark Schwanhausser, and Steve Hamm, "Gentlemen, Start Your Profit Engines!" in the Bits & Bytes column in *San Jose Mercury News,* May 20, 1991, pp. 1F & 2F.
14. Kathy Rebello and Evan I. Schwartz, "MICROSOFT," *Business Week,* February 24, 1992, p. 65.
15. John Schneidawing, "Are Microsoft's Golden Days History?" *USA Today,* April 21, 1992, p. 3B.
16. Toni A. Perry, "Staying with the Basics," *HRMagazine,* November 1990, pp. 73–76.

Index